HEALING OUR DEEPEST WOUNDS:
THE HOLOTROPIC PARADIGM SHIFT

STREAM OF EXPERIENCE PRODUCTIONS

Other books by Stanislav Grof:

The Adventure of Self-Discovery

Ancient Wisdom and Modern Science (editor)

Realms of the Human Unconscious: Observations from LSD Research
(republished in 2009 as *LSD: Doorway to the Numinous*)

LSD Psychotherapy

Beyond the Brain: Birth, Death, and Transcendence in Psychotherapy

Human Survival and Consciousness Evolution (editor)

The Holotropic Mind

Books of the Dead: Manuals for Living and Dying

The Cosmic Game: Explorations of the Frontiers of Human Consciousness

Psychology of the Future: Lessons from Modern Consciousness Research

When the Impossible Happens: Adventures in Non-Ordinary Realities

The Ultimate Journey: Consciousness and the Mystery of Death

Books with Christina Grof:

*The Stormy Search for the Self: A Guide to Personal Growth through
Transformational Crisis*

Spiritual Emergency: When Personal Transformation Becomes a Crisis

Holotropic Breathwork - A New Approach to Self-Exploration and Therapy

Books by Christina Grof:

The Thirst for Wholeness: Attachment, Addiction, and the Spiritual Path

HEALING OUR DEEPEST WOUNDS:

THE HOLOTROPIC PARADIGM SHIFT

STANISLAV GROF

For Albert

CONTENTS

Preface

In 1962, Thomas Kuhn, one of the most influential philosophers of the twentieth century, published his groundbreaking book The Structure of Scientific Revolutions. On the basis of fifteen years of intensive study of the history of science, he was able to demonstrate that the development of knowledge about the universe in various scientific disciplines is not a process of gradual accumulation of data and formulation of ever more accurate theories, as usually assumed. Instead, it shows a clearly cyclical nature with specific stages and characteristic dynamics, which can be understood and even predicted. The central concept of Kuhn's theory, which makes this possible, is that of a paradigm.

A paradigm can be defined as a constellation of beliefs, values, and techniques shared by the members of the community at a particular historical period. It governs the thinking and research activities of scientists until some of its basic assumptions are seriously challenged by new observations. This leads to a crisis and emergence of suggestions for radically new ways of viewing and interpreting the phenomena that the old paradigm is unable to explain. Eventually, one of these alternatives satisfies the necessary requirements to become the new paradigm that then dominates the thinking in the next period of the history of science.

The most famous historical examples of paradigm shifts have been the replacement of the Ptolemaic geocentric system by the heliocentric system of Copernicus, Kepler, and Galileo, the overthrow of Becher's phlogiston theory in chemistry by Lavoisier and Dalton, and the conceptual cataclysms in physics in the first three decades of the twentieth century that undermined the hegemony of Newtonian physics and gave birth to theories of relativity and quantum physics. Paradigm shifts tend to come as a major surprise to mainstream academic community, since its members tend to mistake the leading paradigms for an accurate and definitive description of reality. Thus in 1900 shortly before the advent of quantum-relativistic physics, Lord Kelvin declared: "There is nothing new to be discovered in physics now. All that remains is more and more precise measurements."

In the last five decades, various avenues of modern consciousness research have revealed a rich array of "anomalous" phenomena - experiences and observations that have undermined some of the generally accepted assertions of modern psychiatry, psychology, and psychotherapy concerning the nature and dimensions of the human psyche, the origins of emotional and psychosomatic disorders, and effective therapeutic mechanisms. Many of these observations are so radical that they question the basic metaphysical assumptions of materialistic science concerning the nature of reality and of human beings and the relationship between consciousness and matter.

The most important sources of these revolutionary and paradigm-breaking observations have been psychedelic research, Jungian psychology, new experiential methods of psychotherapy, field anthropology, thanatology, parapsychology, and various laboratory mind-altering techniques, such as sensory deprivation and biofeedback. My own experience with these "anomalous phenomena" and deep interest in them comes from intensive and extensive research of non-ordinary states of consciousness that has been for more than half a century my profession, vocation, and passion.

I spent approximately half of this time conducting therapy with psychedelic substances, first in Czechoslovakia in the Psychiatric Research Institute in Prague and then in the United States, at the Maryland Psychiatric Research Center in Baltimore, where I participated in the last surviving American psychedelic research program. Since 1975, my wife Christina and I have worked with Holotropic Breathwork™, a powerful method of therapy and self-exploration that we jointly developed at the Esalen Institute in Big Sur, California. Over the years, we have also supported many people undergoing spontaneous episodes of non-ordinary states of consciousness - psychospiritual crises or "spiritual emergencies," as Christina and I call them.

The common denominator of these three situations is that they involve non-ordinary states of consciousness or, more specifically, an important subcategory of them that I call holotropic. This composite word literally means "oriented toward wholeness" or "moving in the direction of wholeness" (from the Greek *holos* = whole and *trepo, trepein* = moving toward or in the direction of something). This term suggests that in our everyday state of consciousness we identify with only a small fraction of who we really are. The best way of explaining what holotropic means is to refer to the Hindu distinction between *namarupa* (the name and shape with which we identify in our everyday existence) and *Atman-Brahman* (our deepest identity which is commensurate with the cosmic creative principle). In holotropic states of consciousness, we can transcend the narrow boundaries of the body ego and reclaim our full identity. We can experientially identify with anything that is part of creation and even with the creative principle itself.

Holotropic experiences play an important role in shamanic initiatory crises, healing ceremonies of native cultures, aboriginal rites of passage, and systematic spiritual practice, such as various forms of yoga, Buddhist or Taoist meditation, Sufi dhikers, Kabbalistic exercises, or the Christian Jesus Prayer (*hesychasm*). They have also been described in the literature on the ancient mysteries of death and rebirth, conducted in the Mediterranean area and other parts of the world in the names of various deities. In everyday life, holotropic experiences can occur in near-death situations or spontaneously, without any obvious trigger. They can also be induced by psychedelic substances and by powerful forms of experiential therapy developed in the second half of the twentieth century.

In psychedelic therapy, holotropic states are brought about by administration of mind-altering substances, such as LSD, psilocybin, mescaline, and tryptamine or amphetamine derivatives. In Holotropic Breathwork, consciousness is changed by a combination of faster breathing, evocative music, and energy-releasing bodywork. In spiritual emergencies, holotropic states occur spontaneously, in the middle of everyday life, and their cause is usually unknown. If they are correctly understood and supported, holotropic states have an extraordinary heuristic, healing, transformative, and even evolutionary potential.

In addition to my own research, I have been more peripherally involved in many disciplines that are, more or less directly, related to holotropic states of consciousness. I have spent much time exchanging information with anthropologists and have participated in sacred ceremonies of native cultures in different parts of the world with and without the ingestion of psychedelic plants, such as peyote, ayahuasca, magic mushrooms, and kava kava. This involved contact with various North American, Mexican, South American, and African shamans and healers. I have also had extensive contact with representatives of various spiritual disciplines, including Vipassana, Zen, and Vajrayana Buddhism, Siddha Yoga, Tantra, and the Christian Benedictine order.

Another area that has received much of my attention has been thanatology, the young discipline studying near-death experiences and the psychological and spiritual aspects of death and dying. In the late 1960s and early 1970s I participated in a large research project studying the effects of psychedelic therapy in individuals dying of cancer. I should also add that I have had the privilege of personal acquaintance and experience with some of the great psychics and parapsychologists of our era, pioneers of laboratory consciousness research, and therapists who developed and practiced powerful forms of experiential therapy that induce holotropic states of consciousness.

My study of holotropic experiences has revealed a rich spectrum of "anomalous phenomena" occurring in my clients, workshop participants, trainees, and myself and has convinced me that they represent a paradigm-breaking challenge to the worldview formulated by Western monistic materialistic science. I believe that rigorous unbiased examination of the data from this research would lead to a revolution in many scientific disciplines that in its nature and scope would resemble the conceptual cataclysm brought into scientific thinking by quantum-relativistic physics and, in a sense, would represent its logical completion.

As it has been the case during all previous periods of "abnormal science," as Thomas Kuhn called times of conceptual crises accompanying scientific revolutions, the data from modern consciousness research have encountered determined resistance from the mainstream academic circles, created great controversy, and polarized the scientific community. While its more adventurous and open-minded representatives have shown great interest in pursuing the new avenues of research – often privately or in various workshops and other paraprofessional contexts – the mainstream educational and clinical facilities continue to see the monistic materialistic worldview as a definitive description of reality. The new ideas have been by and large ignored, rejected, and often even ridiculed.

Considering this situation, it came to me as a great surprise when, in summer of 2007, I received a letter from Václav Havel, former president of Czechoslovakia and later the Czech Republic, informing me that I had been granted the prestigious annual award from the Dagmar and Václav Havel "Vision 97" Foundation in Prague. I was very moved by this unusual honor, not only for professional, but also very personal reasons. For many years, I had felt deep admiration and respect for President Havel as philosopher, artist, freedom fighter, statesman with an inspiring spiritual vision, and a man of extraordinary moral values and courage.

Unlike run-of-the-mill politicians, Václav Havel did not have any ambitions to achieve political power and did not strive to become president of Czechoslovakia. He accepted the highest position in the country at the request of the Czech people, who loved and admired him as a symbol of opposition against oppression and tyranny. His inauguration ceremony at the Prague Castle was witnessed by a crowd of hundreds of thousands. For the next five to six years, President Havel enjoyed more than eighty per cent public support. He encouraged social reform and reconciliation, abolished the death penalty, released all political prisoners, and closed the country's arms factories. Shortly after becoming president, he invited His Holiness the Dalai Lama to Czechoslovakia for an official state visit, becoming the first head of state to extend such an invitation to the exiled leader of the Tibetan people. During his presidency, Václav Havel shared his spiritual vision for the world by lecturing in various academic institutions and political forums in many countries of the world.

According to its statement of purpose, the Foundation "Vision 97" that Václav Havel founded jointly with his wife Dagmar strives to "support projects, which are ground-breaking or even visionary, which aim for the future, have pioneering features, attempt to break down conventions, and strengthen those avenues of science and culture which at present do not enjoy support of the majority of people or are not comprehensible to them, but which with their consequences can inspire or otherwise meaningfully influence the future."

Once a year, on Václav Havel's birthday (October 5), the Foundation grants a special award to individuals whose work - according to the members of its board - meets the above criteria. Former laureates included brain researcher Karl Pribram, philosopher and author Umberto Eco, former US Secretary of Labor Robert Reich, scientist and philosopher Zdeněk Neubauer, sociologist Zygmunt Bauman, psychologist Phillip G. Zimbardo, and MIT computer scientist Joseph Weizenbaum. Naturally, I felt extremely honored by joining the list of these extraordinary people and by the recognition of my work expressed by the award.

My wife Christina and I traveled to Prague, accompanied by our son and daughter-in-law, to take part in the award ceremony and returned to California filled with wonderful memories. The ceremony took place in the deconsecrated church of St. Lawrence, beautifully renovated and transformed by the Havels, which is now known as the Crossroads Spiritual Center. The Vision 97 Award consisted of an ornate diploma signed by the Havels and an impressive piece of art – a life-size replica of the staff of St. Adalbert, the tenth century martyred bishop of Prague and patron saint of Bohemia. An important part of the visit was the fact that we got the opportunity to spend some very special private time with the Havels.

All the laureates of the Vision 97 Award are asked to prepare a publication which best represents their work and their specific contributions to science, philosophy, or art. I prepared for this purpose a selection of my papers reflecting the most important areas of my scientific interests and periods of my professional career – psychedelic research, transpersonal psychology, alternative approaches to psychoses, new insights into religion, mysticism, and spirituality, Holotropic Breathwork, roots of human violence and greed, and various avenues of new paradigm in science.

This book was published in Prague by the Dagmar and Václav Havel Foundation and Moravia Press under the title New Perspectives in Psychiatry, Psychology, and Psychotherapy. Because of the broad range of areas and subjects that this work explores, it provides a very useful introduction to the transpersonal field and the revolutionary changes that have occurred in the last several decades in the understanding of the human psyche and of the nature of reality. However, the fact that it was published in the Czech language greatly limited its readership. Kenneth Sloan of the Association for Holotropic Breathwork International (AHBI) suggested that publishing this book in English, the language in which it was originally written, would make this useful information available to larger circles of readers in different parts of the world.

At Kenneth's suggestion, I also decided to change the title of the English edition to Healing Our Deepest Wounds: The Holotropic Paradigm Shift. This title seems to capture the most important theoretical and practical insights from the research of holotropic states of consciousness that this book explores. It shows that the human psyche is not limited to postnatal biography and the individual unconscious described by Freud. In the work with holotropic states induced by psychedelics and various non-drug means, as well as those occurring spontaneously, this model proves to be painfully inadequate. To account for all the phenomena occurring in these states, we must drastically revise our understanding of the dimensions of the human psyche.

Besides the postnatal biographical level that it shares with the traditional model, the new expanded cartography includes two additional large domains. The first of these domains can be referred to as perinatal, because of its close connection with the trauma of biological birth. This region of the unconscious contains the memories of what the fetus experienced in the consecutive stages of the birth process, including all the emotions and physical sensations involved. These memories form four distinct experiential clusters, each of which is related to one of the stages of the birth process. We can refer to them as Basic Perinatal Matrices (BPM I-IV).

The second transbiographical domain of the new cartography can best be called transpersonal, because it contains matrices for a rich array of experiences in which consciousness transcends the boundaries of the body/ego and the usual limitations of linear time and three-dimensional space. This results in experiential identification with other people, groups of people, other life forms, and even elements of the inorganic world. Transcendence of time provides experiential access to ancestral, racial, collective, phylogenetic, and karmic memories. Yet another category of transpersonal experiences can take us into the realm of the collective unconscious that the Swiss psychiatrist C. G. Jung called arche-typal. This region harbors mythological figures, themes, and realms of all the cultures and ages, even those of which we have no intellectual knowledge (Jung 1981).

The new vastly expanded cartography of the psyche is not just a matter of theoretical interest; it has profound implications for the un-derstanding and treatment of emotional and psychosomatic disorders. According to academic psychiatry, the disorders that are not organic in nature have their origin in various periods of postnatal life – infancy, childhood, and adolescence. This can be illustrated by Freud's famous description of the newborn as tabula rasa – clean slate. The work with holotropic states shows that the emotional wounds reach much deeper – to the perinatal and prenatal period and into the historical, karmic, and archetypal collective unconscious. This discouraging recognition of the depth of the roots of emotional disorders is outweighed by a surprising discovery of new extremely effective therapeutic mechanisms operating on the perinatal and transpersonal levels. Responsible work with holo-tropic states of consciousness thus opens new revolutionary therapeutic perspectives of extraordinary power.

The importance of the new understanding of the psyche and of the new therapeutic mechanisms reaches far beyond the benefits offered to individual clients. Current academic psychiatry and psychology with their superficial model of the psyche have not been able to account for the unbridled violence and insatiable greed that the human species has shown throughout history. Such factors as unsatisfactory nursing, prob-lems with forming healthy object relations, strict toilet training, psycho-sexual traumas, and skewed family dynamics cannot provide satisfac-tory explanation of mass sociopolitical pathology – Hitler's Holocaust, Stalin's Gulag Archipelago, Chinese bestiality in Tibet, the global terror-ist threat, and bloody wars, revolutions, and genocide. Current therapies are helpless in dealing with the destructive and self-destructive forces in the human psyche leading to these events and with the posttraumat-ic stress disorders of the people who survived them. Clearly radically new approaches are needed to deal with these problems that currently threaten survival of life on this planet.

I hope that – because of the wide range of topics that it covers – this book will serve as a useful guide for professionals and laypersons inter-ested in psychotherapy, self-exploration, spiritual quest, consciousness research, and the paradigm shift occurring presently in Western science in regard to the understanding of consciousness, the human psyche, and the nature of reality. It might also direct those for whom the transper-sonal vision is new to the rich literature covering various avenues of this exciting chapter of scientific, philosophical, and spiritual quest for knowledge. I believe that deep inner transformation of humanity on a large scale might be necessary for the survival of our species and feel deep respect for those individuals who have recognized that the first step in saving the planet has to be changing ourselves. If this book provides guidance and support for those who decide to undertake this challenging journey or are on it already, it has not been written in vain.

Stanislav Grof
Mill Valley, California 2012

Maslow's Fourth Force:
A Brief History of Transpersonal Psychology

Roundtrip to the Cosmos

The lower picture expresses the astonishment of the artist at the order, harmony, totality, and completeness of the universe. The upper picture reflects the feelings of extreme cold forcing her to leave this cosmic frontier and return. Identification with a pentagon helped her with the grounding and integration of the Holotropic Breathwork session. (Katia Solani)

Maslow's Fourth Force: A Brief History of Transpersonal Psychology

In the middle of the twentieth century, American psychology was dominated by two major schools - behaviorism and Freudian psychoanalysis. Increasing dissatisfaction with these two orientations as adequate approaches to the human psyche led to the development of humanistic psychology. The main spokesperson and most articulate representative of this new field was the well-known American psychologist Abraham Maslow. He offered an incisive critique of the limitations of behaviorism and psychoanalysis, or the First and the Second Force in psychology as he called them, and formulated the principles of a new perspective in psychology (Maslow 1969).

Maslow's main objection against behaviorism was that the study of animals, such as rats and pigeons, can only clarify those aspects of human functioning that we share with these animals. It thus has no relevance for the understanding of higher, specifically human qualities that are unique to human life, such as love, self-consciousness, self-determination, personal freedom, morality, art, philosophy, religion, and science. It is also largely useless in regard to some specifically human negative characteristics, such as greed, lust for power, cruelty, and tendency to "malignant aggression." He also criticized the behaviorists' disregard for consciousness and introspection and their exclusive focus on the study of behavior.

By contrast, the primary interest of humanistic psychology, Maslow's Third Force, was in human subjects and it honored interest in consciousness and introspection as important complements to the objective approach to research. The behaviorists' exclusive emphasis on determination by the environment, stimulus/response, and reward/ punishment was replaced by emphasis on the capacity of human beings to be internally directed and motivated to achieve self-realization and fulfill their human potential.

In his criticism of psychoanalysis, Maslow pointed out that Freud and his followers drew conclusions about the human psyche mainly from the study of psychopathology and he disagreed with their biological reductionism and their tendency to explain all psychological processes in terms of base instincts. By comparison, humanistic psychol-

Abraham Maslow

ogy focused on healthy populations, or even individuals who showed supernormal functioning in various areas (Maslow's "growing tip of the population"), on human growth and potential, and on higher functions of the psyche. It also emphasized that psychology has to be sensitive to practical human needs and serve important interests and objectives of human society.

Within a few years after Abraham Maslow and Anthony Sutich had launched the Association for Humanistic Psychology (AHP) and its journal, the new movement became extremely popular among American mental health professionals and even in the general public. The multidimensional perspective of humanistic psychology and its emphasis on the whole person provided a broad umbrella for the development of a rich spectrum of new effective therapeutic approaches that greatly expanded the range of possibilities for dealing with emotional, psychosomatic, interpersonal, and psychosocial problems.

Among the important characteristics of these new therapies was a decisive shift from the exclusively verbal strategies of traditional psychotherapy to direct expression of emotions and from exploration of individual history and of unconscious motivation to the feelings and thought processes of the clients in the here and now. Another important aspect of this therapeutic revolution was the emphasis on the interconnectedness of the psyche and the body and overcoming of the taboo against touching, which had previously dominated the field of psychotherapy. Various forms of bodywork thus formed an integral part of the new treatment strategies; Fritz Perls' Gestalt therapy, Alexander Lowen's bioenergetics and other neo-Reichian approaches, encounter groups, and marathon sessions can be mentioned here as salient examples of humanistic therapies.

In spite of the popularity of humanistic psychology, its founders Maslow and Sutich themselves grew dissatisfied with the conceptual framework they had originally created. They became increasingly aware that they had left out an extremely important element -- the spiritual dimension of the human psyche (Sutich 1976). The renaissance of interest in Eastern spiritual philosophies, various mystical traditions, meditation, ancient and aboriginal wisdom, as well as the widespread psychedelic experimentation during the stormy 1960s made it absolutely clear that a comprehensive and cross-culturally valid psychology had to include observations from such areas as mystical states, cosmic consciousness, psychedelic experiences, trance phenomena, creativity, and religious, artistic, and scientific inspiration.

In 1967, a small working group, including Abraham Maslow, Anthony Sutich, Stanislav Grof, James Fadiman, Miles Vich, and Sonya Margulies met in Menlo Park, California, with the purpose of creating a new psychology that would honor the entire spectrum of human experience, including various non-ordinary states of consciousness. During these discussions Maslow and Sutich accepted Grof's suggestion and named the new discipline "transpersonal psychology." This term replaced their own original name "transhumanistic," or "reaching beyond humanistic concerns." Soon afterwards, they launched the Association of Transpersonal Psychology (ATP), and started the Journal of Transpersonal Psychology. Several years later, in 1975, Robert Frager founded the (California) Institute of Transpersonal Psychology in Palo Alto, which has remained at the cutting edge of transpersonal education, research and therapy for more than three decades.

Transpersonal psychology, or the Fourth Force, addressed some major misconceptions of mainstream psychiatry and psychology concerning spirituality and religion. It also responded to important observations from modern consciousness research and several other fields for which the existing scientific paradigm had no adequate explanations. Michael Harner, an American anthropologist with good academic credentials, who had experienced a powerful shamanic initiation during his field work in the Amazon, summed up the shortcomings of academic psychology very succinctly in the preface to his book The Way of the Shaman (Harner 1980). He suggested that the understanding of the psyche in the industrial civilization is seriously biased in two important ways: it is *ethnocentric* and *cognicentric* (a better term would probably be *pragmacentric*).

It is *ethnocentric* in the sense that it has been formulated and promoted by Western materialistic scientists who consider their own perspective to be superior to that of any other human group at any time of history. According to them, matter is primary and life, consciousness, and intelligence are its more or less accidental side products. Spirituality of any form and level of sophistication reflects ignorance of scientific facts, superstition, child-like gullibility, self-deception, and primitive magical thinking. Direct spiritual experiences involving the collective unconscious or archetypal figures and realms are seen as pathological products of the brain. Modern mainstream psychiatrists interpret visionary experiences of the founders of great religions, saints, and prophets as manifestations of serious mental diseases, although they lack adequate medical explanations and the laboratory data supporting this position. In their contemptuous dismissal of ritual and spiritual life, they do not distinguish between primitive folk beliefs or the fundamentalists' literal interpretations of scriptures and sophisticated mystical traditions and Eastern spiritual philosophies based on centuries of systematic introspective exploration of the psyche.

Psychiatric literature contains numerous articles and books that discuss what the most appropriate clinical diagnoses would be for many of the great figures of spiritual history. St. Anthony has been called schizophrenic, St. John of the Cross labeled "hereditary degenerate," St. Teresa of Avila has been dismissed as a severe hysterical psychotic, and Mohammed's mystical visions have been attributed to epilepsy. Many other religious and spiritual personages, such as the Buddha, Jesus, Ramakrishna, and Sri Ramana Maharshi have been seen as suffering from psychoses, because of their visionary experiences and "delusions." Similarly, some traditionally trained anthropologists have argued whether shamans should be diagnosed as schizophrenics, ambulant psychotics, epileptics, or hysterics. The famous psychoanalyst Franz Alexander, known as one of the founders of psychosomatic medicine, wrote a paper in which even Buddhist meditation is described in psychopathological terms and referred to as "artificial catatonia" (Alexander 1931).

While Western psychology and psychiatry describe the ritual and spiritual life of ancient and native cultures in pathological terms, dangerous excesses of the industrial civilization potentially endangering life on the planet have become such integral parts of our life that they seldom attract the specific attention of clinicians and researchers and do not receive pathological labels. On a daily basis we witness manifestations of insatiable greed and malignant aggression - plundering non-renewable resources and turning them into industrial pollution; defiling the natural environment critical for survival with nuclear fallout, toxic chemicals, and massive oil spills; abusing scientific discoveries in physics, chemistry, and biology for the development of weapons of mass destruction; invading other countries leading to massacres of civilians and genocide; and designing military operations that if implemented would kill millions of people.

The main engineers and protagonists of such detrimental strategies and doomsday scenarios not only walk freely, but are rich and famous, hold powerful positions in society, and receive various honors. At the same time, people who have potentially life-transforming mystical states, episodes of psychospiritual death and rebirth, or past-life experiences end up hospitalized with stigmatizing diagnoses and suppressive psychopharmacological medication. This is what Michael Harner referred to as the ethnocentric bias in judging what is normal and what is pathological.

According to Michael Harner, Western psychiatry and psychology also show a strong *cognicentric* bias. By this he means that these disciplines formulated their theories on the basis of experiences and observations from ordinary states of consciousness and have systematically avoided or misinterpreted the evidence from non-ordinary states, such as observations from psychedelic therapy, powerful experiential psychotherapies, work with individuals in psychospiritual crises, meditation research, field anthropological studies, or thanatology. The paradigm-breaking data from these areas of research have been either systematically ignored or misjudged and misinterpreted because of their fundamental incompatibility with the leading paradigm.

In the preceding text, I have used the term non-ordinary states of consciousness. Before we continue our discussion, a semantic clarification seems to be appropriate. The term non-ordinary states of consciousness is being used mostly by researchers who study these states and recognize their value. Mainstream psychiatrists prefer the term altered states, which reflects their belief that only the everyday state of consciousness is normal and that all departures from it without exception represent pathological distortions of the correct perception of reality and have no positive potential. However, even the term non-ordinary states is too broad for the purpose of our discussion. Transpersonal psychology is interested in a significant subgroup of these states that have heuristic, healing, transformative and even evolutionary potential. This includes experiences of shamans and their clients, those of initiates in native rites of passage and ancient mysteries of death and rebirth, of spiritual practitioners and mystics of all ages, and individuals in psychospiritual crisis ("spiritual emergencies") (Grof and Grof 1989, 1990).

In the early stages of my research, I discovered to my great surprise that mainstream psychiatry has no name for this important subgroup of non-ordinary states and dismisses all of them as "altered states." Because I felt strongly that they deserve to be distinguished from the rest and placed into a special category, I coined for them the name *holotropic* (Grof 1992). This composite word means literally "oriented toward wholeness" or "moving in the direction of wholeness" (from the Greek *holos* = whole and *trepo, trepein* = moving toward or in the direction of something). This term suggests that in our everyday state of consciousness we identify with only a small fraction of who we really are. In holotropic states, we can transcend the narrow boundaries of the body ego and encounter a rich spectrum of transpersonal experiences that help us to reclaim our full identity. I have described in a different context the basic characteristics of holotropic states and how they differ from conditions that deserve to be referred to as altered states of consciousness (Grof 2000). I have been using this term in discussions of these states for some time now and am happy to report that it has found a growing acceptance.

Transpersonal psychology has made a significant headway toward correcting the ethnocentric and cognicentric bias of mainstream psychiatry and psychology, particularly by its recognition of the genuine nature of transpersonal experiences and their value. In the light of modern consciousness research, the current conceited dismissal and pathologization of spirituality characteristic of monistic materialism appears untenable. In holotropic states, the spiritual dimensions of reality can be directly experienced in a way that is as convincing as our daily experience of the material world, if not more so. Careful study of transpersonal experiences shows that they cannot be explained as products of pathological processes in the brain, but are ontologically real.

To distinguish transpersonal experiences from imaginary products of individual fantasy, Jungian psychologists refer to this domain as *imaginal*. French scholar, philosopher, and mystic, Henri Corbin, who first used the term *mundus imaginalis*, was inspired in this regard by his study of Islamic mystical literature (Corbin 2000). Islamic theosophers call the imaginal world, where everything existing in the sensory world has its analogue, *'alam a mithal,'* or the "eighth climate," to distinguish it from the "seven climates," regions of traditional Islamic geography. The imaginal world possesses extension and dimensions, forms and colors, but these are not perceptible to our senses as they would be when they are properties of physical objects. However, this realm is in every respect as fully ontologically real and susceptible to consensual validation by other people as the material world perceived by the normal senses.

Spiritual experiences appear in two different forms. The first of these, the experience of the *immanent divine*, is characterized by subtly, but profoundly transformed perception of everyday reality. A person having this form of spiritual experience sees people, animals, plants, and inanimate objects in the environment as radiant manifestations of a unified field of cosmic creative energy. He or she has a direct perception of the immaterial nature of the physical world and realizes that the boundaries between objects are illusory and unreal. This type of experience of reality has a distinctly numinous quality and corresponds to Spinoza's *deus sive natura*, or nature as God. Using the analogy with television, this experience could be likened to a situation where a black and white picture would suddenly change into one in vivid, "living colors." When that happens, much of the old perception of the world remains in place, but is radically redefined by the addition of a new dimension.

The second form of spiritual experience, that of the *transcendent divine*, involves manifestation of archetypal beings and realms of reality that are ordinarily transphenomenal, that is, unavailable to perception in the everyday state of consciousness. In this type of spiritual experience, entirely new elements seem to "unfold" or "explicate" - to borrow terms from David Bohm - from another level or order of reality. When we return to the analogy with television, this would be like discovering to our surprise that there exist channels other than the one we have been previously watching, having previously believed that our TV set had only one channel.

The issue of critical importance is, of course, the ontological nature of the spiritual experiences described above. Can they be interpreted and dismissed as meaningless phantasmagoria produced by a pathological process afflicting the brain, yet to be discovered and identified by modern science, or do they reflect objectively existing dimensions of reality, which are not accessible in the ordinary state of consciousness.? Careful systematic study of transpersonal experiences shows that they are ontologically real and contain information about important, ordinarily hidden dimensions of existence, which can be consensually validated (Grof 1998, 2000). In a certain sense, the perception of the world in holotropic states is more accurate than our everyday perception of it.

Quantum-relativistic physics has shown that matter is essentially empty and that all boundaries in the universe are illusory. We know today that what appear to us as discrete static objects are actually condensations within a dynamic unitive energy field. This finding is in direct conflict with the "pedestrian perception" of the world and brings to mind the Hindu concept of maya, a metaphysical principle capable of generating a convincing facsimile of the material world. And the objective nature of the historical and archetypal domains of the collective unconscious has been demonstrated by C.G. Jung and his followers years before psychedelic research and new experiential therapies amassed evidence that confirmed it beyond any reasonable doubt. In addition, it is possible to describe step-by-step procedures and proper contexts that facilitate access to these experiences. These include non-pharmacological procedures, such as meditation practices, music, dancing, breathing exercises, and other approaches that cannot be seen as pathological agents by any stretch of the imagination.

The study of holotropic states confirmed C. G. Jung's insight that the experiences originating on deeper levels of the psyche (in my own terminology "perinatal" and "transpersonal" experiences) have a certain quality that he called (after Rudolph Otto) *numinosity* (Jung 1964 b). The term *numinous* is relatively neutral and thus preferable to other similar names, such as religious, mystical, magical, holy, or sacred, which have often been used in problematic contexts and are easily misleading. The sense of numinosity is based on direct apprehension of the fact that we are encountering a domain that belongs to a superior order of reality, one which is sacred and radically different from the material world.

To prevent misunderstanding and confusion that in the past compromised many similar discussions, it is critical to make a clear distinction between spirituality and religion. Spirituality is based on direct experiences of non-ordinary aspects and dimensions of reality. It does not require a special place or an officially appointed person mediating contact with the divine. The mystics do not need churches or temples. The context, in which they experience the sacred dimensions of reality, including their own divinity, are their bodies and nature. And instead of officiating priests, the mystics need a supportive group of fellow seekers or the guidance of a teacher who is more advanced on the inner journey than they are themselves.

Spirituality involves a special kind of relationship between the individual and the cosmos and is, in its essence, a personal and private affair. By comparison, organized religion involves institutionalized group activity that takes place in a designated location, a temple or a church, and involves a system of appointed officials who might or might not have had personal experiences of spiritual realities. Once a religion becomes organized, it often completely loses the connection with its spiritual source and becomes a secular institution that exploits human spiritual needs without satisfying them.

Organized religions tend to create hierarchical systems focusing on the pursuit of power, control, politics, money, possessions, and other secular concerns. Under these circumstances, religious hierarchy as a rule dislikes and discourages direct spiritual experiences in its members, because these experiences foster independence and cannot be effectively controlled. When this suppression succeeds, genuine spiritual life continues only in the mystical branches, monastic orders, and ecstatic sects of the religions involved. While it is clear that fundamentalism and religious dogma are incompatible with the scientific world view, whether it is Cartesian-Newtonian or based on the new paradigm, there is no reason why we could not seriously study the nature and implications of transpersonal experiences. As Ken Wilber pointed out in his book A Sociable God (Wilber 1983), there cannot possibly be a conflict between genuine science and authentic religion. If there seems to be such a conflict, we are very likely dealing with "bogus science" and/or "bogus religion", where either or both sides have a serious misunderstanding of the other's position and very likely represents a false or fake version of its own discipline.

Transpersonal psychology, as it was born in the late 1960s, was culturally sensitive and treated the ritual and spiritual traditions of ancient and native cultures with the respect that they deserve in view of the findings of modern consciousness research. It also embraced and integrated a wide range of "anomalous phenomena," paradigm-breaking observations that academic science has been unable to account for and explain. However, although comprehensive and well substantiated in and of itself, the new field represented such a radical departure from academic thinking in professional circles that it could not be reconciled with either traditional psychology and psychiatry or with the Newtonian-Cartesian paradigm of Western science.

As a result of this, transpersonal psychology was extremely vulnerable to accusations of being "irrational", "unscientific", and even "flakey," particularly by scientists who were not aware of the vast body of observations and data on which the new movement was based, These critics also ignored the fact that many of the pioneers of this revolutionary movement had impressive academic credentials. Among the pioneers of transpersonal psychology were many prominent psychologists – James Fadiman. Jean Houston, Jack Kornfield, Stanley Krippner, Ralph Metzner, Arnold Mindell, John Perry, Kenneth Ring, Frances Vaughan, Richard Tarnas, Charles Tart, Roger Walsh - and anthropologists, such as Angeles Arrien, Michael and Sandra Harner, Barbara Myerhoff, Peter

Furst, and others. These individuals created and embraced the transpersonal vision of the human psyche not because they were ignorant of the fundamental assumptions of traditional science, but because they found the old conceptual frameworks seriously inadequate and incapable of accounting for their experiences and observations.

The problematic status of transpersonal psychology as viewed from the perspective of the "hard sciences" changed radically during the first two decades of the existence of this fledgling discipline. As a result of revolutionary new concepts and discoveries in various scientific fields, the philosophy of traditional Western science, its basic assumptions, and its Newtonian-Cartesian paradigm were increasingly challenged and undermined. Like many other theoreticians in the transpersonal field, I have followed this development with great interest and described it in the first part of my book Beyond the Brain as an effort to bridge the gap between the findings of my own research and the established scientific worldview (Grof 1985).

The influx of this exciting new information began with the realization of the profound philosophical implications of quantum-relativistic physics, forever changing our understanding of physical reality. The astonishing convergence between the worldview of modern physics and that of the Eastern spiritual philosophies, foreshadowed already in the work of Albert Einstein, Niels Bohr, Werner Heisenberg, Erwin Schroedinger, Wolfgang Pauli, and others, found a full expression in the ground-breaking book by Fritjof Capra, his Tao of Physics (Capra 1975). Capra's pioneering vision was complemented and refined in the following years by the work of Fred Alan Wolf, Nick Herbert, Amit Goswami, and many others (Wolf 1981, Herbert 1979, Goswami 1995). Of particular interest in this regard were the contributions of David Bohm, former co-worker of Albert Einstein and author of prestigious monographs on the theory of relativity and quantum physics. His concept of the explicate and implicate order and his theory of holomovement expounding the importance of holographic thinking in science gained great popular support in the transpersonal field (Bohm 1980), as did Karl Pribram's holographic model of the brain (Pribram 1971).

The same was true for biologist Rupert Sheldrake's theory of morphic resonance and morphogenetic fields, demonstrating the importance of non-physical fields for the understanding of forms, genetics and heredity, order, meaning, and the process of learning (Sheldrake 1981) . Additional exciting contributions were Gregory Bateson's brilliant synthesis of anthropology, cybernetics, information and systems theories, logic, psychology, and other disciplines (Bateson 1979) Ilya Prigogine's studies of dissipative structures and order out of chaos (Prigogine 1980,

Prigogine and Stengers 1984), the chaos theory itself (Gleick 1988), the anthropic principle in astrophysics (Barrow and Tipler 1986), and many others.

Even at this early stage of the development, however, we have more than just a mosaic of unrelated cornerstones of this new vision of reality. At least two major intellectual attempts at integrating transpersonal psychology into a comprehensive new world view deserve to be mentioned. The first of these pioneering ventures has been the work of Ken Wilber. In a series of books beginning with his Spectrum of Consciousness (Wilber 1977), Wilber has achieved a highly creative synthesis of data drawn from a vast variety of areas and disciplines, ranging from psychology, anthropology, sociology, mythology, and comparative religion, through linguistics, philosophy, and history, to cosmology, quantum-relativistic physics, biology, evolutionary theory, and systems theory. His knowledge of the literature is truly encyclopedic, his analytical mind systematic and incisive, and his ability to communicate complex ideas clearly is remarkable. The impressive scope, comprehensive nature, and intellectual rigor of Wilber's work have helped to make it a widely acclaimed and highly influential theory of transpersonal psychology.

However, it would expect too much from an interdisciplinary work of this scope and depth to believe that it could be perfect and flawless in all respects and details. Wilber's writings thus have drawn not just enthusiastic acclaim, but also serious criticism from a variety of sources. The exchanges about the controversial and disputed aspects of his theory have often been forceful and heated. This was partly due to Wilber's often aggressive polemic style that includes strongly worded *ad personam* attacks and is not conducive to productive dialogue. Some of these discussions have been gathered in a volume entitled Ken Wilber in Dialogue (Rothberg and Kelly 1998) and others in numerous articles and Internet websites.

Many of these arguments about Ken Wilber's work focus on areas and disciplines other than transpersonal psychology and discussing them would transcend the nature and scope of this book. However, over the years, Ken and I have exchanged ideas concerning various specific aspects of transpersonal psychology; this involved both mutual compliments and critical comments about our respective theories. I first addressed the similarities and differences between Ken's spectrum psychology and my own observations and theoretical constructs in my book Beyond the Brain (Grof 1985). I later returned to this subject in my contribution to the compendium entitled Ken Wilber in Dialogue (Rothberg and Kelly 1998) and in my own Psychology of the Future (Grof 2000).

In my attempt to critically evaluate Wilber's theories, I approached the task from a clinical perspective, drawing primarily on the data from modern consciousness research, my own and that of others. In my opinion, the main problem of Ken Wilber's writing about transpersonal psychology is that he does not have any clinical experience and the primary sources of his data have been his extensive reading and the experiences from his personal spiritual practice. In addition, he has drawn most of his clinical data from schools that use verbal methods of psychotherapy and conceptual frameworks limited to postnatal biography. He does not take into consideration clinical evidence amassed during the last several decades of experiential therapy, with or without psychedelic substances.

For a theory as important and influential as Ken Wilber's work has become, it is not sufficient that it integrates material from many different ancient and modern sources into a comprehensive philosophical system that shows inner logical cohesion. While logical consistency certainly is a valuable prerequisite, a viable theory has to have an additional property that is equally, if not more important. It is generally accepted among scientists that a system of propositions is an acceptable theory if, and only if, its conclusions are in agreement with observable facts (Frank 1957). I have tried to outline the areas where Wilber's speculations have been in conflict with facts of observation and those that involve logical inconsistencies (Rothberg and Kelly 1998).

One of these discrepancies was the omission of the pre- and perinatal domain from his map of consciousness and from his developmental scheme. Another one was the uncritical acceptance of the Freudian and post-Freudian emphasis on the postnatal origin of emotional and psychosomatic disorders and failure to acknowledge their deeper perinatal and transpersonal roots. Wilber's description of the strictly linear nature of spiritual development, inability to see the paradoxical nature of the pre-trans relationship, and reduction of the problem of death (Thanatos) in psychology to a transition from one developmental fulcrum to another have been additional areas of disagreement.

An issue of considerable dissent between us has been Ken Wilber's insistence that opening to spirituality happens exclusively on the level of the centaur, Wilber's stage of psychospiritual development characterized by full integration of body and mind. I have pointed out, in fundamental agreement with Michael Washburn, that spiritual opening often takes the form of a spiral combining regression and progression, rather than proceeding in a strictly linear fashion (Washburn 1988). Particularly frequent is the opening involving psychospiritual death and rebirth, in which case the critical interface between the personal and transpersonal is the perinatal level. This can be supported not just by clinical observations, but also by the study of the lives of mystics, such as St Teresa of

Shamanic Initiation Part 4

Last of four mandalas from a Holotropic Breathwork session. Fully integrated and transformed, the voyager sits in the center of the picture. She is surrounded by darkness, the three talismans, the Grandmothers, the Snake and the diamond-shaped shamanic reality. The experience is complex but orderly. (Jan Vannatta)

Avila, St. John of the Cross, and others, many of whom Wilber quotes in his books. Particularly problematic and questionable is Wilber's suggestion that we should diagnose clients in terms of the emotional, moral, intellectual, existential, philosophical, and spiritual problems which they show according to his scheme, and assign them to several different therapists specializing in those areas (Wilber 2000). This recommendation might impress a layperson as a sophisticated solution to psychological problems, but it is naive and unrealistic from the point of view of any experienced clinician.

The above problems concerning specific aspects of Wilber's system can be corrected easily and do not invalidate the usefulness of his overall scheme as a comprehensive blueprint for understanding the nature of reality. In recent years, Ken Wilber distanced himself from transpersonal psychology in favor of his own vision that he calls integral psychology. On closer inspection, what he refers to as integral psychology reaches far beyond what we traditionally understand under that name and includes areas that belong to other disciplines. However broad and encompassing our vision of reality is, in practice we have to pare it down to those aspects which are relevant for solving the problems with which we are dealing. With the necessary corrections and adjustments discussed above, Wilber's integral approach will in the future represent a large and useful context for transpersonal psychology rather than a replacement for it; it will also serve as an important bridge to mainstream science.

The second pioneering attempt to integrate transpersonal psychology into a new comprehensive world view has been the work of the Hungarian Ervin Laszlo, the world's foremost system theorist, interdisciplinary scientist, and philosopher, currently living in Italy. A multifaceted individual with a range of interests and talents reminiscent of great figures of the Renaissance, Laszlo achieved international fame as a child prodigy and concert pianist in his teens. A few years later, he turned to science and philosophy, beginning his lifetime search for understanding of human nature and the nature of reality. Where Wilber outlined what an integral theory of everything should look like, Laszlo actually created one (Laszlo 1993, 1996, 2004, Laszlo and Abraham 2004).

In an intellectual *tour de force* and a series of books, Laszlo has explored a wide range of disciplines, including astrophysics, quantum-relativistic physics, biology, and psychology. He pointed out a wide range of phenomena, paradoxical observations, and paradigmatic challenges, for which these disciplines have no explanations. He then examined the attempts of various pioneers of new paradigm science to provide solutions for these conceptual challenges. This included Bohm's theory of holomovement, Pribram's holographic model of the brain, Sheldrake's theory of morphogenetic fields, Prigogine's concept of dissipative structures, and others. He looked at the contributions of these theories and also at the problems that they had not been able to solve.

Drawing on advances in the hard sciences and on mathematics, Laszlo offered a resolution of the current paradoxes in Western science, which transcended the boundaries of individual disciplines. He achieved that by formulating his "connectivity hypothesis," the main cornerstone of which is the existence of what he calls the "psi-field," (Laszlo 1993, 1996, Laszlo and Abraham 2004). He describes it as a subquantum field which holds a holographic record of all the events that have happened in the phenomenal world. Laszlo includes transpersonal psychology and the spiritual philosophies in his all-encompassing theory quite explicitly, as exemplified by his paper on Jungian psychology and my own consciousness research (Laszlo 1996) and his last book Science and the Akashic Field: An Integral Theory of Everything (Laszlo 2004).

It has been very exciting to see that all the new revolutionary developments in science, while irreconcilable with seventeenth century Newtonian-Cartesian thinking and monistic materialism, have been quite compatible with transpersonal psychology. As a result of these conceptual breakthroughs in a number of disciplines, it has become increasingly possible to imagine that transpersonal psychology will be accepted in the future by academic circles and become an integral part of a radically new scientific world view. As scientific progress continues to lift the spell of the outdated seventeenth century materialistic worldview, we can see the general outlines of an emerging radically new comprehensive understanding of ourselves, nature, and the universe we live in. This new paradigm should be able to reconcile science with experientially based spirituality of a non-denominational, universal, and all-embracing nature and bring about a synthesis of modern science and ancient wisdom.

Psychology of the Future:
Lessons from Modern
Consciousness Research

Psychospiritual death and rebirth from a Holotropic Breathwork session, featuring a swan, a powerful spirit bird that plays an important role in Siberian shamanism.

Psychology of the Future: Lessons from Modern Consciousness Research

The objective of this chapter is to summarize my experiences and observations concerning the nature of the human psyche in health and disease that I have amassed during more than fifty years of research of non-ordinary states of consciousness. I will focus specifically on those findings that represent a serious theoretical challenge for academic psychology and psychiatry and suggest the revisions of our current understanding of consciousness and the human psyche that would be necessary to come to terms with the new data, understand them, and explain them.

Holotropic States of Consciousness.

My primary interest is to focus on experiences that have healing, transformative, and evolutionary potential and those that represent a useful source of data about the human psyche and the nature of reality. I will also pay special attention to those aspects of these experiences that reveal the existence of the spiritual dimensions of existence. For this purpose, the term non-ordinary states of consciousness is too general, since it includes a wide range of conditions that are not interesting or relevant from this point of view.

Consciousness can be profoundly changed by a variety of pathological processes -- by cerebral traumas, by intoxications with poisonous chemicals, by infections, or by degenerative and circulatory processes in the brain. Such conditions can certainly result in profound mental changes that would qualify them as "non-ordinary states of consciousness." However, they cause "trivial deliria" or "organic psychoses", states that are very important clinically but are not relevant for our discussion. People suffering from deliriant states are typically disoriented in space and time and might not know who they are. In addition, their mental functioning is significantly impaired. They typically show a disturbance of intellectual functions and have subsequent amnesia for the experiences they have had.

I would, therefore, like to narrow our discussion to a large and important subgroup of non-ordinary states of consciousness for which contemporary psychiatry does not have a specific term. Because I feel strongly that they deserve to be distinguished from the rest and placed into a special category, I have coined for them the name *holotropic* (Grof 1992). This composite word means literally "oriented toward wholeness" or "moving in the direction of wholeness" (from the Greek *holos* = whole and *trepo. trepein* = moving toward or in the direction of something). The full meaning of this term and the justification for its use will become clear later in this book. It suggests that in our everyday state of consciousness we are fragmented and identify with only a small fraction of who we really are.

Holotropic states are characterized by a specific transformation of consciousness associated with dramatic perceptual changes in all sensory areas, intense and often unusual emotions, and profound alterations in the thought processes. They are also usually accompanied by a variety of intense psychosomatic manifestations and unconventional forms of behavior. Consciousness is changed qualitatively in a very profound and fundamental way, but it is not grossly impaired as it is in the deliriant conditions. We are experiencing invasion of other dimensions of existence that can be very intense and even overwhelming. However, at the same time, we typically remain fully oriented and do not completely lose touch with everyday reality. We experience simultaneously two very different realities, have "each foot in a different world." The famous Swiss psychiatrist Eugene Bleuler coined the term "double bookkeeping" (doppelte Buchfuehrung) for this condition.

Extraordinary changes in sensory perception represent a very important and characteristic aspect of holotropic states. Our visual perception of the external world is usually significantly transformed and when we close our eyes we can be flooded with images drawn from our personal history and from the individual and collective unconscious. We can also have visions portraying various aspects of nature, of the cosmos, or of the mythological realms. This can be accompanied by a wide range of experiences engaging other senses - various sounds, physical sensations, smells, and tastes.

The emotions associated with holotropic states cover a very broad spectrum that extends far beyond the limits of our everyday experience. They range from feelings of ecstatic rapture, heavenly bliss, and "peace that passeth all understanding" to episodes of abysmal terror, murderous anger, utter despair, consuming guilt, and other forms of unimaginable emotional suffering that matches the descriptions of the tortures of hell in the great religions of the world.

The content of holotropic states is often spiritual or mystical. We can experience sequences of psychological death and rebirth and a broad spectrum of transpersonal phenomena, such as feelings of oneness with other people, nature, the universe, and God. We might uncover what seem to be memories from other incarnations, encounter powerful archetypal beings, communicate with discarnate entities, and visit numerous mythological landscapes. Holotropic experiences of this kind are the main source of cosmologies, mythologies, philosophies, and religious systems describing the spiritual nature of the cosmos and of existence. They are the key for understanding the ritual and spiritual life of humanity from shamanism and sacred ceremonies of aboriginal tribes to the great religions of the world.

A particularly interesting aspect of holotropic states is their effect on thought processes. The intellect is not impaired, but functions in a way that is significantly different from its everyday mode of operation. While we might not be able to rely on our judgment in ordinary practical matters, we can be literally flooded with remarkable information on a variety of subjects. We can reach profound psychological insights concerning our personal history, unconscious dynamics, emotional difficulties, and interpersonal problems. We can also experience extraordinary revelations concerning various aspects of nature and the cosmos that transcend our educational and intellectual background. However, by far the most interesting insights that become available in holotropic states revolve around philosophical, metaphysical, and spiritual issues.

Holotropic States of Consciousness and Human History

Members of ancient and aboriginal cultures spent much time and energy developing powerful mind-altering techniques that can induce holotropic states. They combine in different ways chanting, breathing, drumming, rhythmic dancing, fasting, social and sensory isolation, extreme physical pain, and other elements. These cultures used them in shamanic procedures, healing ceremonies, and rites of passage -- powerful rituals enacted at the time of important biological and social transitions, such as circumcision, puberty, marriage, or the birth of a child. Many cultures have used psychedelic plants for these purposes. The most famous examples of these are different varieties of hemp, the Mexican cactus peyote, Psilocybe mushrooms, the African shrub iboga, and the Amazonian jungle plants Banisteriopsis caapi and Psychotria viridis, the active ingredients of yagé or ayahuasca.

Additional important triggers of holotropic experiences are various forms of systematic spiritual practice involving meditation, concentration, breathing, and movement exercises that are used in different systems of yoga, Vipassana or Zen Buddhism, Tibetan Vajrayana, Taoism, Christian mysticism, Sufism, or Cabalah. Other techniques were used in the ancient mysteries of death and rebirth, such as the Egyptian temple initiations of Isis and Osiris and the Greek Bacchanalia, rites of Attis and Adonis, and the Eleusinian mysteries. The specifics of the procedures involved in these secret rites have remained for the most part unknown, although it is likely that psychedelic preparations played an important part in them (Wasson, Hofmann, and Ruck 1978).

Among the modern means of inducing holotropic states of consciousness are psychedelic substances in pure form isolated from plants or synthesized in the laboratory and powerful experiential forms of psychotherapy, such as hypnosis, neo-Reichian approaches, primal therapy, and rebirthing. My wife Christina and I have developed Holotropic Breathwork, a method that can facilitate profound holotropic states by very simple means - conscious breathing, evocative music, and focused bodywork. There are also laboratory techniques that are very effective for altering consciousness.

One of these is sensory deprivation, which involves significant reduction of meaningful sensory stimuli. In its extreme form, the individual is deprived of sensory input by total submersion in a dark and soundproof tank filled with water at body temperature. Another well-known laboratory method of changing consciousness is biofeedback, where the individual is guided by electronic feedback signals into holotropic states of consciousness characterized by the preponderance of certain specific frequencies of brainwaves. We could also mention here the techniques of sleep and dream deprivation and lucid dreaming.

It is important to emphasize that episodes of holotropic states of varying duration can also occur spontaneously without any specific identifiable cause and often against the will of the people involved. Since modern psychiatry does not differentiate between mystical or spiritual states and mental diseases, people experiencing these states are often labeled psychotic, hospitalized, and receive routine suppressive psychopharmacological treatment. My wife Christina and I refer to these states as psychospiritual crises or "spiritual emergencies." We believe that properly supported and treated, they can result in emotional and psychosomatic healing, positive personality transformation, and consciousness evolution (Grof and Grof 1989, 1990).

Although I have been deeply interested in all the categories of holotropic states mentioned above, I have done most of my work in the area of psychedelic therapy, Holotropic Breathwork, and spiritual emergency. This book is based predominantly on my observations from these three areas in which I have most personal experience. However, the general conclusions I will be drawing apply to all the situations involving holotropic states.

Holotropic States in the History of Psychiatry.

It is worth mentioning that the history of depth psychology and psychotherapy was deeply connected with the study of holotropic states -- Franz Mesmer's experiments with "animal magnetism," hypnotic sessions with hysterical patients conducted in Paris by Jean Martin Charcot, and the research in hypnosis carried out in Nancy by Hippolyte Bernheim and Ambroise Auguste Liébault. Sigmund Freud's early work was inspired by his work with a client (Miss Anna O.), who experienced spontaneous episodes of non-ordinary states of consciousness. Freud also initially used hypnosis to access his patients' unconscious before he radically changed his strategies.

In retrospect, shifting emphasis from direct experience to free association, from actual trauma to Oedipal fantasies, and from conscious reliving and emotional abreaction of unconscious material to transference dynamics was unfortunate; it limited and misdirected Western psychotherapy for the next fifty years (Ross 1989). While verbal therapy can be very useful in providing interpersonal learning and rectifying interaction and communication in human relationships (e.g. couple and family therapy), it is ineffective in dealing with emotional and bioenergetic blockages and macrotraumas, such as the trauma of birth.

As a consequence of this development, psychotherapy in the first half of the twentieth century was practically synonymous with talking therapy -- face to face interviews, free associations on the couch, and behaviorist deconditioning. At the same time holotropic states, initially seen as an effective therapeutic tool, became associated with pathology rather than healing. This situation started to change in the 1950's with the advent of psychedelic therapy and new developments in psychology and psychotherapy. A group of American psychologists headed by Abraham Maslow, dissatisfied with behaviorism and Freudian psychoanalysis, launched a revolutionary movement -- humanistic psychology. Within a very short time, this movement became very popular and provided the context for a broad spectrum of new therapies.

While traditional psychotherapies used primarily verbal means and intellectual analysis, these new so-called experiential therapies emphasized direct experience and expression of emotions and used various forms of bodywork as an integral part of the process. Probably the most famous representative of these new approaches is Fritz Perls' Gestalt therapy (Perls 1976). However, most experiential therapies still relied to a great degree on verbal communication and required that the client stay in the ordinary state of consciousness. The most radical innovations in the therapeutic field are approaches which are so powerful that they profoundly change the state of consciousness, such as psychedelic therapy, Holotropic Breathwork, primal therapy, rebirthing, and others. The therapeutic use of holotropic states is the most recent development in Western psychotherapy. Paradoxically, it is also the oldest form of healing, one that can be traced back to the dawn of human history. Therapies using holotropic states actually represent a rediscovery and modern reinterpretation of the elements and principles that have been documented by historians and anthropologists studying the sacred mysteries of death and rebirth, rites of passage, and ancient and aboriginal forms of spiritual healing, particularly various shamanic procedures. Shamanism is the most ancient spiritual system and healing art of humanity; its roots reach far back into the Paleolithic era.

Among the beautiful images of primeval animals painted and carved on the walls of the great caves in Southern France and northern Spain, such as Lascaux, Font de Gaume, Les Trois Frères, Niaux, Altamira, and others, are figures combining human and animal features that very likely represent ancient shamans. In some of the caves, the discoverers also found footprints in circular arrangements suggesting that their inhabitants conducted dances, similar to those still performed by some aboriginal cultures for the induction of holotropic states. Shamanism is not only ancient, it is also universal; it can be found in North and South America, in Europe, Africa, Asia, Australia, and Polynesia.

The fact that so many different cultures throughout human history have found shamanic techniques useful and relevant suggests that they address the "primal mind"-- a basic and primordial aspect of the human psyche that transcends race, culture, and time. All the cultures with the exception of Western industrial civilization have held holotropic states in great esteem and spent much time and effort to develop various ways of inducing them. They used them to connect with their deities, other dimensions of reality, and with the forces of nature, for healing, for cultivation of extrasensory perception, and for artistic inspiration. For pre-industrial cultures, healing always involved holotropic states of consciousness -- either for the client, for the healer, or for both of them at the same time. In many instances, a large group or even an entire tribe enters a non-ordinary state of consciousness together, as it is, for example, among the !Kung Bushmen in the African Kalahari Desert (Lee and DeVore 1976).

Most western psychiatrists and psychologists do not see holotropic states (with the exception of dreams that are not recurrent or frightening) as potential sources of healing or of valuable information about the human psyche, but rather as pathological phenomena. Traditional psychiatry tends to use indiscriminately pathological labels and suppressive

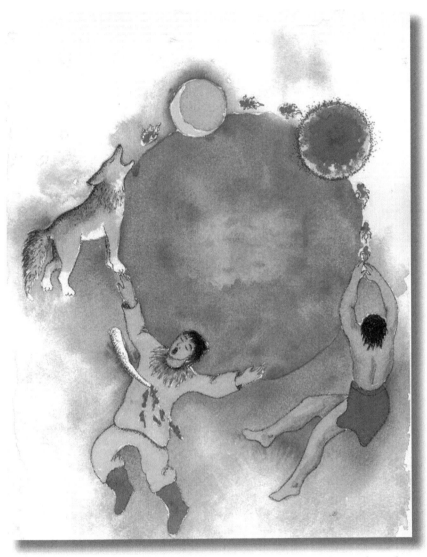

The shaman's heart is pierced by a walrus tusk and his spirit travels to the wolf, to the moon, to the sun, and to another shaman. Mandala from a Holotropic Breathwork session. (Tai Hazard)

medication whenever these states occur spontaneously. Michael Harner (Harner 1980), an anthropologist of good academic standing who underwent a shamanic initiation during his fieldwork in the Amazonian jungle and practices shamanism, suggests that Western psychiatry is seriously biased in at least two significant ways.

It is *ethnocentric*, which means that it considers its own view of the human psyche and of reality to be the only correct one and superior to all others. It is also *cognicentric* (a more accurate word might be *pragmacentric*), meaning that it takes into consideration only experiences and observations in the ordinary state of consciousness. Psychiatry's disinterest in holotropic states and disregard for them has resulted in a culturally insensitive approach and a tendency to pathologize all activities that cannot be understood in its own narrow context. This includes the ritual and spiritual life of ancient and pre-industrial cultures and the entire spiritual history of humanity.

Implications of Modern Consciousness Research for Psychiatry

If we subject the experiences and observations associated with holotropic states to systematic scientific scrutiny we are led to a radical revision of our understanding of consciousness, the human psyche, and the nature of reality. The resulting revolution in our thinking resembles in its scope and depth the conceptual cataclysm that the physicists faced in the first three decades of the twentieth century, when they had to move from Newtonian to quantum-relativistic physics. In a sense, the new insights from consciousness research concerning the psyche represent a logical completion of the revolution that has already occurred in our understanding of matter. The changes we would have to make in our thinking about psychiatry, psychology, psychotherapy and even the nature of reality itself fall into several large categories:

1. *New understanding and cartography of the human psyche*
2. *The nature and architecture of emotional and psychosomatic disorders*
3. *Therapeutic mechanisms and the process of healing*
4. *The strategy of psychotherapy and self-exploration*
5. *The role of spirituality in human life*
6. *The nature of reality*

1. NEW UNDERSTANDING AND CARTOGRAPHY OF THE HUMAN PSYCHE

The phenomena encountered in the study of holotropic states cannot be explained in the context of the traditional model of the psyche limited to postnatal biography and the Freudian individual unconscious. The dimensions of the human psyche are infinitely larger than what is described in handbooks of academic psychology and psychiatry. In an effort to account for the experiences and observations from holotropic states I have suggested a cartography or model of the psyche that contains, in addition to the usual *biographical level*, two transbiographical realms: *the perinatal domain*, related to the trauma of biological birth; and *the transpersonal domain*, which is the source of such phenomena as experiential identification with other people or with animals, visions of archetypal and mythological beings and realms, ancestral, racial, and karmic experiences, and identification with the Universal Mind or the Supracosmic Void. These are experiences that have been described throughout ages in the religious, mystical, and occult literature and oral traditions of different countries of the world.

Postnatal Biography and the Individual Unconscious

The biographical level of the psyche does not require much discussion, since it is well known from traditional psychology and psychotherapy; as a matter of fact, it is what traditional psychology is all about. However, there are a few important differences between exploring this domain through verbal psychotherapy and through approaches using holotropic states. First, one does not just remember emotionally significant events or reconstruct them indirectly from dreams, slips of the tongue, or from transference distortions. One experiences the original emotions, physical sensations, and even sensory perceptions in full age regression.

That means that during the reliving of an important trauma from infancy or childhood the individual actually has the body image, the naive perception of the world, sensations, and the emotions corresponding to the age he or she was at that time. The authenticity of this regression is supported by the fact that the wrinkles in the face of these people temporarily disappear, giving them an infantile expression, the postures and gestures become childlike, and their neurological reflexes take the form characteristic for children (e.g., the sucking reflex and Babinski's reflex).

The second difference between the work on the biographical material in holotropic states, as compared to verbal psychotherapy is that, beside confronting the usual psychotraumas known from handbooks of psychology, people often have to relive and integrate traumas that were primarily of a physical nature. Many people have to process experiences of near drowning, operations, accidents, and children's diseases, particularly those that were associated with suffocation, such as diphtheria, whooping cough, or aspiration of a foreign object.

This material emerges quite spontaneously and without any programming. As it surfaces, people realize that these physical traumas have played a significant role in the psychogenesis of their emotional and psychosomatic problems, such as asthma, migraine headaches, a variety of psychosomatic pains, phobias, sadomasochistic tendencies, or depression and suicidal tendencies. Reliving of such traumatic memories and their integration can then have very far-reaching therapeutic consequences. This contrasts sharply with the attitudes of academic psychiatry and psychology, which do not recognize the direct psychotraumatic impact of physical traumas.

Another new information about the biographical-recollective level of the psyche that emerged from my research was the discovery that emotionally relevant memories are not stored in the unconscious as a mosaic of isolated imprints, but in the form of complex dynamic constellations. I have coined the name *COEX systems* for them, which is short for systems of condensed experience. A COEX system consists of emotionally charged memories from different periods of our life that resemble each other in the quality of emotion or physical sensation that they share. Each COEX has a basic theme that permeates all its layers and represents their common denominator. The individual layers then contain variations on this basic theme that occurred at different periods of the person's life.

The nature of the central theme varies considerably from one COEX to another. The layers of a particular system can, for example contain all the major memories of humiliating, degrading, and shaming experiences that have damaged our self-esteem. In another COEX, the common denominator can be anxiety experienced in various shocking and terrifying situations or claustrophobic and suffocating feelings evoked by oppressive and confining circumstances. Another common motif is rejection and emotional deprivation which damage our ability to trust men, women, or people in general. Situations that have generated profound feelings of guilt and a sense of failure in us, events that have left us with a conviction that sex is dangerous or disgusting, and encounters with indiscriminate aggression and violence are also characteristic examples. COEX systems that contain memories of encounters with situations endangering life, health, and integrity of the body are particularly important.

The above discussion could easily leave the impression that COEX systems always contain painful and traumatic memories. However, it is the intensity of the experience and its emotional relevance that determines whether a memory will be included into a COEX, not its unpleasant nature. In addition to negative constellations there are also those that comprise memories of very pleasant or even ecstatic moments. The concept of COEX dynamics emerged from clinical work with clients suffering from serious forms of psychopathology where the work on traumatic aspects of life plays a very important role. The spectrum of negative COEX systems is also much richer and more variegated than that of the positive ones; it seems that the misery in our life can have many different forms, while happiness depends on the fulfillment of a few basic conditions. However, a general discussion requires that we emphasize that the COEX dynamics is not limited to constellations of traumatic memories.

When I first described the COEX systems in the early stages of my LSD research, I thought that they governed the dynamics of the bio-graphical level of the unconscious. At that time, my understanding of psychology was based on a superficial model of the psyche limited to postnatal biography that I had inherited from my teachers. In addition, in the initial psychedelic sessions, particularly when lower dosages are used, the biographical material often predominates. As my experience with holotropic states became richer and more extensive, I realized that the roots of COEX systems reach much deeper. Each of the COEX con-stellations seems to be superimposed over and anchored in a particular aspect of the trauma of birth.

As we will see later in the discussion of the perinatal level of the unconscious, the experience of birth is so complex and rich in emotions and physical sensations that it contains the elementary themes of all conceivable COEX systems in a prototypical form. In addition, a typical COEX reaches even further and has its deepest roots in various forms of transpersonal phenomena, such as past life experiences, Jungian ar-chetypes, conscious identification with various animals, and others. At present, I see the COEX systems as general organizing principles of the human psyche. The similarities and differences between the concept of COEX systems and Jung's concept of complexes have been discussed elsewhere (Grof 1975, 2000).

The COEX systems play an important role in our psychological life. They can influence the way we perceive ourselves, other people, and the world and how we feel about them. They are the dynamic forces behind our emotional and psychosomatic symptoms, difficulties in relation-ships with other people, and irrational behavior. There exists a dynamic interplay between the COEX systems and the external world. External events in our life can specifically activate corresponding COEX systems and, conversely, active COEX systems can make us perceive the world and behave in such a way that we recreate their core themes in our pres-ent life. This mechanism can be observed very clearly in experiential work. In holotropic states, the content of the experience, the perception of the environment, and the behavior of the client are determined in general terms by the COEX system that dominates the session and more specifically by the layer of this system that is momentarily emerging into consciousness.

All the characteristics of COEX systems can best be demonstrated by a practical example. I have chosen the example of Peter, a thirty-seven-year-old teacher who had been, prior to his psychedelic therapy, intermittently hospitalized and treated without success in our psychiatric department in Prague, for this purpose.

At the time when we began LSD psychotherapy, Peter could barely function in his everyday life. Almost all the time, he was obsessed by the idea to find a man of a certain physical appearance and preferably clad in black. He wanted to befriend this man and tell him about his urgent desire to be locked in a dark cellar and exposed to various diabolic physical and mental tortures. He hoped to find a man who would be willing to participate in this scheme. Unable to concentrate on anything else, he wandered aimlessly through the city, visiting public parks, lavatories, bars, and railroad stations searching for the "right man."

He succeeded on several occasions to persuade or bribe various men who met his criteria to promise to do what he asked. Having a special gift for finding persons with sadistic traits, he was almost killed twice, was several times seriously hurt, and was once robbed of all his money. On those occasions when he was able to experience what he craved for, he was extremely frightened and actually strongly disliked the tortures. In addition to this main problem, Peter suffered from suicidal depressions, impotence, and infrequent epileptiform seizures.

Reconstructing his history, I found out that his major problems started at the time of his compulsory employment in Germany during World War II. The Nazis referred to this form of slave labor using people from occupied territories in hard dangerous work situations as Totaleinsetzung. At that time, two SS officers forced Peter at gun point to engage in their homosexual practices. When the war was over, Peter realized that these experiences led him to have a preference for homosexual intercourse experienced in the passive role. This gradually changed into fetishism for black clothes and finally into the complex obsession described above.

Fifteen consecutive psychedelic sessions revealed an important COEX system underlying this problem. In its most superficial layers were Peter's more recent traumatic experiences with his sadistic partners. One of the accomplices whom he managed to recruit bound him with ropes, locked him in a cellar without food and water, and tortured him by flagellation and strangulation, as per his wish. Another one of these men hit Peter on the head, bound him with a rope, and left him lying in a forest after having stolen his money.

Peter's most dramatic adventure happened with a man who promised to take him to his cabin in the woods that he claimed had just the cellar Peter wanted. When they were traveling by train to this man's weekend house, Peter was struck by his companion's strange-looking bulky backpack. When the latter left the compartment and went to the bathroom, Peter stepped up on the seat and checked the suspect baggage. He discovered a complete set of murder weapons, including a gun, a large butcher knife, a freshly sharpened hatchet, and a surgical saw used for amputations. Panic-stricken, he jumped out of the moving train and suffered serious injuries. Elements of the above episodes formed the most superficial layers of Peter's most important COEX system.

A deeper layer of the same system contained Peter's memories from the Third Reich. In the sessions where this part of the COEX constellation manifested, he relived in detail his experiences with the homosexual SS officers with all the complicated feelings involved. In addition, he relived several other traumatic memories from WW II and dealt with the entire oppressive atmosphere of this period. He had visions of pompous Nazi military parades and rallies, banners with swastikas, ominous giant eagle emblems, scenes from concentration camps, and many others.

Then came layers related to Peter's childhood, particularly those involving punishment by his parents. His alcoholic father was often violent when he was drunk and used to beat him in a sadistic way with a large leather strap. His mother's favorite method of punishing him was to lock him in a dark cellar without food for long periods of time. All through Peter's childhood, she always wore black dresses; he did not remember her ever wearing anything else. At this point, Peter realized that one of the roots of his obsession seemed to be craving for suffering that would combine elements of punishment by both parents.

However, that was not the whole story. As we continued with the sessions, the process deepened and Peter confronted the trauma of his birth with all its biological brutality. This situation had all the elements that he expected from the sadistic treatment he was so desperately trying to receive: dark enclosed space, confinement and restriction of the body movements, and exposure to extreme physical and emotional tortures. Reliving of the trauma of birth finally resolved his difficult symptoms to such an extent that he could again function in life. The above COEX system also had some connections to elements of a transpersonal nature.

Although the above example is more dramatic than most, it effectively illustrates the basic features characteristic for other COEX constellations. In experiential work, the COEX systems operate as functional wholes. While the person involved experiences the emotions and physical feelings characteristic of a particular constellation, the content of its individual layers emerges successively into consciousness and determines the specific nature of the experience.

Before we continue our discussion of the new extended cartography of the human psyche it seems appropriate to emphasize a very important and remarkable property of holotropic states that played an important role in charting the unconscious and that is also invaluable for the process of psychotherapy. Holotropic states tend to engage something like an "inner radar," automatically bringing the contents from the unconscious that have the strongest emotional charge, are currently most psychodynamically relevant, and are currently available for processing into consciousness. This is a great advantage in comparison with verbal psychotherapy, where the client presents a broad array of information of various kinds and the therapist has to decide what is important, what is irrelevant, where the client is blocking, etc.

Since there is no general agreement about basic theoretical issues among different schools, such assessments will always reflect the personal bias of the therapist, as well as the specific views of his or her school. The holotropic states save the therapist such difficult decisions and eliminate much of the subjectivity and professional idiosyncrasy of the verbal approaches. This "inner radar" often surprises the therapist by detecting emotionally strongly charged memories of physical traumas and brings them to the surface for processing and conscious integration. This automatic selection of relevant topics also spontaneously leads the process to the perinatal and transpersonal levels of the psyche, transbiographical domains not recognized and acknowledged in academic psychiatry and psychology. The phenomena originating in these deep recesses of the psyche were well-known to ancient and pre-industrial cultures of all ages and greatly honored by them. In the Western world they have been erroneously attributed to pathology of unknown origin and considered to be meaningless and erratic products of cerebral dysfunction.

The Perinatal Level of the Unconscious

The domain of the psyche that lies immediately beyond (or beneath) the recollective-biographical realm has close connections with the beginning of life and its end, with birth and death. Many people identify the experiences that originate on this level as the reliving of their biological birth trauma. This is reflected in the name *perinatal* that I have suggested for this level of the psyche. It is a Greek-Latin composite word where the prefix *peri-*, means "near" or "around," and the root *natalis* "pertaining to childbirth." This word is commonly used in medicine to describe various biological processes occurring shortly before, during, and immediately after birth. Thus the obstetricians talk, for example, about perinatal hemorrhage, infection, or brain damage. However, since traditional medicine denies that the child can consciously experience birth and claims that the event is not recorded in memory, one does not ever hear about perinatal *experiences*. The use of the term perinatal in connection with consciousness reflects my own findings and is entirely new (Grof 1975).

Academic psychiatry generally denies the possibility of a psychotraumatic impact from biological birth, unless the trauma is so serious that it causes irreversible damage to the brain cells. This is usually attributed to the fact that the cerebral cortex of the newborn is not myelinized, which means its neurons are not fully protected by sheaths of fatty substance called *myelin*. The assumption that the child does not experience anything during all the hours of this extremely painful and stressful event and that the birth process does not leave any record in the brain is astonishing, since it is known that the capacity for memory exists in many lower life forms that do not have a cerebral cortex at all. However, it is particularly striking in view of the fact that many current theories attribute great significance to nuances of nursing and to the early interaction between the mother and the child, including bonding. Such blatant logical contradiction appearing in rigorous scientific thinking is unbelievable and has to be the result of a profound emotional repression to which the memory of birth is subjected.

People who reach the perinatal level in their inner explorations experience emotions and physical sensations of extreme intensity, often surpassing anything they had previously considered humanly possible. These experiences represent a very strange mixture and combination of two critical aspects of human life -- birth and death. They combine a sense of severe, life-threatening confinement with a desperate and determined struggle to free oneself and survive. The intimate connection between birth and death on the perinatal level reflects the fact that birth is in fact a potentially life-threatening event. The child and the mother can actually lose their lives during this process and children can be born blue from asphyxiation or even dead and in need of resuscitation.

As their name indicates, an important core of perinatal experiences is the reliving of various aspects of the biological birth process. It often involves photographic details and occurs even in people who have no intellectual knowledge about their birth. The replay of the original birth situation can be very convincing. We can, for example, discover through direct experience that we had a breech birth, that a forceps was used during our delivery, or that we were born with the umbilical cord twisted around the neck. We can feel the anxiety, biological fury, physical pain, and suffocation associated with this terrifying event and even accurately recognize the type of anesthesia used when we were born.

This is often accompanied by various physical manifestations that an external observer can notice. The postures and movements of the body, arms, and legs, as well as the rotations, flections, and deflections of the head can accurately recreate the mechanics of a particular type of delivery, even in people without elementary obstetric knowledge. Bruises, swellings, and other vascular changes can unexpectedly appear on the skin in the places where the forceps was applied, the wall of the birth canal was pressing on the head, or where the umbilical cord was constricting the throat. The accuracy of all these details can be confirmed if good birth records or reliable personal witnesses are available.

The spectrum of perinatal experiences is not limited to the elements that can be derived from the biological processes involved in childbirth. The perinatal domain of the psyche also represents an important gateway to the collective unconscious in the Jungian sense. Identification with the infant facing the ordeal of the passage through the birth canal seems to provide access to experiences involving people from other times and cultures, various animals, and even mythological figures. It is as if by connecting with the fetus struggling to be born, one reaches an intimate, almost mystical connection with other sentient beings who are in a similar difficult predicament.

Experiential confrontation with birth and death seems to result automatically in a spiritual opening and discovery of the mystical dimensions of the psyche and of existence. It does not seem to make a difference whether it happens symbolically, as in psychedelic and holotropic sessions and in the course of spontaneous psychospiritual crises ("spiritual emergencies") or in actual life situations, for example, in delivering women or in the context of near-death experiences (Ring 1985). The specific symbolism of these experiences comes from the Jungian collective unconscious, not from the individual's memory banks. It can thus draw on any spiritual tradition of the world, quite independently from the subject's cultural or religious background and intellectual knowledge.

Perinatal phenomena occur in four distinct experiential patterns characterized by specific emotions, physical feelings, and symbolic images. Each of them is closely related to one of the four consecutive periods of biological delivery. At each of these stages, the baby undergoes a specific and typical set of experiences. In turn, these experiences form distinct matrices or psychospiritual blueprints whose content can manifest in holotropic states of consciousness and that we find echoing in individual and social psychopathology, religion, art, philosophy, politics, and other areas of our life. We can talk about these four dynamic constellations of the deep unconscious that are associated with the trauma of birth as Basic Perinatal Matrices (BPMs).

Each perinatal matrix has its specific biological, psychological, archetypal, and spiritual aspects. In addition to having specific content of their own, BPMs also function as organizing principles for experiences from other levels of the unconscious. They have specific connections with related postnatal memories arranged in COEX systems and with the archetypes of the Great Mother Goddess, Terrible Mother Goddess, Hell, and Heaven, as well as racial, collective, and karmic memories, and phylogenetic experiences.

BPM I (Primal Union with Mother)

This matrix can be referred to as the "amniotic universe;" it is related to the intrauterine existence before the onset of delivery. The fetus does not have an awareness of boundaries or the ability to differentiate between the inner and outer. This is reflected in the nature of the experiences associated with the reliving of the memory of the prenatal state. During episodes of undisturbed embryonal existence, people can have feelings of vast regions with no boundaries or limits. They can identify with galaxies, interstellar space, or the entire cosmos. A related experience is that of floating in the sea, identifying with various aquatic animals, such as fish, dolphins, or whales, or even becoming the ocean. This seems to reflect the fact that the fetus is essentially an aquatic creature. One might also have archetypal visions of Mother Nature - nature that is beautiful, safe, and unconditionally nourishing, like a good womb. This can involve visions of luscious orchards, fields of ripe corn, agricultural terraces in the Andes, or unspoiled Polynesian islands. Mythological images from the collective unconscious that often appear in this context portray various celestial realms and paradises.

The persons reliving episodes of intrauterine disturbances, or "bad womb" experiences, have a sense of dark and ominous threat and often feel that they are being poisoned. They might see images that portray polluted waters and toxic dumps, reflecting the fact that many prenatal disturbances are caused by toxic changes in the body of the pregnant mother. Sequences of this kind can be associated with visions of frightening demonic entities. Those who relive more violent interferences with prenatal existence, such as imminent miscarriage or attempted abortion, usually experience some form of universal threat or bloody apocalyptic visions of the end of the world. This again reflects the intimate interconnections between events in one's biological history and Jungian archetypes.

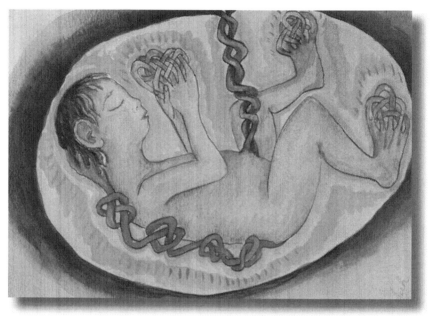

Undisturbed intrauterine life (BPM I)
The entanglement and interconnectedness of the fingers and toes represents the experience of the fetal body image that is different from that of an adult.

The following account of a high dose psychedelic session can be used as a typical example of a BPM I experience, opening at times into the transpersonal realm.

All that I was experiencing was an intense sense of malaise resembling a flu. I could not believe that a high dose of LSD that in my previous sessions had produced dramatic changes — to the point that on occasions I was afraid that my sanity or even my life was at stake — could evoke such a minimal response. I decided to close my eyes and observe carefully what was happening. At this point, the experience seemed to deepen, and I realized that what with my eyes open appeared to be an adult experience of a viral disease now changed into a realistic situation of a fetus suffering some strange toxic insults during its intrauterine existence.

I was greatly reduced in size, and my head was disproportionately larger than the rest of my body and extremities. I was suspended in a liquid milieu and some harmful chemicals were being channeled into my body through the umbilical area. Using some unknown receptors, I was detecting these influences as noxious and hostile to my organism. While this was happening, I was aware

Amniotic universe
*A painting representing a blissful episode of intrauterine life (BPM I) in
a high-dose LSD session. Regression to prenatal life mediates access to the
experience of oneness with the cosmos. The shape of the galaxy resembling a
female breast ("Milky Way") suggest simultaneous experiential connection
with the memories of the "good breast."*

that these toxic "attacks" had something to do with the condition and activity of the maternal organism. Occasionally, I could distinguish influences that
appeared to be due to ingestion of alcohol, inappropriate food, or smoking and
others that I perceived as chemical mediators of my mother's emotions —anxiet-
ies, nervousness, anger, conflicting feelings about pregnancy, and even sexual
arousal.

Then the feelings of sickness and indigestion disappeared, and I was experiencing an ever-increasing state of ecstasy. This was accompanied by a clearing
and brightening of my visual field. It was as if multiple layers of thick, dirty
cobwebs were being magically torn and dissolved, or a poor-quality movie projection or television broadcast were being brought into focus by an invisible
cosmic technician. The scenery opened up, and an incredible amount of light
and energy was enveloping me and was streaming in subtle vibrations through
my whole being.

On one level, I was a fetus experiencing the ultimate perfection and bliss

Prenatal Bliss
Experience of the good womb in an LSD session with
simultaneous identification with the archetype of the
Divine Child.

of a good womb and could also switch to the experience of a newborn fusing
with a nourishing and life-giving breast of my mother. On another level, I was
witnessing the spectacle of the macrocosm with countless pulsating and vibrat-
ing galaxies and, at the same time, I could actually become it and be identical
with it. These radiant and breathtaking cosmic vistas were intermingled with
experiences of the equally miraculous microcosm from the dance of atoms and
molecules to the origins of life and the biochemical world of individual cells. For
the first time, I was experiencing the universe for what it really is — an unfath-
omable mystery, a divine play of energy. Everything in this universe appeared
to be conscious and alive.

For some time, I was oscillating between the state of a distressed, sickened
fetus and blissful and serene intrauterine existence. At times, the noxious influ-
ences took the form of insidious demons or malevolent creatures from the world
of fairy tales. During the undisturbed episodes of fetal existence, I experienced
feelings of basic identity and oneness with the universe. It was the Tao, the

Hostile Womb
*A painting from an LSD session depicting the experience of a womb that is
actively attacking the fetus. The aggressive immunological forces take the
form of archetypal animals. (Robin Maynard-Dobbs)*

Descent into the Maelstrom

A painting representing the onset of delivery experienced in a high-dose LSD session as engulfment by a giant whirlpool. The little boat with a skeleton suggests the impending encounter with death.

Beyond that is Within, the Tat tvam asi (Thou art That) of the Upanishads. I lost my sense of individuality; my ego dissolved, and I became all of existence.

Sometimes this experience was intangible and contentless, sometimes it was accompanied by many beautiful visions —archetypal images of Paradise, the ultimate cornucopia, golden age, or virginal nature. I became a dolphin playing in the ocean, a fish swimming in crystal-clear waters, a butterfly floating in mountain meadows, and a seagull gliding by the sea. I was the ocean, animals, plants, and the clouds — sometimes all these at the same time.

Nothing concrete happened later in the afternoon and in the evening hours. I spent most of this time feeling one with nature and the universe, bathed in golden light that was slowly decreasing in intensity.

BPM II (Cosmic Engulfment and No Exit or Hell)

Individuals reliving the onset of biological birth typically feel that they are being sucked into a gigantic whirlpool or swallowed by some mythic beast. They might also experience that the entire world or cosmos is being engulfed. This can be associated with images of devouring archetypal monsters, such as leviathans, dragons, giant snakes, tarantulas, and octopuses. The sense of overwhelming vital threat can lead to intense anxiety and general mistrust bordering on paranoia. Another experiential variety involves the theme of descending into the depths of the underworld, the realm of death, or hell. As Joseph Campbell so eloquently described, this is a universal motif in the mythologies of the hero's journey (Campbell 1956).

A fully developed first stage of biological birth is characterized by a situation where the uterine contractions periodically constrict the fetus and the cervix is not yet open. Each contraction causes compression of the uterine arteries, and the fetus is threatened by lack of oxygen. Reliving this stage is one of the worst experiences a human being can have. One feels caught in a monstrous claustrophobic nightmare, exposed to agonizing emotional and physical pain, and has a sense of utter helplessness and hopelessness. Feelings of loneliness, guilt, the absurdity of life, and existential despair reach metaphysical proportions. A person in this predicament often becomes convinced that this situation will never end and that there is absolutely no way out.

Reliving this stage of birth is typically accompanied by sequences that involve people, animals, and even mythological beings in a similar painful and hopeless predicament. One experiences identification with prisoners in dungeons and inmates of concentration camps or insane asylums, and senses the pain of animals caught in traps. He or she may even feel the intolerable tortures of sinners in hell and the agony of Jesus on the cross or of Sisyphus rolling his boulder up the mountain in the deepest pit of Hades. It is only natural that someone facing this aspect of the psyche would feel a great reluctance to confront it. Going deeper into this experience seems like accepting eternal damnation. However, this state of darkness and abysmal despair is known from the spiritual literature as the Dark Night of the Soul, a stage of spiritual opening that can have an immensely purging and liberating effect.

The most characteristic features of BPM II in its extreme form can be illustrated by the following account from a high-dosage LSD session.

The atmosphere seemed increasingly ominous and fraught with hidden danger. It seemed that the entire room started to turn and I felt drawn into the very center of a threatening whirlpool. I had to think about Edgar Allan Poe's chilling description of a similar situation in "A Descent into the Maelstrom." As the objects in the room seemed to be flying around me in a rotating motion, another image from literature emerged in my mind — the cyclone that in Frank Baum's Wonderful Wizard of Oz sweeps Dorothy away from the monotony of her life in Kansas and sends her on a strange journey of adventure. There was no doubt in my mind that my experience also had something to do with entering the rabbit hole in Alice in Wonderland, and I awaited with great trepidation what world I would find on the other side of the looking glass. The entire universe seemed to be closing in on me and there was nothing I could do to stop this apocalyptic engulfment.

As I was sinking deeper and deeper into the labyrinth of my own unconscious, I felt an on-slaught of anxiety, turning to panic. Everything became dark, oppressive, and terrifying. It was as if the weight of the whole world was encroaching on me exerting incredible hydraulic pressure that threatened to crack my skull and reduce my body to a tiny compact ball. A rapid fugue of memories from my past cascaded through my brain showing me the utter futility and meaninglessness of my life and existence in general. We are born naked, frightened, and in agony and we will leave the world the same way. The existentialists were right! Everything is impermanent, life is nothing else but waiting for Godot! Vanity of vanities, all is vanity!

The discomfort I felt turned to pain and the pain increased to agony. The torture intensified to the point where every cell in my body felt like it was being bored open with a diabolic dentist's drill. Visions of infernal landscapes and devils torturing their victims suddenly brought to me the awareness that I was in Hell. I thought of Dante's Divine Comedy: "Abandon all hope ye who enter!" There seemed to be no way out of this diabolical situation; I was forever doomed without the slightest hope for redemption.

BPM III (The Death-Rebirth Struggle)

Many aspects of this rich and colorful experience can be understood from its association with the second clinical stage of delivery, the propulsion through the birth canal after the cervix opens and the head descends. Beside the elements that are easily comprehensible as natural derivatives of the birth situation, such as sequences of titanic struggle involving strong pressures and energies or scenes of bloody violence and torture, there are others that require special explanation. Sexual imagery, satanic scenes, and encounters with fire are all motifs that are typically associated with this matrix.

There seems to be a mechanism in the human organism that transforms extreme suffering, particularly when it is associated with suffocation, into a strange form of sexual arousal. This explains why a large variety of sexual experiences and visions often occur in connection with the reliving of birth. One can feel a combination of sexual excitement with pain, aggression, or fear, experience various sadomasochistic sequences, rapes, and situations of sexual abuse, or see pornographic images. The fact that, in the final stages of birth, the fetus can encounter various forms of biological material — blood, mucus, urine, and even

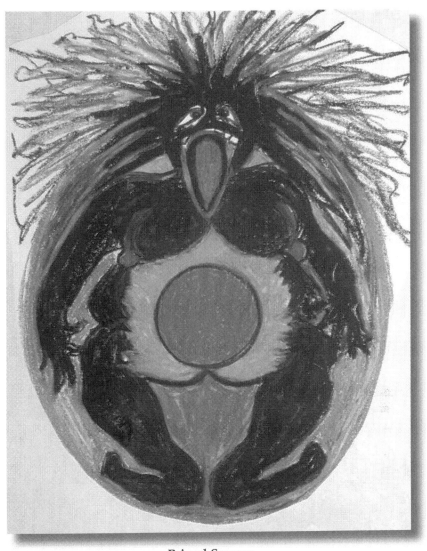

Primal Scream

Powerful release of deep emotions in a Holotropic Breathwork session in which the artist experienced rebirth. (Anne Høivik)

A painting from a high-dose LSD session, in which uterine contractions are represented as attacks by giant predatory birds.

feces — seems to account for the fact that these elements also play a role in death-rebirth sequences.

Another category of motifs associated with BPM III includes archetypal elements from the collective unconscious, particularly those related to heroic figures and deities representing death and rebirth. At this stage, many people have visions of Jesus, his suffering and humiliation, the Way of the Cross, and the Crucifixion, or even actually experience full identification with his hanging on the cross. Others connect with such mythological themes and figures as the Egyptian divine couple Isis and Osiris, the Greek deities Dionysus, Attis, and Adonis, the Sumerian goddess Inanna and her descent into the underworld, the Aztec god Quetzalcoatl, or the Mayan Hero Twins from the Popol Vuh.

The frequent appearance of motifs related to various satanic rituals such as the Witches' Sabbath seems to be related to the fact that reliving this stage of birth involves the same strange combination of emotions, sensations, and elements that characterizes the archetypal scenes of the Black Mass and of Walpurgis' Night: sexual arousal, aggression, pain, sacrifice, and encounters with ordinarily repulsive biological material — all associated with a peculiar sense of sacredness or numinosity.

Just before the experience of (re)birth, people often encounter the motif of fire. This is a somewhat puzzling symbol. Its connection with biological birth is not as direct and obvious as are many of the other symbolic elements. One can experience fire either in its ordinary form or in the archetypal variety of purifying flames. At this stage of the process, the person can have the feeling that his or her body is on fire, have visions of burning cities and forests, or identify with immolation victims. In the archetypal version, the burning seems to have a purgatorial quality. It seems to radically destroy whatever is corrupted and prepare the individual for spiritual rebirth.

Many of the symbolic themes associated with BPM III are described in the following account from a psychedelic session.

Although I never really clearly saw the birth canal, I felt its crushing pressure on my head and all over, and I knew with every cell of my body that I was involved in a birth process. The tension was reaching dimensions that I had not imagined were humanly possible. I felt unrelenting pressure on my forehead, temples, and occiput, as if I were caught in the steel jaws of a vise. The tensions in my body also had a brutally mechanical quality. I imagined myself passing through a monstrous meat grinder or a giant press full of cogs and cylinders. The image of Charlie Chaplin victimized by the world of technology in Modern Times briefly flashed through my mind.

Incredible amounts of energy seemed to be flowing through my entire body, condensing and releasing in explosive discharges. I felt an amazing mixture of feelings: I was suffocated, frightened, and helpless, but also furious and strangely sexually aroused. Another important aspect of my experience was a sense of utter confusion. While I felt like an infant involved in a vicious struggle for survival and realized that what was about to happen was my birth, I was also experiencing myself as my delivering mother. I knew intellectually that being a man I could never have an experience of delivering, yet I felt that I was somehow crossing that barrier and that the impossible was becoming reality.

There was no question that I was connecting with something primordial — an ancient feminine archetype, that of the delivering mother. My body image included a large pregnant belly and female genitals with all the nuances of biological sensations. I felt frustrated by not being able to surrender to this elemental process — to give birth and be born, to let go and to let the baby out. An enormous reservoir of murderous aggression emerged from the underworld of my psyche. It was as if an abscess of evil had suddenly been punctured by the cut of a cosmic surgeon. A werewolf or a berserker was taking me over; Dr. Jekyll was turning into Mr. Hyde. There were many images of the murderer and the victim as being one and the same person, just as earlier I could not distinguish between the child who was being born and the delivering mother.

I was a merciless tyrant, a dictator exposing his subordinates to unimaginable cruelties, and also a revolutionary, leading the furious mob to overthrow the tyrant. I became the mobster who murders in cold blood and the policeman who kills the criminal in the name of law. At one point, I experienced the horrors of the Nazi concentration camps. When I opened my eyes, I saw myself as an SS officer. I had a profound sense that he, the Nazi, and I, the Jew, were the same person. I could feel the Hitler and the Stalin in me and felt fully responsible for the atrocities in human history. I saw clearly that humanity's problem is not the existence of vicious dictators, but this Hidden Killer that we all find within our own psyche, if we look deep enough.

Then the nature of the experience changed and reached mythological proportions. Instead of the evil of human history, I now sensed the atmosphere of witchcraft and the presence of demonic elements. My teeth were transformed into long fangs filled with some mysterious poison, and I found myself flying on large bat wings through the night like an ominous vampire. This changed soon into wild, intoxicating scenes of a Witches' Sabbath. In this strange, sensuous ritual, all the usually forbidden and repressed impulses seemed to surface and found their full expression. I was aware of participating in some mysterious sacrificial ceremony celebrating the Dark God.

As the demonic quality gradually disappeared from my experience, I felt tremendously erotic and was engaged in endless sequences of the most fantastic orgies and sexual fantasies, in which I played all the roles. All through these experiences, I simultaneously continued being also the child struggling through

Psychospiritual Death and Rebirth

Experience from a Holotropic Breathwork session, in which the vision of the peacock tail (like the famous cauda pavonic in the alchemical process) appears as a symbol of transformation and transfiguration. (Anne Høivik)

the birth canal and the mother delivering it. It became very clear to me that sex, birth, and death were deeply connected and that satanic forces had important links with the propulsion through the birth canal. I struggled and fought in many different roles and against many different enemies. Sometimes I wondered if there would ever be an end to my awful predicament.

Then a new element entered my experience. My entire body was covered with some biological filth, which was slimy and slippery. I could not tell if it was the amniotic fluid, urine, mucus, blood, or vaginal secretions. The same stuff seemed to be in my mouth and even in my lungs. I was choking, gagging, making faces, and spitting, trying to get it out of my system and off my skin. At the same time, I was getting a message that I did not have to fight. The process had its own rhythm and all I had to do was surrender to it. I remembered many situations from my life, where I felt the need to fight and struggle and, in retrospect, that too felt unnecessary. It was as if I had been somehow programmed by my birth to see life as much more complicated and dangerous than it actually is. It seemed to me that this experience could open my eyes in this regard and make my life much easier and more playful than before.

BPM IV (The Death-Rebirth Experience)

This matrix is related to the third stage of delivery, to the final emergence from the birth canal and the severing of the umbilical cord. Here the fetus completes the preceding difficult process of propulsion through the birth canal and achieves explosive liberation as it emerges into light. Reliving of this stage of birth often involves various specific concrete and realistic memories, such as the experience of anesthesia, the pressures of the forceps, and the sensations associated with various obstetric maneuvers or postnatal interventions.

To understand why the reliving of biological birth is experienced as death and rebirth, one has to realize that what happens is more than just a replay of the original event. Because the fetus is completely confined during the birth process and has no way of expressing the extreme emotions and sensations involved, the memory of this event remains psychologically undigested and unassimilated. The way we in later life experience ourselves and the world is heavily tainted by this constant reminder of the vulnerability, inadequacy, and weakness that we experienced at birth. In a sense, we were born anatomically but have not caught up with this fact emotionally. The "dying" and the agony during the struggle for rebirth reflect the actual pain and vital threat of the biological birth process. However, the ego death that precedes rebirth is related to the extinction of our old concepts of who we are and what the world is like, which were forged by the traumatic imprint of birth.

Peacock Heaven

The final stage of the psychospiritual process of death and rebirth from a psychedelic session. The body of the newborn is still in the birth canal consumed by flames, but its head emerges into a peacock heaven of a Great Mother Goddess.

As we are purging these old programs by letting them emerge into consciousness, they are becoming irrelevant and are, in a sense, dying. As frightening as this process is, it is actually very healing and transforming. Approaching the moment of the ego death might feel like the end of the world. Paradoxically, when only a small step separates us from an experience of radical liberation, we have a sense of all-pervading anxiety and impending catastrophe of enormous proportions. It feels as if we are losing all that we are; at the same time, we have no idea of what is on the other side, or even if there is anything there at all. This fear drives many people to resist the process at this stage; as a result, they can remain psychologically stuck in this problematic experiential territory.

When the individual overcomes the metaphysical fear encountered at this important juncture and decides to let things happen, he or she experiences total annihilation on all levels. It involves a sense of physical destruction, emotional disaster, intellectual and philosophical defeat, ultimate moral failure, and even spiritual damnation. During this experience, all reference points — everything that is important and meaningful in the individual's life — seem to be mercilessly destroyed. Immediately following the experience of total annihilation — hitting "cosmic bottom"— one is overwhelmed by visions of light that has a supernatural radiance and beauty and is usually perceived as divine.

The survivor of what seemed like the ultimate apocalyptic destruction experiences only seconds later visions of divine light, radiant celestial beings, paradisean landscapes, fantastic displays of rainbows, and peacock designs. He or she feels redeemed and blessed by salvation, reclaiming his or her divine nature and cosmic status. At this time, one is frequently overcome by a surge of positive emotions toward oneself, other people, nature, and existence in general. This kind of healing and life-changing experience occurs when birth was not too debilitating or confounded by heavy anesthesia. If the latter was the case, the individual has to do psychological work on the specific traumatic issues involved.

The following account of a death-rebirth experience from a psychedelic session describes a typical sequence characteristic of BPM IV.

However, the worst was yet to come. All of a sudden, I seemed to be losing all my connections to reality, as if some imaginary rug was pulled from under my feet. Everything was collapsing and I felt that my entire world was shattered to pieces. It was like puncturing a monstrous metaphysical balloon of my existence; a gigantic bubble of ludicrous self-deception had burst open and exposed the lie of my life. Everything that I ever believed in, everything that I did or pursued, everything that seemed to give my life meaning suddenly appeared utterly false. These were all pitiful crutches without any substance with which I tried to patch up the intolerable reality of existence. They were now blasted and blown away like the frail feathered seeds of a dandelion, exposing a frightening abyss of ultimate truth — the meaningless chaos of the existential Emptiness.

In the next moment, I was facing a terrifying giant figure of a dark goddess whom I identified as the Indian Goddess Kali. My face was being pushed by an irresistible force toward her gaping vagina that was full of what seemed to be menstrual blood or repulsive afterbirth. I sensed that what was demanded of me was absolute surrender to the forces of existence and to the feminine principle represented by the goddess. I had no choice but to kiss and lick her bleeding vulva in utmost submission and humility. At this moment, which was the ultimate and final end of any feeling of male supremacy and machismo I had ever harbored, I connected with the memory of the moment of my biological birth. My head was emerging from the birth canal with my mouth in close contact with the bleeding vagina of my mother.

Filled with indescribable horror, I saw a gigantic figure of a deity towering over me in a threatening pose. I somehow instinctively recognized that this was Bhairava, the Hindu god Shiva in his destructive aspect. I felt the thunderous impact of his enormous foot that crushed me, shattered me to smithereens, and smeared me like an insignificant piece of excrement all over what I felt was the bottom of the cosmos. Just as I experienced total annihilation, there appeared divine light of supernatural radiance and beauty whose rays exploded into thousands of exquisite peacock designs. From this brilliant golden light emerged a figure of a Great Mother Goddess who seemed to embody love and protection through the ages. She spread her arms and reached toward me, enveloping me into her essence. I merged with this incredible energy field, feeling purged, healed, and nourished. What seemed to be some divine nectar and ambrosia, some archetypal essence of milk and honey, was pouring through me in absolute abundance.

Then the figure of the goddess gradually disappeared, absorbed by an even more brilliant light. It was abstract, yet endowed with definite personal characteristics, conscious, and radiating infinite intelligence. It became clear to me that what I was experiencing was the merging with and absorption into the Universal Self, or Brahman, as I have read about it in books of Indian philosophy. This experience subsided after about ten minutes of clock-time; however, it transcended any concept of time and felt like eternity. The flow of the healing and nourishing energy and the visions of golden glow with peacock designs lasted through the night. The resulting sense of wellbeing stayed with me for many days. The memory of the experience has remained vivid for years and has profoundly changed my entire life philosophy.

The Transpersonal Domain of the Psyche

The second major domain that has to be added to mainstream psychiatry's cartography of the human psyche when we work with holotropic states is now known under the name *transpersonal,* meaning literally "beyond the personal" or "transcending the personal." The experiences that originate on this level involve transcendence of the usual boundaries of the individual (his or her body and ego) and of the usual limitations of three-dimensional space and linear time that restrict our perception of the world in the ordinary state of consciousness. The transpersonal experiences are best defined by describing first the everyday experience of ourselves and the world - how we have to experience ourselves and the environment to pass for "normal" according to the standards of our culture and of traditional psychiatry.

In the ordinary or "normal" state of consciousness, we experience ourselves as Newtonian objects existing within the boundaries of our skin. The American writer and philosopher Alan Watts referred to this experience of oneself as identifying with the "skin-encapsulated ego." Our perception of the environment is restricted by the physiological limitations of our sensory organs and by physical characteristics of the environment. For example, we cannot see objects from which we are separated by a solid wall, ships that are beyond the horizon, or the other side of the moon. If we are in Prague, we cannot hear what our friends are talking about in San Francisco. We cannot feel the softness of the lambskin unless the surface of our body is in direct contact with it. In addition, we can experience vividly and with all our senses only the events that are happening in the present moment. We can recall the past and anticipate future events or fantasize about them; however, these are very different experiences from the immediate and direct experience of the present moment. In transpersonal states of consciousness none of these limitations are absolute; any of them can be transcended.

Transpersonal experiences can be divided into three large categories. The first of these involves primarily transcendence of the usual spatial barriers, or the limitations of the "skin-encapsulated ego. Here belong experiences of merging with another person into a state that can be called "dual unity," assuming the identity of another person, identifying with the consciousness of an entire group of people (e.g. all mothers of the world, the entire population of India, or all the inmates of concentration camps), or even experiencing an extension of consciousness that seems to encompass all of humanity. Experiences of this kind have been repeatedly described in the spiritual literature of the world.

In a similar way, one can transcend the limits of the specifically human experience and identify with the consciousness of various animals, plants, or even with a form of consciousness that seems to be associated with inorganic objects and processes. In the extremes, it is possible to experience consciousness of the entire biosphere, of our planet, or the entire material universe. Incredible and absurd as it might seem to a Westerner committed to materialistic philosophy and to the Cartesian-Newtonian paradigm, these experiences suggest that everything that we can experience in our everyday state of consciousness as an object, has in the holotropic states of consciousness a corresponding subjective representation. It is as if everything in the universe has its objective and subjective aspect, the way it is described in the great spiritual philosophies of the East. For example, in Hinduism all that exists is seen as a manifestation of Brahman and in Taoism as a transformation of the Tao.

The second category of transpersonal experiences is characterized primarily by the overcoming of temporal rather than spatial boundaries, by transcendence of linear time. We have already talked about the possibility of vivid reliving of important memories from infancy and of the trauma of birth. This historical regression can continue farther and involve authentic fetal and embryonal memories from different periods of intrauterine life. It is not even unusual to experience, on the level of cellular consciousness, full identification with the sperm and the ovum at the time of conception. But the historical regression does not stop even here; it is possible to have experiences from the lives of one's human or animal ancestors, and those that seem to be coming from the racial and collective unconscious as described by C. G. Jung. Quite frequently, the experiences that seem to be happening in other cultures and historical periods are associated with a sense of personal remembering (déjà vu); people then talk about reliving of memories from past lives, from previous incarnations.

In the transpersonal experiences described so far, the content reflected various phenomena existing in space-time. They involved elements of the everyday familiar reality - other people, animals, plants, materials, and events from the past. What is surprising about these experiences is not their content, but the fact that we can witness or fully identify with something that is not ordinarily accessible to our experience. We know that there are pregnant whales in the world, but we should not be able to have an authentic experience of being one. The fact that there was once a French revolution is readily acceptable, but we should not be able to have a vivid experience of being there and lying wounded on the barricades of Paris. We know that there are many things happening in the world in places where we are not present, but it is usually considered impossible to actually experience or observe something that is hap-

The Dragon Mother
The artist's traumatic childhood memory in a Holotropic Breathwork session reflecting her mother's intolerance of strong emotions. The Dragon Mother shakes and frightens the infant to make her stop crying. Her message is: "If you cry, you die." (Jan Vannatta)

pening in remote locations (without the mediation of the television and a satellite). We may also be surprised to find consciousness associated with lower animals, plants, and with inorganic objects and processes.

The third category of transpersonal experiences is even stranger; here consciousness seems to extend into realms and dimensions that the Western industrial culture does not even consider to be "real." Here belong numerous encounters or even identification with deities and demons of various cultures and other archetypal figures, visits to mythological landscapes, and communication with discarnate beings, spirit guides, suprahuman entities, extraterrestrials, and inhabitants of parallel universes. Additional examples in this category are visions and intuitive understanding of universal symbols, such as the cross, the Nile cross or ankh, the swastika, the pentacle, the six-pointed star, or the yin-yang sign.

In its farther reaches, individual consciousness can identify with cosmic consciousness or the Universal Mind known under many different names - Brahman, Buddha, the Cosmic Christ, Keter, Allah, the Tao, the Great Spirit, and many others. The ultimate of all experiences appears to be identification with the Supracosmic and Metacosmic Void, the mysterious and primordial emptiness and nothingness that is conscious of itself and is the ultimate cradle of all existence. It has no concrete content, yet it contains all there is in a germinal and potential form.

Transpersonal experiences have many strange characteristics that shatter the most fundamental metaphysical assumptions of the Newtonian-Cartesian paradigm and of the materialistic world view. Researchers who have studied and/or personally experienced these fascinating phenomena realize that the attempts of mainstream science to dismiss them as irrelevant products of human fantasy and imagination or as hallucinations - erratic products of pathological processes in the brain - are naive and inadequate. Any unbiased study of the transpersonal domain of the psyche has to come to the conclusion that these observations represent a critical challenge not only for psychiatry and psychology, but for the entire philosophy of Western science.

Although transpersonal experiences occur in the process of deep individual self-exploration, it is not possible to interpret them simply as intrapsychic phenomena in the conventional sense. On the one hand, they appear on the same experiential continuum as the biographical and perinatal experiences and are thus coming from within the individual psyche. On the other hand, they seem to be tapping directly, without the mediation of the senses, into sources of information that are clearly far beyond the conventional reach of the individual. Somewhere on the perinatal level of the psyche, a strange flip seems to occur and what was up to that point deep intrapsychic probing becomes experiencing of the universe at large through extrasensory means. Some people have compared this to an "experiential Moebius strip," since it is impossible any more to say what is inside and what is outside.

These observations indicate that we can obtain information about the universe in two radically different ways: besides the conventional possibility of learning through sensory perception and analysis and synthesis of the data, we can also find out about various aspects of the world by direct identification with them in a holotropic state of consciousness. Each of us thus appears to be a microcosm containing in a holographic way the information about the macrocosm. In the mystical traditions, this was expressed by such phrases as: "as above so below" or "as without, so within."

The reports of subjects who have experienced episodes of embryonal existence, the moment of conception, and elements of cellular, tissue, and organ consciousness abound in medically accurate insights into the anatomical, physiological, and biochemical aspects of the processes involved. Similarly, ancestral, racial and collective memories and past incarnation experiences frequently provide very specific details about architecture, costumes, weapons, art forms, social structure, and religious and ritual practices of the culture and historical period involved, or even concrete historical events.

People who have phylogenetic experiences or experience identification with existing life forms not only find them unusually authentic and convincing, but often acquire in the process extraordinary insights concerning animal psychology, ethology, specific habits, or unusual reproductive cycles. In some instances, this is accompanied by archaic muscular innervations not characteristic for humans, or even such complex behaviors as enactment of a courtship dance of a particular animal species.

The philosophical and scientific challenge associated with the already described observations, as formidable as it is all by itself, is further augmented by the fact that transpersonal experiences correctly reflecting the material world often appear on the same continuum as and intimately interwoven with others that contain elements which the Western industrial world does not consider to be real. Here belong, for example, experiences involving deities and demons from various cultures, mythological realms such as heavens and paradises, and legendary or fairytale sequences.

For example, one can have an experience of Shiva's heaven, of the paradise of the Aztec rain god Tlaloc, of the Sumerian underworld, or of one of the Buddhist hot hells. It is also possible to communicate with Jesus, have a shattering encounter with the Hindu goddess Kali, or identify with the dancing Shiva. Even these episodes can impart accurate new information about religious symbolism and mythical motifs that were previously unknown to the person involved. *Observations of this kind confirm C. G. Jung's idea that beside the Freudian individual unconscious we can also gain access to the collective unconscious that contains the cultural heritage of all humanity.*

It is not an easy task to convey in a few sentences conclusions from daily observations from over fifty years of research of holotropic states of consciousness and make this statement believable. It is not realistic to expect that a few sentences would be able to override the deeply culturally ingrained worldview in those readers who are not familiar with the transpersonal dimension and who cannot relate what I say to their own personal experiences. Although I myself had many experiences of holotropic states and the opportunity to observe them closely in thousands of other people, it took me years to fully absorb the impact of this cognitive shock.

Because of space considerations, I cannot present detailed case histories that could help to illustrate the nature of transpersonal experiences and the insights which they make available. I have to refer those readers who would like to explore this area further to my books The Adventure of Self-Discovery, Psychology of the Future, and When the Impossible Happens (Grof 1988, 2000, 2006 a), where I discuss in detail various types of transpersonal experiences and give many illustrative examples of situations where they provided unusual new information about different aspects of the universe. The book Holotropic Breathwork: A New Approach to Self-Exploration and Therapy (Grof and Grof, 2010) co-written with Christina Grof describes the method of Holotropic Breathwork, which opens the access to the perinatal and transpersonal realms for anybody who is interested in personal verification of the above observations. Comparable information focusing specifically on psychedelic sessions can be found in my book LSD Psychotherapy that has now been available for several years in a new edition (Grof 2001).

The existence and nature of transpersonal experiences violates some of the most basic assumptions of mechanistic science. They imply such seemingly absurd notions as the relative and arbitrary nature of all physical boundaries, non-local connections in the universe, communication through unknown means and channels, memory without a material substrate, nonlinearity of time, or consciousness associated with all living organisms, and even inorganic matter. Many transpersonal experiences involve events from the microcosm and the macrocosm, realms that cannot normally be reached by unaided human senses, or from historical periods that precede the origin of the solar system, formation of planet earth, appearance of living organisms, development of the nervous system, and emergence of homo sapiens.

The research of holotropic states thus reveals an astonishing paradox concerning the nature of human beings. It clearly shows that, in a mysterious and yet unexplained way, each of us harbors the information about the entire universe and all of existence, has potential experiential access to all of its parts, and in a sense is the whole cosmic network, as much as he or she is just an infinitesimal part of it, a separate and insignificant biological entity. The new cartography reflects this fact and portrays the individual human psyche as being essentially commensurate with the entire cosmos and the totality of existence. As absurd and implausible as this idea might seem to a traditionally trained scientist and to our common sense, it can be relatively easily reconciled with new revolutionary developments in various scientific disciplines usually referred to as the new or emerging paradigm.

I firmly believe that the expanded cartography, which I have outlined above, is of critical importance for any serious approach to such phenomena as shamanism, rites of passage, mysticism, religion, mythology, parapsychology, near-death experiences, and psychedelic states. This new model of the psyche is not just a matter of academic interest. As I will try to show in the remaining pages of this chapter, it has deep and revolutionary implications for the understanding of emotional and psychosomatic disorders and offers new and revolutionary therapeutic possibilities.

2. The Nature and Architecture of Emotional and Psychosomatic Disorders

Traditional psychiatry uses the medical model and the disease concept not only for disorders of a clearly organic nature, but also for emotional and psychosomatic disorders for which no biological cause has been found. Psychiatrists use the term "mental disease" quite loosely and try to assign various emotional disorders to specific diagnostic categories comparable to those of somatic medicine. Generally, the time of the onset of symptoms is seen as the beginning of the "disease" and the intensity of the symptoms is used as the measure of the seriousness of the pathological process. Alleviation of the symptoms is considered "clinical improvement" and their intensification is seen as "worsening of the clinical condition. "

The observations from the study of holotropic states suggest that thinking in terms of disease, diagnosis, and allopathic therapy is not appropriate for most psychiatric problems that are not clearly organic in nature, including some of the conditions currently labeled as psychoses. We have all experienced the vicissitudes and challenges of embryological development, birth, infancy and childhood. This has left traumatic imprints in the unconscious of all of us, although we certainly differ as to the intensity, extensity, and also availability of these memories for conscious experience. Every person also carries a variety of more or less latent emotional and bioenergetic blockages which interfere with full physiological and psychological functioning.

The manifestation of emotional and psychosomatic symptoms is the beginning of a healing process through which the organism is trying to free itself from these traumatic imprints and simplify its functioning. The only way this can happen is by emergence of the traumatic material into consciousness and its full experience and emotional and motor expression. If the trauma that is being processed is of major proportions, such as a difficult birth that lasted many hours and seriously threat-

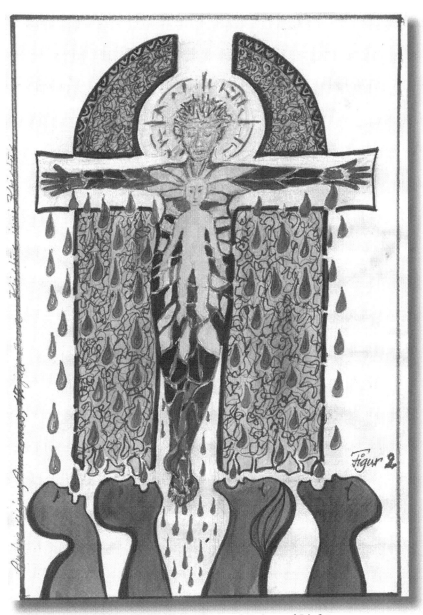

Vision of the Transformed Being of Light
inside the body of a Female Christ from a Holotropic Breathwork session.
(Anne Høivik)

ened biological survival, the emotions and behavioral expressions can be extremely dramatic. Under these circumstances, it might seem more plausible to conclude that these manifestations are the result of some exotic yet unknown pathology rather than realize that they represent a potentially beneficial process. However, properly understood and supported, even such extreme symptoms can be conducive to healing, spiritual opening, personality transformation, and consciousness evolution.

The emergence of symptoms thus represents not only a problem, but also a therapeutic opportunity; this insight is the basis of most experiential psychotherapies. Symptoms manifest in the area where the defense system is at its weakest, making it possible for the healing process to begin. According to my experience, this is true not only for neuroses and psychosomatic disorders, but also for many conditions traditionally labeled functional psychoses. It is interesting to mention in this context that the Chinese pictogram for "crisis" is composed of two simpler ones, one meaning "danger" and the other "opportunity." The idea that the symptoms are not manifestations of disease but are expressions of a healing process and should be supported is the basic tenet of a therapeutic system called homeopathy (Vithoulkas 1980).

In traditional psychotherapy, emotional and psychosomatic symptoms that are not of organic but rather psychogenic origin are seen as resulting from postnatal biographical traumas, especially those that occurred in infancy and childhood. Therapeutic work using holotropic states reveals that they usually have additional deeper roots on the perinatal and transpersonal levels. Thus, for example, someone suffering from psychogenic asthma can discover that the biographical material underlying this disorder consists of memories of suffocation during a near-drowning accident in childhood and an episode of diphtheria in infancy. On a deeper level, the same problem is also connected with choking in the birth canal. And its deepest root can be a past life experience of being strangled or hanged. To fully resolve this symptom, it is necessary to work through all the layers of unconscious problems with which it is associated. New insights concerning this multilevel dynamic structure of the major forms of emotional and psychosomatic disorders were described in detail elsewhere (Grof 1985, 2000).

3. THERAPEUTIC MECHANISMS AND THE PROCESS OF HEALING

The work with holotropic states has thus shown that emotional and psychosomatic problems are much more complex than is usually assumed and that their roots reach incomparably deeper into the psyche. However, it has also revealed the existence of deeper and more effective therapeutic mechanisms. Traditional schools of psychotherapy recognize only therapeutic mechanisms related to postnatal biographical material and the individual unconscious. For example, they value the lifting of psychological repression and the remembering of events from infancy and childhood; reconstructing such events from free associations, dreams, and neurotic symptoms; emotional and intellectual insights into one's life history; and analysis of transference.

The new observations show that these approaches fail to recognize and appreciate the extraordinary healing potential of the deeper dynamics of the psyche. Thus, for example, the reliving of birth and the experience of ego death and psychospiritual rebirth can have far-reaching therapeutic impact on a broad spectrum of emotional disorders. Effective therapeutic mechanisms are also associated with various forms of transpersonal phenomena, such as past life experiences, encounters with archetypal figures and motifs, and identification with various animals. Of particular importance in this respect are ecstatic feelings of oneness with other people, nature, the universe, and God. If they are allowed to run their full course and are properly integrated, such experiences represent a healing mechanism of extraordinary power.

These observations show that the conceptual framework of psychotherapy has to be extended as vastly as the cartography of the unconscious. Freud once used a metaphor of the iceberg to describe the human psyche. What was generally thought to be the totality of the psyche was just like the tip of the iceberg showing above the water surface. The bulk of this iceberg hidden under water corresponded to the unconscious realms revealed by psychoanalysis. In view of the discoveries of modern consciousness research, we can paraphrase this simile and say that all that Freudian psychoanalysis has discovered about the human psyche represents at best the exposed part of the iceberg, while vast domains of the unconscious resisted Freud's efforts and remained hidden even for him. Mythologist Joseph Campbell, using his incisive Irish humor, put it very succinctly: "Freud was fishing while sitting on a whale."

4. THE STRATEGY OF PSYCHOTHERAPY AND SELF-EXPLORATION

Modern psychotherapy is plagued by an astonishing lack of agreement among its different schools about the most fundamental questions concerning the functioning and the main motivating forces of the human psyche; the cause, nature, and dynamics of symptoms; and the strategy and technique of psychotherapy. This does not apply only to the schools based on entirely different philosophical assumptions, such as behaviorism, psychoanalysis, and existential therapy, but also to the various branches of depth psychology that evolved historically from the same source, the original work of Sigmund Freud - the Adlerian, Rankian,

Jungian, Kleinian, Reichian, and Lacanian schools, ego psychology, and many others.

The world of modern psychotherapy resembles a large busy market place, in which it is difficult to orient oneself. Each of the many schools offers a different explanation for the same emotional and psychosomatic disorder and uses a different therapeutic technique. Each of these approaches is presented as the scientific way to understand and treat these problems. It is difficult to envision a similar degree of disagreement in one of the hard sciences. Yet in psychology, we have somehow learned to live with this situation and do not usually even question it or consider it strange.

There are no convincing statistical studies showing that one form of psychotherapy is superior to others. The differences seem to be within the schools rather than between them. Psychotherapy is generally as good as the therapist; good therapists of all schools tend to get better results and bad therapists are less successful without regard to their orientation. Clearly, the results of psychotherapy have very little to do with the theoretical concepts of a particular school and with what the therapists think they are doing -- the content and the timing of interpretations, analysis of transference, strategic use of silence, and so on.

It seems that the factors which play a critical role in psychotherapy are very different from those that are usually discussed in professional books. They are also very difficult to describe in scientific terms, as exemplified by such descriptions as "the quality of human encounter between the therapist and the client" or "the client's feeling of being unconditionally accepted by another human being, often for the first time in his or her life." Under these circumstances, if we opt as beginning professionals for a certain school of psychotherapy, for example Freudian, Reichian, Jungian, or Sullivanian, it is because we are attracted to it for very personal reasons. It is a purely subjective choice reflecting our own personality structure and it has very little to do with the objective value and scientific accuracy of that particular approach.

The work with holotropic states suggests a very interesting alternative: if the experts cannot reach agreement, why not trust one's own healing intelligence, one's own inner healer? This approach was first suggested by C. G. Jung. He was aware of the fact that it is impossible to reach intellectual understanding of how the psyche functions and why the symptoms develop and derive from it a technique that makes it possible to correct the psychological functioning of other people. According to Jung, the psyche is not a product of the brain; it is a cosmic principle (*anima mundi*) that permeates all of existence and our individual psyche partakes in this cosmic matrix.

The intellect is just a partial function of the psyche which makes it possible for us to orient ourselves in practical situations and to solve everyday problems; it is incapable of fathoming and manipulating the psyche. Jung saw the task of the therapist in helping to establish a dynamic interaction between the client's conscious ego and the Self, a higher aspect of the client's personality; this interaction takes the form of a dialectic exchange using the language of symbols. The healing then comes from the collective unconscious and it is guided by an inner intelligence whose immense wisdom surpasses the knowledge of any individual therapist or therapeutic school. This is the essence of what Jung called the *individuation process.*

Therapeutic work with holotropic states, as exemplified by psychedelic therapy or Holotropic Breathwork, generally supports Jung's understanding of the therapeutic process. However, it is much more effective than the therapeutic techniques which were available to Jung such as the analysis of dreams and the method of active imagination. Holotropic states tend to activate the spontaneous healing potential of the psyche and of the body and initiate a transformative process guided by deep inner intelligence. In this process, unconscious material with strong emotional charge and relevance will automatically emerge into consciousness and become available for full experience and integration.

The task of the therapist is to offer a method that induces a holotropic state of consciousness (e.g. a psychedelic substance or faster breathing and evocative music), to create a safe environment, and to support unconditionally and with full trust the spontaneous unfolding of the process. This trust has to extend even to situations where the therapist does not understand intellectually what is happening. Healing and resolution can often occur in ways that transcend rational understanding. In this form of therapy, the therapist thus is not the doer, the agent who is instrumental in the healing process, but a sympathetic supporter and co-adventurer. This attitude is in consonance with the original meaning of the Greek word *therapeutes,* which means attendant or assistant in the healing process.

5. THE ROLE OF SPIRITUALITY IN HUMAN LIFE

Traditional psychology and psychiatry are dominated by materialistic philosophy and have no recognition of spirituality in any form. From the point of view of Western science, the material world represents the only reality and any form of spiritual belief is seen as reflecting a lack of education, primitive superstition, magical thinking, or regression to infantile patterns of functioning. Direct experiences of spiritual realities are then relegated to the world of gross psychopathology and serious mental disorders. Western psychiatry makes no distinction between a mystical experience and a psychotic experience and sees both as manifestations of mental disease. In its rejection of religion, it does not differentiate primitive folk beliefs or fundamentalists' literal interpretations of scriptures from sophisticated mystical traditions and Eastern spiritual philosophies based on centuries of systematic introspective exploration of the psyche. It pathologizes spirituality of any kind and together with it the entire spiritual history of humanity.

The observations from the study of holotropic states confirm an important insight of C.G. Jung. According to him, the experiences originating in deeper levels of the psyche (in my own terminology perinatal and transpersonal experiences) have a certain quality that he called (after Rudolph Otto) *numinosity*. They are associated with the feeling that one is encountering a dimension which is sacred, holy, and radically different from everyday life, and which belongs to a superior order of reality. The term *numinous* is relatively neutral and thus preferable to others, such as religious, mystical, magical, holy, or sacred, which have often been used incorrectly and are easily misleading.

To prevent confusion and misunderstandings that in the past have compromised many similar discussions, it is critical to make a clear distinction between spirituality and religion. Spirituality is based on direct experiences of other realities. It does not necessarily require a special place or a special person mediating contact with the divine, although mystics can certainly benefit from spiritual guidance and a community of fellow seekers. Spirituality involves a special relationship between the individual and the cosmos and is in its essence a personal and private affair. At the cradle of all great religions were visionary (perinatal and/or transpersonal) experiences of their founders, prophets, saints, and even ordinary followers. All major spiritual scriptures -- the Vedas, the Buddhist Pali Canon, the Bible, the Koran, the Book of Mormon, and many others are based on revelations in holotropic states of consciousness.

By comparison, the basis of organized religion is institutionalized group activity that takes place in a designated location (temple, church), and involves a system of appointed officials. Ideally, religions should provide for their members access to and support for direct spiritual experiences. However, it often happens that an organized religion sooner or later completely loses the connection with its spiritual source and becomes a secular institution exploiting human spiritual needs without satisfying them. Instead, it creates a hierarchical system focusing on the pursuit of power, control, politics, money, and other possessions. Under these circumstances, religious hierarchy tends to actively discourage and suppress direct spiritual experiences in its members, because they foster independence and cannot be effectively controlled. When this happens, genuine spiritual life continues only in the mystical branches and monastic orders.

From the scientific point of view, the main question is the ontological status of transpersonal experiences. While mainstream psychiatry and psychology see them as indications of pathology, transpersonal psychology considers them important phenomena *sui generis* that have great heuristic and therapeutic value and deserve to be seriously studied. While much of what is found in mainstream religions and their theologies is certainly in serious conflict with science, this is not true in regard to spirituality based on direct transpersonal experiences. The findings of modern consciousness research show remarkable convergence with many revolutionary developments in Western science referred to as the emerging paradigm. As Ken Wilber has noted, there cannot possibly be a conflict between genuine science and authentic religion. If there seems to be a conflict, we are very likely dealing with "bogus science" and/or "bogus religion," where either side has a serious misunderstanding of the other's position and very likely represents a false or fake version of its own discipline (Wilber 2000 a).

6. The Nature of Reality

As we have seen, the observations from the research of holotropic states represent a serious challenge to contemporary psychiatry and psychology and require a drastic revision of our thinking in these fields. However, many of them are of such a fundamental nature that they transcend the narrow frame of these disciplines and challenge the most basic metaphysical assumptions of Western science and its Newtonian-Cartesian paradigm. They seriously undermine the belief that consciousness is a product of neurophysiological processes in the brain and thus an epiphenomenon of matter; they strongly suggest that it is a primary attribute of all existence.

The scope of this chapter does not allow me to offer a comprehensive discussion of this important subject and illustrate it by clinical examples. I have done it in my books Beyond the Brain (Grof 1985), The Cosmic Game (Grof 1998), and Psychology of the Future (Grof 2000) and can thus refer the interested reader to these publications. I will mention here a set of astonishing observations from thanatology, a relatively young science studying death and dying; most readers will probably be familiar with these paradigm-breaking findings.

It has now been established beyond any reasonable doubt that the consciousness of individuals experiencing clinical death or involved in near-death situations can detach from their bodies and is able to perceive the environment without the mediation of the physical senses. It is capable of observing from the area of the ceiling the resuscitation procedures performed on the body in the operating room, watching from the bird's eye view the site of the accident, or perceiving events in adjacent rooms and various remote locations (Moody 1975, Ring 1982, Sabom 1982). This occurs even in people who are congenitally blind for organic reasons. When their consciousness leaves their bodies, they are not only able to see, but what they see at this time can be later verified by individuals with intact vision. Ring and Cooper, who conducted extensive studies of such individuals call such experiences "veridical" and refer to the capacity of disembodied consciousness to see the environment as "mindsight" (Ring and Cooper 1999).

When confronted with the challenging observations from modern consciousness research, we have only two choices. The first one is to reject the new observations simply because they are incompatible with the traditional scientific belief system. This involves a presumptuous assumption that we already know what the universe is like and can tell with certainty what is possible and what is not possible. With this kind of approach, there cannot be any great surprises, but there is also very little real progress. In this context, everybody who brings critically challenging data is accused of being a bad scientist, a fraud, or a mentally deranged person.

This is an approach that characterizes pseudoscience or scientistic fundamentalism and has very little to do with genuine science. There exist many historical examples of such an approach: people who refused to look into Galileo Galilei's telescope, because they "knew" there could not possibly be craters on the moon; those who fought against the atomic theory of chemistry and defended the concept of a non-existing royal substance called flogiston; those who called Einstein a psychotic when he proposed his special theory of relativity, and many others.

The second reaction to these challenging new observations is characteristic of true science. It is excitement about the occurrence of anomalies and intense research interest in them combined with healthy critical skepticism. Major scientific progress has always occurred when the leading paradigm was unable to account for some significant findings and its adequacy was seriously questioned. In the history of science, paradigms come, dominate the field for some time, and then are replaced by new ones (Kuhn 1962). If instead of doubting, rejecting, and ridiculing the new observations from consciousness research, we would accept their challenge, conduct our own study, and subject them to rigorous scrutiny, we might be able to move psychiatry and psychology to a new level.

It is hard to imagine that Western academic circles will continue indefinitely ignoring, censoring, and misinterpreting all the extraordinary evidence that has been amassed in the study of various forms of holotropic states of consciousness. Sooner or later, they will have to face the challenge of the new data and accept their far-reaching theoretical and practical implications. I firmly believe that in the not too distant future the old materialistic world view will be replaced by a new comprehensive vision of reality, which will integrate modern science with spirituality and Western pragmatism with ancient wisdom. I have no doubt that it will include as an important element the new revolutionary understanding of consciousness, human nature, and the nature of reality that has emerged from the study of holotropic states.

Holotropic Breathwork:
New Perspectives in Psychotherapy and Self-Exploration

The Universal Heart
The little individual heart finding its way back to the big Universal Heart, from a Holotropic Breathwork session. (Anne Høivik)

Holotropic Breathwork: New Perspectives in Psychotherapy and Self-Exploration

Holotropic Breathwork is an experiential method of self-exploration and psychotherapy that my wife Christina and I developed at the Esalen Institute in Big Sur, California, in the mid -1970s. This approach induces deep holotropic states of consciousness by a combination of very simple means - accelerated breathing, evocative music, and a technique of bodywork that helps to release residual bioenergetic and emotional blocks. The sessions are usually conducted in groups; participants work in pairs and alternate in the roles of "breathers" and "sitters."

The process is supervised by trained facilitators who assist participants whenever special intervention is necessary. Following the breathing sessions, participants express their experiences by painting mandalas and sharing accounts of their inner journeys in small groups. Follow-up interviews and various complementary methods are used, if necessary, to facilitate the completion and integration of the breathwork experience.

In its theory and practice, Holotropic Breathwork combines and integrates various elements from modern consciousness research, depth psychology, transpersonal psychology, Eastern spiritual philosophies, and native healing practices. It differs significantly from traditional forms of psychotherapy, which use primarily verbal means, such as psychoanalysis and various other schools of depth psychology derived from it. It shares certain common characteristics with the experiential therapies of humanistic psychology, such as Gestalt practice and the neo-Reichian approaches, which emphasize direct emotional expression and work with the body. However, the unique feature of Holotropic Breathwork is that it utilizes the therapeutic potential of holotropic states of consciousness.

The extraordinary healing power of holotropic states - which ancient and native cultures used for centuries or even millennia in their ritual, spiritual, and healing practices - was confirmed by modern consciousness research conducted in the second half of the twentieth century. This research has also shown that the phenomena occurring during these states and associated with them represent a critical challenge for current

Mother Kundalini
Identification in a Holotropic Breathwork session with a small child resting in a papoose on the back of a woman with a fiery garment, wrapped in a star mantle. The artist wrote: "I was both the mother and the child. I loved this Great Mother deeply, I loved my mother, I loved every creature, every sentient being" (Katia Solani).

conceptual frameworks used by academic psychiatry and psychology and for their basic metaphysical assumptions. The work with Holotropic Breathwork thus requires a new understanding of consciousness and of the human psyche in health and disease. The basic principles of this new psychology were discussed in another context (Grof 2000, 2007).

Essential Components of Holotropic Breathwork

Holotropic Breathwork combines very simple means - faster breathing, evocative music, and releasing bodywork - to induce intense holotropic states of consciousness; it uses the remarkable healing and transformative power of these states. This method provides access to biographical, perinatal, and transpersonal domains of the unconscious and thus to deep psychospiritual roots of emotional and psychosomatic disorders. It also makes it possible to utilize the mechanisms of healing and personality transformation that operate on these levels of the psyche. The process of self-exploration and therapy in Holotropic Breathwork is spontaneous and autonomous; it is governed by inner healing intelligence rather than following the instructions and guidelines of a particular school of psychotherapy.

Most of the recent revolutionary discoveries concerning consciousness and the human psyche on which Holotropic Breathwork is based are new only for modern psychiatry and psychology. They have a long history as integral parts of the ritual and spiritual life of many ancient and native cultures and their healing practices. Basic principles of Holotropic Breathwork thus represent rediscovery, validation, and modern reformulation of ancient wisdom and procedures, some of which can be traced to the dawn of human history. As we will see, the same is true for the principal constituents used in the practice of Holotropic Breathwork – breathing, instrumental music and chanting, bodywork, and mandala drawing or other forms of artistic expression. They have been used for millennia in the healing ceremonies and ritual practices of all pre-industrial human groups.

The Healing Power of Breath

In ancient and pre-industrial societies, breath and breathing have played a very important role in cosmology, mythology, and philosophy, as well as being an important tool in ritual and spiritual practice. Various breathing techniques have been used since time immemorial for religious and healing purposes. Since earliest times, virtually every major psychospiritual system seeking to comprehend human nature has viewed breath as a crucial link between nature, the human body, the psyche, and the spirit. This is clearly reflected in the words many languages use for breath.

In the ancient Indian literature, the term *prana* meant not only physical breath and air, but also the sacred essence of life. Similarly, in traditional Chinese medicine, the word *chi* refers to the cosmic essence and the energy of life, as well as to the natural air we breathe using our lungs. In Japan, the corresponding word is *ki*. Ki plays an extremely important role in Japanese spiritual practices and martial arts. In ancient Greece, the word *pneuma* meant both air or breath and spirit or the essence of life. The Greeks also saw breath as being closely related to the psyche. The term *phren* was used both for the diaphragm, the largest muscle involved in breathing, and mind (as we see in the term *schizophrenia* = literally split mind).

In the old Hebrew tradition, the same word, *ruach,* denoted both breath and creative spirit, which were seen as identical. The following quote from Genesis shows the close relationship between God, breath, and life: "Then the Lord God formed man {Hebrew *adam*} from the dust of the ground, and breathed into his nostrils the breath of life; and the man became a living being." In Latin the same name was used for breath and spirit - *spiritus*. Similarly, in Slavic languages, spirit and breath have the same linguistic root.

In the native Hawaiian tradition and medicine (kanaka maoli lapa'au), the word *ha* means the divine spirit, wind, air, and breath. It is contained in the popular Hawaiian *aloha*, an expression that is used in many different contexts. It is usually translated as presence (*alo*) of the Divine Breath (*ha*). Its opposite, *ha'ole*, meaning literally without breath or without life, is a term that native Hawaiians have applied to white-skinned foreigners since the arrival of the infamous British sea captain James Cook in 1778. The kahunas, "Keepers of Secret Knowledge," have used breathing exercises to generate spiritual energy (*mana*).

It has been known for centuries that it is possible to influence consciousness by techniques that involve breathing. The procedures that have been used for this purpose by various ancient and non-Western cultures cover a very wide range from drastic interference with breathing to subtle and sophisticated exercises of various spiritual traditions. Thus the original form of baptism practiced by the Essenes involved forced submersion of the initiate under water for an extended period of time. This resulted in a powerful experience of death and rebirth. In some other groups, the neophytes were half-choked by smoke, by strangulation, or by compression of the carotid arteries.

Profound changes in consciousness can be induced by both extremes in the breathing rate, hyperventilation and prolonged withholding of breath, as well as by using them in an alternating fashion. Very sophisticated and advanced methods of this kind can be found in the ancient

Indian science of breath, or *pranayama*. William Walker Atkinson, American writer, who was influential in the turn-of-the-century (1890s-1900s) spiritual/philosophical movement wrote under the pseudonym Yogi Ramacharaka a comprehensive treatise on the Hindu science of breath (Ramacharaka 1903).

Specific techniques involving intense breathing or withholding of breath are also part of various exercises in Kundalini Yoga, Siddha Yoga, the Tibetan Vajrayana, Sufi practice, Burmese Buddhist and Taoist meditation, and many other spiritual systems. Indirectly, the depth and rhythm of breathing is profoundly influenced by ritual artistic performances such as the the Balinese monkey chant or Ketjak, the Inuit Eskimo throat music, the Tibetan and Mongolian multivocal chanting, and the singing of kirtans, bhajans, or Sufi chants.

More subtle techniques, which emphasize special awareness in relation to breathing rather than changes of the respiratory dynamics, have a prominent place in Buddhism. Anāpānasati is a basic form of meditation taught by the Buddha; it means literally "mindfulness of breathing" (from the Pali *anāpāna* = inhalation and exhalation and *sati* = mindfulness). Buddha's teaching of anāpāna was based on his experience using it as a means of achieving his own enlightenment. He emphasized the importance of being mindful not only of one's breath, but using the breath to become aware of one's entire body and of all of one's experience. According to the Anāpānasati Sutta (*sutra*), practicing this form of meditation leads to the removal of all defilements (*kilesa*). The Buddha taught that systematic practice of anāpānasati would lead to the final release (*nirvāna* or *nibāna*).

Anāpānasati is practiced in connection with Vipassana (insight meditation) and Zen meditation (*shikantaza*, literally *"just sitting"*). The essence of anāpānasati as the core meditation practice in Buddhism, especially the Theravada school, is to be a passive observer of the natural involuntary breathing process. This is in sharp contrast with the yogic pranayama practices, which employ breathing techniques that aim for rigorous control of breath. Anāpānasati is not, however, the only Buddhist form of breathing meditation. In the Buddhist spiritual practices used in Tibet, Mongolia, and Japan, the control of breathing plays an important role. Cultivation of special attention to breathing also represents an essential part of certain Taoist and Christian practices.

In the development of materialistic science, breathing lost its sacred meaning and was stripped of its connection to the psyche and spirit. Western medicine reduced it to an important physiological function. The physical and psychological manifestations that accompany various respiratory maneuvers, have all been pathologized. The psychosomat-

Imprisoned Aggression *(above)* and **Rage** *(below)*
Suppressed anger trying to find release and expression, and then experienced in identification with an archetypal feline predator in a Holotropic Breeathwork session. (Albrecht Mahr)

ic response to faster breathing, the so-called *hyperventilation syndrome*, is considered a pathological condition, rather than what it really is, a process that has an enormous healing potential. When hyperventilation occurs spontaneously, it is routinely suppressed by administration of tranquilizers, injections of intravenous calcium, and application of a paper bag over the face to increase the concentration of carbon dioxide and combat the alkalosis caused by faster breathing.

In the last few decades, Western therapists rediscovered the healing potential of breath and developed techniques that utilize it. We have ourselves experimented with various approaches involving breathing in the context of our month-long seminars at the Esalen Institute in Big Sur, California. These included both breathing exercises from ancient spiritual traditions under the guidance of Indian and Tibetan teachers and techniques developed by Western therapists. Each of these approaches has a specific emphasis and uses breath in a different way. In our own search for an effective method of using the healing potential of breath, we tried to simplify this process as much as possible.

We came to the conclusion that it is sufficient to breathe faster and more effectively than usual and with full concentration on the inner process. Instead of emphasizing a specific technique of breathing, we follow even in this area the general strategy of holotropic work - to trust the intrinsic wisdom of the body and follow the inner clues. In Holotropic Breathwork, we encourage people to begin the session with faster and somewhat deeper breathing, tying inhalation and exhalation into a continuous circle of breath. Once in the process, they find their own rhythm and way of breathing.

We have been able to confirm repeatedly Wilhelm Reich's observation that psychological resistances and defenses are associated with restricted breathing (Reich 1949, 1961). Respiration is an autonomous function, but it can also be influenced by volition. Deliberate increase of the pace of breathing typically loosens psychological defenses and leads to a release and emergence of unconscious (and superconscious) material. Unless one has witnessed or experienced this process personally, it is difficult to believe on theoretical grounds alone the power and efficacy of this technique.

The Therapeutic Potential of Music

In Holotropic Breathwork, the consciousness-expanding effect of breath is combined with evocative music. Like breathing, music and other forms of sound technology have been used for millennia as powerful tools in ritual and spiritual practice. Monotonous drumming, rattling, chanting, instrumental music, and other forms of sound-produc-

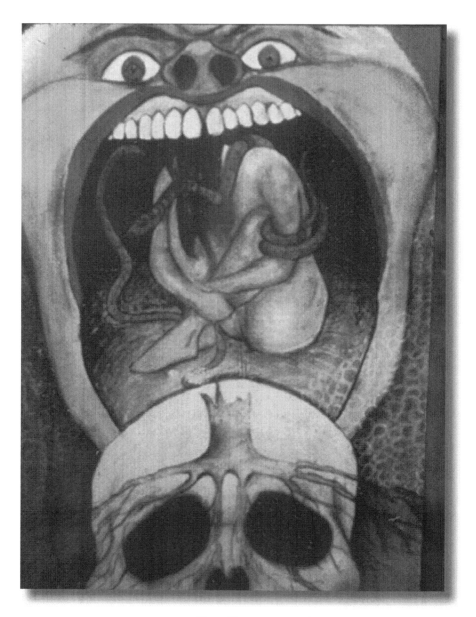

Engulfment
The onset of the process of psychospiritual death and rebirth experienced as engulfment by a grotesque archetype figure in a Holotropic Breathwork session. The skull represents the imminence of death, the root system and the snake, the placental circulatory system.
(Peg Holms).

ing techniques have always been the principle tools of shamans in many different parts of the world. Many pre-industrial cultures have quite independently developed drumming rhythms that in laboratory experiments have remarkable effects on the electric activity of the brain (Goldman 1952, Jilek 1974, 1982; Neher 1961, 1962). The archives of cultural anthropologists contain countless examples of trance-inducing methods of extraordinary power combining instrumental music, chanting, and dancing.

In many cultures, sound technology has been used specifically for healing purposes in the context of intricate ceremonies. The Navajo healing rituals conducted by trained singers have astounding complexity that has been compared to that of the scripts of Wagnerian operas. The trance dance and extended drumming of the !Kung Bushmen of the African Kalahari Desert have enormous healing power, as has been documented in many anthropological studies and movies (Lee and DeVore 1976; Katz 1976). The healing potential of the syncretistic religious rituals of the Caribbean and South America, such as the Cuban *santeria* or Brazilian *umbanda* is recognized by many professionals in these countries who have traditional Western medical training. Remarkable instances of emotional and psychosomatic healing occur in the meetings of Christian groups using music, singing, and dance, such as the Snake Handlers (Holy Ghost People), and the revivalists or members of the Pentecostal Church.

Some spiritual traditions have developed sound technologies that do not just induce a general trance state but have a specific effect on consciousness and the human psyche and body. Thus the Indian teachings postulate a specific connection between certain acoustic frequencies and the individual chakras or energy centers of the human body. With systematic use of this knowledge it is possible to influence the state of consciousness in a predictable and desirable way. The ancient Indian tradition called *nada yoga* or the way to union through sound is known to maintain, improve, and restore emotional, psychosomatic, and physical health and well-being.

Examples of extraordinary vocal performances used for ritual, spiritual, and healing purposes are the multivocal chanting of the Tibetan Gyotso monks and of the Mongolian and Tuva shamans, the Hindu bhajans and kirtans, the Santo Daime chants (Ikaros) used in the ayahuasca ceremonies, the throat music of the Inuit Eskimo people, and the sacred chants (*dhikrs*) of various Sufi orders. These are just a few examples of the extensive use of instrumental music and chanting for healing, ritual, and spiritual purposes.

Journey into and Through Mother Fear
Drawings from a Holotropic Breathwork session in which the artist - as a child and also as an older, wiser accompanying adult - relived her birth, from entering the mouth of the Mother Dragon (above) through through fully facing the fear, and then the dissolving of the Dragon's head allowing safe passage (below).
(Jan Vannatta)

We used music systematically in the program of psychedelic therapy at the Maryland Psychiatric Research Center in Baltimore, Maryland, and have learned much about its extraordinary potential for psychotherapy. Carefully selected music seems to be of particular value in holotropic states of consciousness, where it has several important functions. It mobilizes emotions associated with repressed memories, brings them to the surface, and facilitates their expression. It helps to open the door into the unconscious, intensifies and deepens the therapeutic process, and provides a meaningful context for the experience. The continuous flow of music creates a carrier wave that helps the subject move through difficult experiences and impasses, overcome psychological defenses, surrender, and let go. In Holotropic Breathwork sessions, which are usually conducted in groups, music has an additional function: it masks the noises made by the participants and weaves them into a dynamic esthetic gestalt.

In order to use music as a catalyst for deep self-exploration and experiential work it is necessary to learn a new way of listening to music and relating to it that is alien to our culture. In the West, we employ music frequently as an acoustic background that has little emotional relevance. Typical examples would be use of popular music in cocktail parties or piped music (*muzak*) in shopping areas and workspaces. A different approach used by sophisticated audiences is the disciplined and attentive listening to music in theaters and concert halls. The dynamic and elemental way of using music characteristic of rock concerts comes closer to the use of music in Holotropic Breathwork. However, the attention of participants in such events is usually extroverted and the experience lacks an element that is essential in holotropic therapy or self-exploration - sustained focused introspection.

In holotropic therapy, it is essential to surrender completely to the flow of music, to let it resonate in one's entire body, and to respond to it in a spontaneous and elemental fashion. This includes manifestations that would be unthinkable in a concert hall, where even crying or coughing is seen as a disturbance and causes annoyance and embarrassment. In holotropic work, one should give full expression to whatever the music is bringing out, whether it is loud screaming or laughing, baby talk, animal noises, shamanic chanting, or talking in tongues. It is also important not to control any physical impulses, such as bizarre grimacing, sensual movements of the pelvis, violent shaking, or intense contortions of the entire body. Naturally, there are exceptions to this rule; destructive behavior directed toward oneself, others, and the physical environment is not permissible.

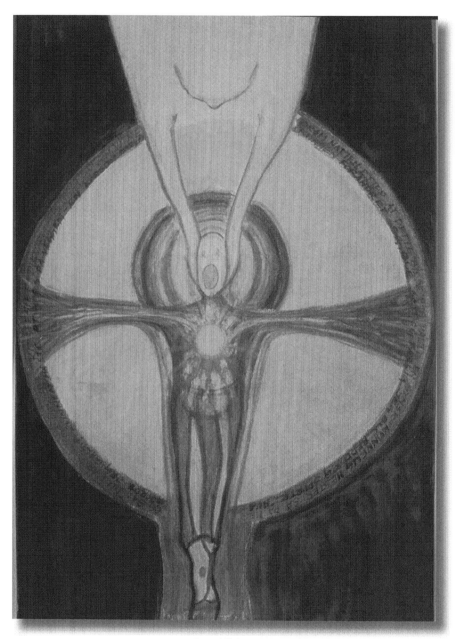

Crucifixion
Vision of crucifixion in the final stage of the birth process in a Holotropic Breath-work session. The artist said "The experience showed me clearly how many levels of reality can be woven together and that God or The Great Spirit is behind it all."
(Anne Høivik)

We also encourage participants to suspend any intellectual activity, such as trying to guess the composer of the music or the culture from which the music comes. Other ways of avoiding the emotional impact of the music involve engaging one's professional expertise - judging the performance of the orchestra, guessing which instruments are playing, and criticizing the technical quality of the recording or of the music equipment in the room. When we can avoid these pitfalls, music can become a very powerful tool for inducing and supporting holotropic states of consciousness. For this purpose, the music has to be of superior technical quality and played at a sufficient volume to drive the experience. The combination of music with faster breathing has a remarkable mind-manifesting and consciousness-expanding power.

As far as the specific choice of music is concerned, we will outline here only the general principles and give a few suggestions based on our experience. After a certain time, each therapist or therapeutic team develops a list of their favorite pieces for various stages of the sessions. The basic rule is to respond sensitively to the phase, intensity, and content of the participants' experience, rather than trying to program it. This is in congruence with the general philosophy of holotropic therapy, particularly the deep respect for the wisdom of the inner healer, for the collective unconscious, and for the autonomy and spontaneity of the healing process.

In general, it is important to use music that is intense, evocative, and conducive to a positive experience. We try to avoid selections that are jarring, dissonant, and anxiety - provoking. Preference should be given to music of high artistic quality that is not well known and has little concrete content. One should avoid playing songs and other vocal pieces in languages known to the participants, which would through their verbal content convey a specific message or suggest a specific theme. When vocal compositions are used, they should be in foreign languages so that the human voice is perceived just as another musical instrument. For the same reason, it is preferable to avoid pieces which evoke specific intellectual associations and tend to program the content of the session, such as Wagner's or Mendelssohn-Bartholdy's wedding marches and overtures to Bizet's Carmen or Verdi's Aida.

The session typically begins with activating music that is dynamic, flowing, and emotionally uplifting and reassuring. As the session continues, the music gradually increases in intensity and moves to powerful rhythmic pieces, preferably drawn from ritual and spiritual traditions of various native cultures. Although many of these performances can be esthetically pleasing, the main purpose of the human groups that developed them is not entertainment, but induction of holotropic experiences.

Death and Rebirth
Death and rebirth followed by the experience of hieros gamos - sacred union - of the Feminine and Masculine in a Holotropic Breathwork session. (Anne Høivik)

An example here could be the dance of the whirling dervishes accompanied by beautiful music and chants. It is not designed to be admired but to take people to the experience of God.

About an hour and a half into the session of Holotropic Breathwork, when the experience typically culminates, we introduce what we call "breakthrough music." The selections used at this time range from sacred music - masses, oratoria, requiems, and other strong orchestral pieces - to excerpts from dramatic movie soundtracks. In the second half of the session, the intensity of the music gradually decreases and we bring in loving and emotionally moving pieces ('heart music'). Finally, in the termination period of the session, the music has a soothing, flowing, timeless, and meditative quality.

Most practitioners of Holotropic Breathwork collect musical recordings and tend to create their own favorite sequences for the five consecutive phases of the session: (1) opening music, (2) trance-inducing music, (3) breakthrough music, (4) heart music, and (5) meditative music. Some of them use music programs prerecorded for the entire session; this allows the facilitators to be more available for the group, but makes it impossible to flexibly adjust the selection of the music to the energy of the group.

The Use of Releasing Bodywork

The physical response to Holotropic Breathwork varies considerably from one person to another. Most commonly, faster breathing brings, at first, more or less dramatic psychosomatic manifestations. The textbooks of respiratory physiology refer to this response to accelerated breathing as the "hyperventilation syndrome." They describe it as a stereotypical pattern of physiological responses that consists primarily of tensions in the hands and feet ("carpopedal spasms"). We have now conducted over thirty-five thousand holotropic breathing sessions and have found the current medical understanding of the effects of faster breathing to be incorrect.

There are many individuals for whom fast breathing carried over a period of several hours does not lead to a classical hyperventilation syndrome but to progressive relaxation, intense sexual feelings, or even mystical experiences. Others develop tensions in various parts of the body but do not show signs of the carpopedal spasms. Moreover, in those who develop tensions, continued faster breathing does not lead to progressive increase of the tensions, but tends to be self-limited. It typically reaches a climactic culmination followed by profound relaxation. The pattern of this sequence has a certain resemblance to sexual orgasm.

In repeated holotropic sessions, this process of intensification of tensions and subsequent relaxation tends to move from one part of the body to another in a way that varies from person to person. The overall amount of muscular tensions and of intense emotions tends to decrease with the number of sessions. What happens in this process is that faster breathing extended for a long period of time changes the chemistry of the organism in such a way that blocked physical and emotional energies associated with various traumatic memories are released and become available for peripheral discharge and processing. This makes it possible for the previously repressed content of these memories to emerge into consciousness and be integrated. It is thus a healing process that should be encouraged and supported and not a pathological process that needs to be suppressed, as is common in medical practice.

Physical manifestations that develop during the breathing in various areas of the body are not simple physiological reactions to faster breathing. They show a complex psychosomatic structure and usually have specific psychological meaning for the individuals involved. Sometimes they represent an intensified version of tensions and pains which the person knows from everyday life, either as a chronic problem or as symptoms that appear at times of emotional or physical stress, fatigue, lack of sleep, weakening by an illness, or the use of alcohol or marijuana. Other times, they can be recognized as reactivation of old latent symptoms that the individual suffered from in infancy, childhood, puberty, or some other time of his or her life.

The tensions that we carry in our body can be released in two different ways. The first of them involves *catharsis* and *abreaction* - discharge of pent-up physical energies through tremors, twitches, dramatic body movements, coughing, and vomiting. Both catharsis and abreaction also typically include release of blocked emotions through crying, screaming, or other types of vocal expression. These are mechanisms that are well known in traditional psychiatry since the time when Sigmund Freud and Joseph Breuer published their studies in hysteria (Freud and Breuer 1936). Various abreactive techniques have been used in traditional psychiatry in the treatment of traumatic emotional neuroses, and abreaction also represents an integral part of the new experiential psychotherapies, such as the neo-Reichian work, Gestalt practice, and primal therapy.

The second mechanism that can mediate release of physical and emotional tensions plays an important role in Holotropic Breathwork, rebirthing, and other forms of therapy using breathing techniques. It represents a new development in psychiatry and psychotherapy and seems to be more effective than abreaction. Here the deep tensions surface in the form of *unrelenting muscular contractions of various duration*

Liberation

Experience of psychospiritual death and rebirth in a Holotropic Breathwork session . The old personality structure has fallen apart, out of it emerges a new self (or Self), connected to the spiritual domain. Dismemberment is a frequent motif in the initiatory experiences of novice shamans. (Jaryna Moss) ("tetany"). By sustaining these muscular tensions for extended periods of time, the organism consumes enormous amounts of previously pent-up energy and simplifies its functioning by disposing of them. The deep relaxation that typically follows the temporary intensification of old tensions or appearance of previously latent ones bears witness to the healing nature of this process.

These two mechanisms have their parallels in sport physiology, where it is well known that it is possible to do work and train the muscles in two different ways, by *isotonic* and *isometric* exercises. As the names suggest, during isotonic exercises the tension of the muscles remains constant while their length oscillates. During isometric exercises, the tension of the muscles changes, but their length remains the same all the time. A good example of isotonic activity is boxing, while weight-lifting or bench-pressing are distinctly isometric exercises. Both of these mechanisms are extremely effective in releasing and resolving deep-seated chronic muscular tension. In spite of their superficial differences, they have much in common and in Holotropic Breathwork complement each other very effectively.

In many instances the difficult emotions and physical sensations that emerge from the unconscious during Holotropic Breathwork sessions are spontaneously resolved and the breathers end up in a deeply relaxed meditative state. In this case, no external interventions are necessary and the breathers remain in this state until they return to the ordinary state of consciousness. After getting clearance from the facilitators, they move to the art room to draw mandalas.

If the breathing in and of itself does not lead to a good completion and there are residual tensions or unresolved emotions, facilitators may offer participants a specific form of bodywork which helps them to reach a better closure for the session. The general strategy of this work is to ask the breather to focus his or her attention on the area where there is unreleased tension and to do whatever is necessary to intensify the existing physical sensations. The facilitators then help to intensify these feelings even further by appropriate external intervention.

While the attention of the breather is focused on the energetically charged problem area, he or she is encouraged to find a spontaneous reaction to this situation. This response should not reflect a conscious choice of the breather, but be fully determined by the unconscious process. It often takes an entirely unexpected and surprising form - animal-like vocalizations, talking in tongues or an unknown foreign language, shamanic chant from a particular culture, gibberish, or baby talk.

Equally frequent are completely unexpected physical reactions, such as violent tremors, jolts, coughing, and vomiting, as well as various characteristic animal movements – climbing, flying, digging, crawling, slithering, and others. It is essential that the facilitators encourage and support what is spontaneously emerging, rather than apply some technique offered by a particular school of therapy. This work should be continued until the facilitator and the breather reach an agreement that the session has been adequately closed. The breather should end the session in a comfortable and relaxed state.

Supportive and Nourishing Physical Contact

In Holotropic Breathwork we also use a different form of physical intervention that is designed to provide support on a deep preverbal level. This is based on the observation that there exist two fundamentally different forms of trauma that require diametrically different approaches. The first of these can be referred to as *trauma by commission.* This form of trauma results from external intrusions that damaged the future development of the individual, such as physical, emotional, or sexual abuse; frightening situations; destructive criticism; or ridicule. These traumas represent foreign elements in the unconscious that can be brought into consciousness, energetically discharged, and resolved.

Although this distinction is not recognized in conventional psychotherapy, the second form of trauma, *trauma by omission,* is radically different. It actually involves the opposite mechanism - lack of positive experiences that are essential for a healthy emotional development. The infant, as well as an older child, have strong primitive needs for instinctual satisfaction and security that pediatricians and child psychiatrists call *anaclitic* (from the Greek *anaklinein* meaning to lean upon). These involve the need to be held and experience skin contact, be caressed, comforted, played with, and be the center of human attention. When these needs are not met it has serious negative consequences for the future of the individual.

Many people have a history of emotional deprivation, abandonment, and neglect in infancy and childhood that resulted in serious frustration of the anaclitic needs. The only way to heal this type of trauma is to offer a corrective experience in the form of supportive physical contact in a holotropic state of consciousness. For this approach to be effective, the individual has to be deeply regressed to the infantile stage of development, otherwise the corrective measure would not reach the developmental level on which the trauma occurred. Depending on circumstances and on previous agreement, this physical support can range from simple holding of the hand or touching the forehead to full body contact.

Use of nourishing physical contact is a very effective way of healing early emotional trauma, but using it requires following strict ethical rules. We have to explain the rationale of this technique to the breathers and sitters before the session and get their approval to use it. Under no circumstances can this approach be practiced without previous consent and no pressures can be used to obtain this permission. For many people with a history of sexual abuse, physical contact is a very sensitive and charged issue. Very often those who most need such healing touch have the strongest resistance against it. It can sometimes take a long time and many sessions before a person develops enough trust toward the facilitators and the group to be able to accept this technique and benefit from it.

Supportive physical contact has to be used exclusively to satisfy the needs of the breathers and not those of the sitters or facilitators. By this I do not mean only sexual needs or needs for intimacy which, of course, are the most obvious issues. Equally problematic can be the sitter's strong need to be needed, loved, or appreciated; unfulfilled maternal needs; and other less extreme forms of emotional wants and desires. An incident from one of our workshops at the Esalen Institute in Big Sur, California, can serve here as a good example.

At the beginning of our five-day seminar, one of the participants, a postmenopausal woman, shared with the group how much she had always wanted to have children and how much she suffered because this had not happened. In the middle of the Holotropic Breathwork session, in which she was the sitter for a young man, she suddenly pulled the upper part of her partner's body into her lap and started to rock and comfort him.

Her timing could not have been worse; as we found out later during the sharing, he was at the time in the middle of a past-life experience that featured him as a powerful Viking warrior on a military expedition. He described with a great sense of humor how he initially tried to experience her rocking as the movement of the boat on the ocean; however, when she added comforting babytalk, that made it impossible for him to continue and brought him back to reality.

It is usually quite easy to recognize when a breather is regressed to early infancy. In a deep age regression the wrinkles in the face disappear and the individual actually looks and behaves like an infant. This can involve various infantile postures and gestures, as well as copious salivation and thumb-sucking. At other times, the appropriateness of offering physical contact is obvious from the context; for example, when the breather has just finished reliving biological birth and looks lost and forlorn. The maternal needs of the woman in the Esalen workshop were

Journey
Overcoming the fear of darkness and the unknown and following a guide deeper and deeper into the underworld in a Holotropic Breathwork session. (Tai Hazard)

so strong that they took over and she was unable to objectively assess the situation and act appropriately.

The use of nourishing physical contact in holotropic states to heal traumas caused by abandonment, rejection, and emotional deprivation was developed by two London psychoanalysts, Pauline McCririck and Joyce Martin; they used this method with their LSD patients under the name of *fusion therapy*. During their sessions, their clients spent several hours in a deep age regression, lying on a couch covered with a blanket, while Joyce or Pauline lay by their side, holding them in close embrace, as a good mother would do to comfort her child (Martin 1965).

Their revolutionary method effectively divided and polarized the community of LSD therapists. Some of the practitioners realized that this was a very powerful and logical way to heal "traumas by omission" - emotional problems caused by emotional deprivation and bad mothering. Others were horrified by this radical "anaclitic therapy." They warned that close physical contact between therapist and client in a non-ordinary state of consciousness would cause irreversible damage to the transference/countertransference relationship.

At the Second International Conference on the use of LSD in psychotherapy held in May 1965 in Amityville, New York, Joyce and Pauline showed their fascinating film on the use of the fusion technique in psychedelic therapy. In a heated discussion that followed, most of the questions revolved around the transference/countertransference issues. Pauline provided a very interesting and convincing explanation of why this approach presented fewer problems in this regard than an orthodox Freudian approach. She pointed out that most patients who come to therapy experienced a lack of affection from their parents in their infancy and childhood. The cold attitude of the Freudian analyst tends to reactivate the resulting emotional wounds and triggers desperate attempts on the part of the patients to get the attention and satisfaction that had been denied to them (Martin 1965).

By contrast, according to Pauline, fusion therapy provided a corrective experience by satisfying the old anaclitic cravings. Having their emotional wounds healed, the patients recognized that the therapist was not an appropriate sexual object and were able to find suitable partners outside of the therapeutic relationship. Pauline explained that this paralleled the situation in the early development of object relationships. Individuals who receive adequate mothering in infancy and childhood are able to emotionally detach from their mothers and find mature relationships. By contrast, those who experienced emotional deprivation remain pathologically attached and go through life craving and seeking satisfaction of primitive infantile needs. We occasionally used fusion therapy in

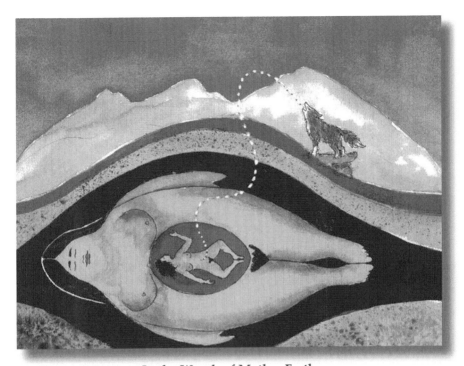

In the Womb of Mother Earth
Resting deep in the womb of the earth and listening to the wolf chanting stories.
Mandala from a Holotropic Breathwork session. (Tai Hazard)

the psychedelic research program at the Maryland Psychiatric Research Center, particularly in the work with terminal cancer patients (Grof 2006 b). In mid-1970s, when we developed Holotropic Breathwork, anaclitic support became an integral part of our workshops and training.

Before closing this section on bodywork, I would like to address one question that often comes up in the context of holotropic workshops or lectures on experiential work: "Why should reliving of traumatic memories be therapeutic rather than represent a retraumatization?" The best answer can be found in the article "Unexperienced Experience" by the Irish psychiatrist Ivor Browne (Browne 1990). He suggested that we are not dealing here with an exact replay or repetition of the original traumatic situation, but with the first full experience of the appropriate emotional and physical reaction to it. This means that the traumatic events are recorded in the organism at the time when they happen but not fully consciously experienced, processed, and integrated.

In addition, the person who is confronted with the previously repressed traumatic memory is no longer the helpless and vitally dependent child or infant that he or she was in the original situation, but a grown-up adult. The holotropic state induced in powerful experiential forms of psychotherapy thus allows the individual to be present and operate simultaneously in two different sets of space-time coordinates. Full age regression makes it possible to experience all the emotions and physical sensations of the original traumatic situation from the perspective of the child, but at the same time analyze and evaluate the memory in the therapeutic situation from a mature adult perspective. This understanding is supported by breathers reliving various traumatic memories who, from the viewpoint of an outside observer, appear to be in a lot of pain and suffering immensely, but who typically afterwards report a subjective feeling of purging pain from their bodies and experience relief rather than the emotional and physical pain itself.

Mandala Drawing: Expressive Power of Art

Mandala is a Sanskrit word meaning literally "circle" or "completion." In the most general sense, this term can be used for any design showing complex geometrical symmetry, such as a spiderweb, arrangement of petals in a flower or blossom, sea shell (e.g. a sand dollar), image in a kaleidoscope, stained glass window in a Gothic cathedral or labyrinth design on its floor. The mandala is a visual construct that can be easily grasped by the eye, since it corresponds to the structure of the organ of visual perception. The pupil of the eye has itself a simple mandala form.

In ritual and spiritual practice, the term mandala refers to images which can be drawn, painted, modeled, or danced. In the Tantric branches of Hinduism, Buddhism, Vajrayana, and Jainism this word refers to elaborate cosmograms composed of elementary geometrical forms (points, lines, triangles, squares, and circles), lotus blossoms, and complex archetypal figures and sceneries. They are used as important meditation aids which help practitioners to focus attention inside and lead them to specific states of consciousness.

Although the use of mandalas in the tantric branches of Hinduism, Buddhism, and Jainism has been particularly refined and sophisticated, the art of mandala drawing as a part of spiritual practice can be found in many other cultures. Examples of particularly beautiful mandalas are the nierikas, yarn paintings of the Huichol Indians from Central Mexico, portraying visions induced by ritual ingestion of peyote. Elaborate sand paintings used in the healing and other rituals of the Navajo people and the bark paintings of the Australian Aborigines also include many intricate mandala patterns.

Sahasrara

*Snake energy (Kundalini) rising from the most physical root chakra (muladhara)
to the most ethereal crown chakra (sahasrara) and triggering a cosmic experience
in a Holotropic Breathwork session. (Jan Vannatta)*

The use of mandalas in spiritual and religious practice of various
cultures and in alchemy attracted the attention of the Swiss psychiatrist
C. G. Jung, who noticed that similar patterns appeared in the paintings
of his patients at a certain stage of their psychospiritual development.
According to him, the mandala is a "psychological expression of the totality of the self." In his own words: "The severe pattern imposed by a
circular image of this kind compensates for the disorder and confusion
of the psychic state - namely, through the construction of a central point
to which everything is related." (Jung 1959).

Our own use of mandala drawing was inspired by the work of Joan
Kellogg, who was a member of the team at the Maryland Psychiatric
Research Center in Baltimore, MD, conducting psychedelic therapy. In
her work as art therapist in psychiatric hospitals in Wycoff and Pater-

son, New Jersey, Joan had given hundreds of patients a piece of paper with an outline of a circle and painting supplies and asked them to paint whatever came into their mind. She was able to find significant correlations between their psychological problems and clinical diagnosis and specific aspects of their paintings, such as choice of colors, preference for sharp or round shapes, use of concentric circles, dividing the mandala into sections, and respecting or not respecting boundaries of the circle.

At the Maryland Psychiatric Research Center, Joan compared the mandalas the experimental subjects were painting before and after their psychedelic sessions, looking for significant correlations between the basic features of the mandalas, content of psychedelic experiences, and outcome of therapy. We have found her method to be extremely useful in our work with Holotropic Breathwork. Joan herself saw the mandala drawing as a psychological test and described in several papers the criteria for interpretations of their various aspects (Kellogg 1977, 1978). In our work we do not interpret the mandalas, but use them in the sharing groups simply as a source of information about the breathers' experiences. We will describe the work with the mandalas in a later section of this chapter.

An interesting alternative to mandala drawing is the method of "SoulCollage" developed by Seena B. Frost (Frost 2001). Many participants in holotropic workshops, training, and therapy, experience psychological blocks when they are confronted with the task of drawing or painting. This usually has its roots in some traumatic experiences that they had as children with their teachers and/or peers in art classes or in their generally low self-esteem that makes them doubt their abilities and paralyzes their performance. SoulCollage helps these people overcome their emotional blocks and resistances; it is a creative process which almost anyone can do since it uses already existing paintings or photographs.

Instead of drawing and painting supplies participants receive a rich selection of illustrated magazines, catalogs, calendars, greeting cards, and postcards. They can also bring their personal photos from the family album or pictures of people, animals, and landscapes they have themselves taken. Using scissors, they cut out pictures or fragments thereof that seem appropriate to portray their experience; they fit them together and glue them on pre-cut mat board cards. If they participate in ongoing groups, they end up eventually with a deck of cards which have deep personal meaning for them. They can take these cards to a friend's house, to sessions of individual therapy or support groups, or use them as decorations in their home.

The Course of Holotropic Sessions

The nature and course of holotropic sessions varies considerably from person to person and also for the same person from session to session. Some individuals remain entirely quiet and almost motionless. They may be having very profound experiences but give the impression to an external observer that nothing is happening or that they are asleep. Others are agitated and show rich motor activity. They experience violent shaking and complex twisting movements, roll and flail around, assume fetal positions, behave like infants struggling in the birth canal, or look and act like newborns. Also crawling, slithering, swimming, digging, or climbing movements are quite common.

Occasionally, the movements and gestures can be extremely refined, complex, quite specific, and differentiated. They can take the form of strange animal movements emulating snakes, birds, or feline predators and be associated with corresponding sounds. Sometimes breathers spontaneously assume various yogic postures and make gestures (*asanas* and *mudras*) with which they are not intellectually familiar. Occasionally, the automatic movements and/or sounds resemble ritual or theatrical performances from different cultures - shamanic practices, Javanese dances, the Balinese monkey chant, Japanese Kabuki, or talking in tongues reminiscent of Pentecostal meetings.

The emotional qualities observed in holotropic sessions cover a very wide range. On one side of the spectrum participants can encounter feelings of extraordinary well-being, profound peace, tranquility, serenity, bliss, cosmic unity, or ecstatic rapture. On the other side of the same spectrum are episodes of indescribable terror, all-consuming guilt, murderous aggression, or eternal doom. The intensity of these emotions can transcend anything that can be experienced or even imagined in the everyday state of consciousness. These extreme emotional states are usually associated with experiences that are perinatal or transpersonal in nature.

In the middle band of the experiential spectrum observed in Holotropic Breathwork sessions are less extreme emotional qualities that are closer to what we know from our daily existence - episodes of anger, anxiety, sadness, hopelessness, and feelings of failure, inferiority, shame, guilt or disgust. These are typically linked to biographical memories; their sources are traumatic experiences from infancy, childhood, and later periods of life. Their positive counterparts are feelings of happiness, emotional fulfillment, joy, sexual satisfaction, and general increase in zest.

In some instances faster breathing does not induce any physical tensions or difficult emotions, but leads directly to increasing relaxation, a sense of expansion and well-being, and visions of light. The breather can feel flooded with feelings of love and experiences of mystical connection to other people, nature, the entire cosmos, and God. These positive emotional states arise most often at the end of the holotropic sessions after the challenging and turbulent parts of the experience have been worked through.

It is surprising how many people in our culture, because of strong Protestant ethics or for some other reasons, have great difficulty accepting ecstatic experiences unless they follow suffering and hard work, or even then. They often respond to them with a strong sense of guilt or with a feeling that they do not deserve them. It is also common, particularly in mental health professionals, to react to positive experiences with mistrust and suspicion that they hide and mask some particularly painful and unpleasant material. It is very important under these circumstances to assure the breathers that positive experiences are extremely healing and encourage them to accept them without reservation as unexpected grace.

A typical result of a Holotropic Breathwork session is profound emotional release and physical relaxation. After a successful and well-integrated session, many people report that they feel more relaxed than they have ever felt in their life. Continued accelerated breathing thus represents an extremely powerful and effective method of stress reduction and it is conducive to emotional and psychosomatic healing. Another frequent result of this work is connection with the numinous dimensions of one's own psyche and of existence in general. This is also a frequent occurrence in ritual and spiritual practices of many cultures and ages.

The healing potential of breath is particularly strongly emphasized in Kundalini yoga. There episodes of faster breathing are used in the course of meditative practice (*bastrika*) or occur spontaneously as part of the emotional and physical manifestations known as *kriyas*. This is consistent with my own view that similar spontaneous episodes occurring in psychiatric patients, referred to as the *hyperventilation syndrome*, are attempts at self-healing. They should be encouraged and supported rather than routinely suppressed as is the common medical practice.

Holotropic Breathwork sessions vary in their duration from individual to individual and, in the same individual, also from session to session. It is essential, for the best possible integration of the experience that the facilitators and sitters stay with the breather as long as he or she is in process. In the terminal stage of the session good bodywork can

Riding through the Air

Experience following a major breakthrough in a Holotropic Breathwork session -
"feeling like a baby in the arms of the Great Mother of the Void, completely safe
and loved for who I am, and riding with her through the air into eternity."
(Anne Høivik)

significantly facilitate emotional and physical resolution. Intimate contact with nature can also have a very calming and grounding effect and help the integration of the session. Particularly effective in this regard is exposure to water, such as a stay in a hot tub or a swim in a pool, a lake, or in the ocean.

Mandala Drawing and the Sharing Groups

When the session is completed and the breather returns to the ordinary state of consciousness the sitter accompanies him or her to the mandala room. This room is equipped with a variety of art supplies such as pastels, magic markers, and watercolors, as well as large drawing pads. On the sheets of these pads are pencil drawings of circles about the size of dinner plates. The breathers are asked to sit down, meditate on their experience, and then find a way of expressing what happened to them during the session by using these tools.

There are no specific guidelines for the mandala drawing. Some people simply produce color combinations, others construct geometrical mandalas or figurative drawings or paintings. The latter might represent a vision that occurred during the session or a pictorial travelogue with

Oneness with the Ocean and Setting Sun at Big Sur
Experience toward the end of a Holotropic Breathwork session.

several distinct sequences. On occasion, the breather decides to document a single session with several mandalas reflecting different aspects or stages of the session. In rare instances, the breather has no idea what he or she is going to draw and produces an automatic drawing.

We have seen instances when the mandala did not illustrate the immediately preceding session, but actually anticipated the session that followed. This is in congruence with C. G. Jung's idea that the products of the psyche cannot be fully explained from preceding historical events. In many instances, they have not just a retrospective, but also a prospective aspect. Some mandalas thus reflect a movement in the psyche that Jung called *the individuation process* and reveal its forthcoming stage. A possible alternative to mandala drawing is sculpting with clay. We introduced this method when we had participants in a group who were blind and could not draw a mandala. It was interesting to see that some of the other participants preferred to use this medium, when it was available, or opted for a combination of mandala and three-dimensional figure.

Later during the day, breathers bring their mandalas to a sharing session in the course of which they talk about their experiences. The strategy of the facilitators who lead the group is to encourage maximum openness and honesty in sharing the experience. Willingness of participants to reveal the content of their sessions, including various intimate details, is conducive to bonding and development of trust in the group. It encourages others to share with equal honesty, which deepens, intensifies, and accelerates the therapeutic process.

In contrast to the practice of most psychotherapeutic schools, facilitators abstain from interpreting the experiences of participants. The reason for it is the lack of agreement among the existing schools concerning the functioning of the psyche, its principal motivating forces, and the cause and meaning of the symptoms. Under these circumstances any interpretations are questionable and arbitrary. Another reason for staying away from interpretations is the fact that psychological contents are typically overdetermined and are meaningfully related to several levels of the psyche. Giving a supposedly definitive explanation or interpretation carries the danger of freezing the process and interfering with therapeutic progress.

A more productive alternative is to ask questions that help to elicit additional information from the perspective of the client who, being the experiencer, is the ultimate expert as far as his or her experience is concerned. When we are patient and resist the temptation to share our own impressions, participants very often find their own explanations that best fit their experiences. On occasion, it can be very helpful to share our observations from the past concerning similar experiences or point out connections with experiences of other members of the group. When the experiences contain archetypal material it can be helpful to use C. G. Jung's method of *amplification* – pointing out parallels between a particular experience and similar mythological motifs from various cultures - or to consult a good dictionary of symbols.

Follow-Up and Use of Complementary Techniques

On the days following intense sessions that involved a major emotional breakthrough or opening a wide variety of complementary approaches can facilitate good integration. Among them are discussions about the session with an experienced facilitator, writing down the content of the experience, drawing additional mandalas, meditation, and movement meditation, such as hatha yoga, tai-chi, or qi-gong. Good bodywork with a practitioner who allows emotional expression, jogging, swimming, and other forms of physical exercise, or expressive dancing can be very useful, if the holotropic experience freed excess previously pent-up physical energy. A session of Dora Kalff's Jungian sandplay (Kalff and Kalff 2004), Fritz Perls' Gestalt therapy (Perls 1976), Jacob Moreno's psychodrama (Moreno 1948), or Francine Shapiro's eye movement desensitization and reprocessing (EMDR) (Shapiro 2001), can be of great help in refining insights into the holotropic experience and understanding its content.

Therapeutic Potential of Holotropic Breathwork

Christina and I developed and practiced Holotropic Breathwork outside of the professional setting - in our month-long seminars and shorter workshops at the Esalen Institute, in various breathwork workshops in many other parts of the world, and in our training program for facilitators. I have not had the opportunity to test the therapeutic efficacy of this method in the same way I had been able to do in the past when I conducted psychedelic therapy. The psychedelic research at the Maryland Psychiatric Research Center involved controlled clinical studies with psychological testing and a systematic, professionally conducted follow-up.

However, the therapeutic results of Holotropic Breathwork have often been so dramatic and meaningfully connected with specific experiences in the sessions that I have no doubt Holotropic Breathwork is a viable form of therapy and self-exploration. We have seen numerous instances over the years when participants in the workshops and the training were able to break out of depression that had lasted several years, overcome various phobias, free themselves from consuming irrational feelings, and radically improve their self-confidence and self-esteem. We have also witnessed on many occasions disappearance of severe psychosomatic pains, including migraine headaches, and radical and lasting improvements or even complete clearing of psychogenic asthma. On many occasions, participants in the training or workshops favorably compared their progress in several holotropic sessions to years of verbal therapy.

When we talk about evaluating the efficacy of powerful forms of experiential psychotherapy, such as work with psychedelics or Holotropic Breathwork, it is important to emphasize certain fundamental differences between these approaches and verbal forms of therapy. Verbal psychotherapy often extends over a period of years and major exciting breakthroughs are rare exceptions rather than commonplace events. When changes of symptoms occur, it happens on a broad time scale and it is difficult to prove their causal connection with specific events in therapy or the therapeutic process in general. By comparison, in a psychedelic or holotropic session, powerful changes can occur in the course of a few hours and they can be convincingly linked to a specific experience.

The changes observed in holotropic therapy are not limited to conditions traditionally considered emotional or psychosomatic. In many cases, Holotropic Breathwork sessions led to dramatic improvement of physical conditions that in medical handbooks are described as organic diseases. Among them was clearing of chronic infections (sinusitis, pharyngitis, bronchitis, and cystitis) after bioenergetic unblocking opened blood circulation in the corresponding areas. Unexplained to this day remains solidification of bones in a woman with osteoporosis that occurred in the course of holotropic training.

We have also seen restitution of full peripheral circulation in twelve people suffering from Raynaud's disease, a disorder that involves coldness of hands and feet accompanied by dystrophic changes of the skin. In several instances, Holotropic Breathwork led to striking improvement of arthritis. In all these cases, the critical factor conducive to healing seemed to be release of excessive bioenergetic blockage in the afflicted parts of the body followed by vasodilation. The most astonishing observation in this category was a dramatic remission of advanced symptoms of Takayasu arteritis, a disease of unknown etiology, characterized by progressive occlusion of arteries in the upper part of the body. It is a condition that is usually considered progressive, incurable, and potentially lethal.

In many cases the therapeutic potential of Holotropic Breathwork was confirmed in clinical studies conducted by practitioners who had been trained by us and independently use this method in their work. A significant number of clinical studies was also conducted by psychiatrists and psychologists in Russia who have not participated in our training for facilitators. A list of studies involving or related to Holotropic Breathwork is included in a special section of the bibliography in our book on Holotropic Breathwork (Grof and Grof 2010).

On many occasions, we have also had the opportunity to receive informal feedback from people years after their emotional, psychosomatic, and physical symptoms had improved or disappeared after holotropic sessions in our training or in our workshops. This has shown us that the improvements achieved in holotropic sessions are often lasting. I hope that the efficacy of this interesting and promising method of self-exploration and therapy will be confirmed in the future by well-designed extensive clinical research.

Following is a description of experiences in a Holotropic Breathwork session which included related perinatal, biographical, and transperson-

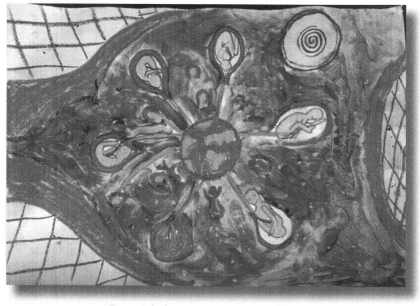

From Birth Unto Birth Unto Birth
Holotropic Breathwork mandala of a session including related perinatal, biographic, and transpersonal elements. (Paul Browde)

al elements. It shows the deep influence that the nature and circumstances of our birth can have on our postnatal life.

The corresponding mandala is entitled "From Birth Unto Birth Unto Birth."

This session was in keeping with my actual birth, in which I lay in an occipital posterior position, so that delivery did not proceed as it is supposed to. My mother was given Pitocin, which resulted in a tonic uterine contraction that continued for many minutes. I have always known that this was one of the most excruciating experiences of my mother's life, but only during this breathwork session did I recognize the pain it must have caused me. Ultimately a forceps was required to pull me out.

I realized during this session that there are many current emotional patterns that correspond to this birth process, and that perhaps I am repeating the birth experience again and again as I move from one stage of life to another. It then dawned on me that we are all in a process of birth, as we move from one state to another. Birth is a birth, aging is a birth, and death itself is a birth. On seeing this I felt greatly connected to all other people. I experienced myself as part of a collective, going through our birth experiences alone, yet connected through our common experience of being human. This showed up in the mandala as connection to mother earth through our umbilical cords.

I also saw that the earth itself, and indeed the universe is in a constant state of birth or evolution, moving from one state to another. This shows up in the mandala as the universe depicted as a giant womb floating on a matrix of consciousness.

The yellow spiral represents a passageway from this realm of consciousness to other realms as yet undiscovered. I am passionate about exploring these other realms and finding the passages to reach them. (Paul Browde)

Physiological Mechanisms Involved In Holotropic Breathwork

In view of the powerful effect Holotropic Breathwork has on consciousness, it is interesting to consider the physiological and biochemical mechanisms that might be involved. Many people believe that when we breathe faster, we simply bring more oxygen into the body and the brain. But the situation is actually much more complicated. It is true that faster breathing brings more air and thus oxygen into the lungs, but it also eliminates carbon dioxide (CO_2) and causes vasoconstriction in certain parts of the body.

Since CO_2 is acidic, reducing its content in blood increases the alkalinity of the blood (so called pH) and in an alkaline setting relatively less oxygen is being transferred to the tissues. This in turn triggers a homeostatic mechanism that works in the opposite direction: the kidneys excrete urine that is more alkaline to compensate for this change. The brain is also one of the areas in the body that can respond to faster breathing by vasoconstriction. Since the degree of gas exchange does not depend only on the rate of breathing, but also on its depth, the situation is quite complex and it is not easy to assess the overall situation in an individual case without a battery of specific laboratory examinations.

However, if we take all the above physiological mechanisms into consideration, the situation of people during Holotropic Breathwork very likely resembles that in high mountains, where there is less oxygen and the CO_2 level is decreased by compensatory faster breathing. The cerebral cortex, being the youngest part of the brain from an evolutionary point of view, is generally more sensitive to a variety of influences (such as alcohol and anoxia) than the older parts of the brain. This situation would thus cause inhibition of the cortical functions and intensified activity in the archaic parts of the brain, making the unconscious processes more available.

It is interesting that many individuals, and entire cultures, who lived in extreme altitudes, were known for their advanced spirituality. We can think in this context of the yogis in the Himalayas, the Tibetan Buddhists in the Quinzang high plateau, and the Incas in the Peruvian Andes. It is tempting to attribute it to the fact that, in an atmosphere with a lower content of oxygen, they had easy access to transpersonal experiences. However, an extended stay in high elevations leads to physiological adaptations, for example, hyperproduction of red blood cells in the spleen. The acute situation during Holotropic Breathwork might, therefore, not be directly comparable to an extended stay in high mountains.

In any case, it is a long way from the description of the physiological changes in the brain to the extremely rich array of phenomena induced by Holotropic Breathwork, such as authentic experiential identification with animals, archetypal visions, or past life memories. This situation is similar to the problem of the psychological effects of LSD. The fact that both of these methods can induce transpersonal experiences in which there is access to accurate new information about the universe through extrasensory channels makes it difficult to accept that such experiences are stored in the brain.

Aldous Huxley, after having experienced psychedelic states, came to the conclusion that our brain cannot possibly be the source of the rich and fantastic array of phenomena that he had experienced. He suggested that it is more likely that the brain functions like a reducing valve that shields us from an infinitely larger cosmic input. The concepts, such as "memory without a material substrate" (Foerster 1965), Sheldrake's "morphogenetic fields" (Sheldrake 1981), and Laszlo's "psi field" or "akashic field" (Laszlo 1993) bring important support for Huxley's idea and make it increasingly plausible.

In conclusion, I would like to compare psychotherapy using holotropic states of consciousness, in general, and Holotropic Breathwork, in particular, with talking therapies. Verbal methods of psychotherapy attempt to get to the roots of emotional and psychosomatic problems indirectly by helping the clients to remember relevant forgotten and repressed events from their life or reconstruct them indirectly by analysis of dreams, symptoms, or distortions of the therapeutic relationship (transference).

Most of verbal psychotherapies also use a model of the psyche which is limited to postnatal biography and to the Freudian individual unconscious. They also employ techniques that cannot reach the perinatal and transpersonal domains of the psyche and thus the deeper roots of the disorders they are trying to heal. The limitations of verbal therapies are particularly obvious in relation to memories of traumatic events that have a strong physical component, such as difficult birth, episodes of near-drowning, and injuries or diseases. Traumas of this kind cannot be worked through and resolved by talking about them; they have to be relived and the emotions and blocked physical energies attached to them have to be fully expressed.

Other advantages of Holotropic Breathwork are of economic nature; they are related to the ratio between the number of participants in breathwork groups and the number of facilitators. It was estimated that a classical psychoanalyst was able to treat about eighty patients in his or her entire lifetime. In spite of all the changes psychotherapy has undergone since Freud's times, the ratio between the number of clients needing treatment and the number of professional therapists required for this task continues to be very unfavorable.

By comparison, Holotropic Breathwork utilizes the healing potential of group members, who alternate in the roles of breathers and sitters. Participants need no special training to be good sitters. A typical group requires one trained facilitator per eight to ten group participants. Although it might be objected that traditional group psychotherapy has a similar or even better therapist/client ratio, it is important to take into consideration that in breathwork groups each participant has a personal experience focused specifically on his or her problems. Sitters also repeatedly report what a profound experience it was for them to assist others and how much they had learned from it.

We have also observed that a significant number of people who have attended Holotropic Breathwork sessions tend to become very interested in the process and decide to enroll in the training for facilitators. The number of people from different countries of the world who have completed our training and have become certified as facilitators has recently exceeded one thousand. This "chain reaction" effect of Holotropic Breathwork is a very hopeful sign for the future.

In addition, many people who had experienced verbal psychotherapy before they came to Holotropic Breathwork often compared the results of a small number of breathwork sessions with what they had achieved in years of talk therapy. I hope that in the near future these impressions will be confirmed by well-designed controlled clinical studies.

Understanding
and
Treatment of
Psychospiritual Crises -
"Spiritual Emergencies"

Painting from an LSD session depicting the experience of psychospiritual rebirth – emerging in fire from the vagina of the Great Mother Goddess and feeling supported by nourishing cosmic hands. While the upper part of the painting represents BPM IV, the lower part – the star-filled sky and the nourishing hands - represent BPM I, the time when the uterus meant nourishment and safety.

Understanding and Treatment of Psychospiritual Crises - "Spiritual Emergencies"

One of the most important implications of the research of holotropic states is the realization that many of the conditions which are currently diagnosed as psychotic and indiscriminately treated by suppressive medication are actually difficult stages of a radical personality transformation and of spiritual opening. If they are correctly understood and supported, these psychospiritual crises can result in emotional and psychosomatic healing, remarkable psychological transformation, and consciousness evolution (Grof and Grof 1989, 1990).

Episodes of this nature can be found in the life stories of shamans, founders of the great religions of the world, famous spiritual teachers, mystics, and saints. The mystical literature of the world describes these crises as important signposts of the spiritual path and confirms their healing and transformative potential. Because of their narrow conceptual framework, mainstream psychiatrists do not differentiate psychospiritual crises, or even episodes of uncomplicated mystical experiences, from serious mental diseases, .

Academic psychiatry, being a subdiscipline of medicine, has a strong preference for biological interpretations and uses a model of the psyche limited to postnatal biography and the Freudian individual unconscious. These are serious obstacles in understanding the nature and content of mystical states and the ability to distinguish them from manifestations of mental disease.

The term "spiritual emergency" (psychospiritual crisis), which my wife Christina and I coined for these states alludes to their positive potential. In English, this term is a play on words reflecting the similarity between the word "emergency" (a suddenly appearing acute crisis) and "emergence" (surfacing or rising). It thus suggests both a problem and opportunity to rise to a higher level of psychological functioning and spiritual awareness. We often refer in this context to the Chinese pictogram for crisis that illustrates the basic idea of spiritual emergency. This ideogram is composed of two images, one of which means danger and the other opportunity.

Among the benefits that can result from psychospiritual crises that receive expert support and are allowed to run their natural course are improved psychosomatic health, increased zest for life, a more rewarding life strategy, and an expanded worldview that includes the spiritual dimension. Successful completion and integration of such episodes also involves a substantial reduction of aggression, increase of racial, political, and religious tolerance, ecological awareness, and deep changes in the hierarchy of values and existential priorities. It is not an exaggeration to say that successful completion and integration of psychospiritual crisis can move the individual to a higher level of consciousness evolution.

In recent decades we have seen a rapidly growing interest in spiritual matters that has led to extensive experimentation with ancient, aboriginal, and modern "technologies of the sacred" - consciousness-expanding techniques that can mediate spiritual opening. Among them are various shamanic methods, Eastern meditative practices, use of psychedelic substances, effective experiential psychotherapies, and laboratory methods developed by experimental psychiatry. According to public polls, the number of Americans who have had spiritual experiences significantly increased in the second half of the twentieth century and continues to grow. It seems that this has been accompanied by a parallel increase of psychospiritual crises.

More and more people seem to realize that genuine spirituality based on profound personal experience is a vitally important dimension of life. In view of the escalating global crisis brought about by the materialistic orientation of Western technological civilization, it has become obvious that we are paying a great price for having rejected spirituality. We have banned from our life a force that nourishes, empowers, and gives meaning to human existence.

On the individual level, the toll for the loss of spirituality is an impoverished, alienated, and unfulfilling way of life and an increase of emotional and psychosomatic disorders. On the collective level, the absence of spiritual values leads to strategies of existence that threaten the survival of life on our planet, such as plundering of nonrenewable resources, polluting the natural environment, disturbing ecological balance, and using violence as a principal means of international problem-solving.

It is, therefore, in the interest of all of us to find ways of bringing spirituality back into our individual and collective life. This would have to include not only theoretical recognition of spirituality as a vital aspect of existence but also encouragement and social sanctioning of activities that mediate experiential access to spiritual dimensions of reality. An

Shiva Nataraja Lord of the Cosmic Dance
*Depiction of a Holotropic Breathwork session vision during a month-long
Esalen seminar.*

important part of this effort would have to be development of an appropriate support system for people undergoing crises of spiritual opening, therefore making it possible to utilize the positive potential of these states.

In 1980, Christina founded the Spiritual Emergency Network (SEN), an organization that connects individuals undergoing psychospiritual crises with professionals, who are able and willing to provide assistance based on the new understanding of these states. Filial branches of SEN now exist in many countries of the world.

Triggers of Spiritual Emergency

In many instances, it is possible to identify the situation that precipitated the psychospiritual crisis. It can be a primarily physical factor, such as a disease, accident, or operation. At other times, extreme physical exertion or prolonged lack of sleep may appear to be the most immediate trigger. In women, it can be childbirth, miscarriage, or abortion. We have also seen situations where the onset of the process coincided with an exceptionally powerful sexual experience.

In other cases, the psychospiritual crisis begins shortly after a traumatic emotional experience. This can be the loss of an important relationship, such as the death of a child or another close relative, divorce, or the end of a love affair. Similarly, a series of failures or loss of a job or property can immediately precede the onset of spiritual emergency. In predisposed individuals, the "last straw" can be an experience with psychedelic substances or a session of experiential psychotherapy.

One of the most important catalysts of psychospiritual crisis seems to be deep involvement in various forms of meditation and spiritual practice. This should not come as a surprise, since these methods have been specifically designed to facilitate spiritual experiences. We have been repeatedly contacted by persons in whom extended periods of holotropic states were triggered by the practice of Zen, Vipassana, or Vajrayana Buddhist meditation, yogic practices, Sufi ceremonies, monastic contemplation, or Christian prayer.

The wide range of triggers of spiritual crises clearly suggests that the individual's readiness for inner transformation plays a far more important role than the external stimuli. When we look for a common denominator or final common pathway of the situations described above, we find that they all involve a radical shift in the balance between the unconscious and conscious processes. Weakening of psychological defenses or, conversely, increase of the energetic charge of the unconscious dynamics, makes it possible for the unconscious (and superconscious) material to emerge into consciousness.

It is well known that psychological defenses can be weakened by a variety of biological insults, such as physical trauma, infection, intoxication, exhaustion, or sleep deprivation. Psychological traumas can mobilize the unconscious, particularly when they involve elements that are reminiscent of earlier traumas and are part of a significant COEX system. The strong potential of childbirth as a trigger of psychospiritual crisis seems to reflect the fact that delivering a child combines biological weakening with specific reactivation of the mother's own perinatal memories.

Failures and disappointments in professional and personal life can undermine and thwart the outward-oriented motivations and ambitions of the individual. This makes it more difficult to use external activities as an escape from emotional problems and leads to psychological withdrawal and turning of attention to the inner world. As a result, unconscious contents can emerge into consciousness and interfere with the individual's everyday experience or even completely override it.

Diagnosis of Spiritual Emergency

When we emphasize the need to recognize the existence of psychospiritual crises, this does not mean indiscriminate rejection of the theories and practices of traditional psychiatry. Not all states that are currently diagnosed as psychotic are crises of psychospiritual transformation or have a healing potential. Episodes of nonordinary states of consciousness cover a very broad spectrum from purely spiritual experiences to conditions that are clearly biological in nature and require medical treatment. While modern psychiatrists generally tend to pathologize mystical states, there also exists the opposite error of romanticizing and glorifying psychotic states or, even worse, overlooking a serious medical problem.

Many mental health professionals who encounter the concept of psychospiritual crisis want to know the exact criteria by which one can make the "differential diagnosis" between a crisis of this kind ("spiritual emergency") and psychosis. Unfortunately, it is in principle impossible to make such differentiation according to the standards used in somatic medicine. Unlike diseases treated by somatic medicine, psychotic states that are not obviously organic in nature - "functional psychoses" or "endogenous" psychoses - are not medically defined. It is actually highly questionable whether they should be called diseases at all.

Functional psychoses certainly are not diseases in the same sense as diabetes, typhoid fever, or pernicious anemia. They do not yield any specific clinical or laboratory findings that would support the diagnosis and justify the assumption that they are of biological origin. The diagnosis of these states is based entirely on the observation of unusual experiences and behaviors for which contemporary psychiatry lacks adequate explanation. The meaningless attribute "endogenous" (literally "generated from within") used for these conditions is tantamount to admission of this ignorance. At present, there is no reason to refer to these conditions as "mental diseases" and assume that the experiences involved are products of a pathological process in the brain yet to be discovered by future research.

If we give it some thought, we realize it is highly unlikely that a pathological process afflicting the brain could, in and of itself, generate the incredibly rich experiential spectrum of the states currently diagnosed as psychotic. How could abnormal processes in the brain generate such experiences as culturally specific sequences of psychospiritual death and rebirth, convincing identification with Christ on the cross or with the dancing Shiva, an episode involving death on the barricades in Paris during the French revolution, or complex scenes of alien abduction?

When similar experiences manifest under circumstances in which the biological changes are accurately defined, such as administration of specific dosages of chemically pure LSD-25, the nature and origin of their content remain a deep mystery. The spectrum of possible reactions to LSD is very broad and includes reliving of various biographical events, experiences of psychospiritual death and rebirth, episodes of mystical rapture, feelings of cosmic unity, sense of oneness with God, and past-life memories, as well as paranoid states, manic episodes, apocalyptic visions, exclusively psychosomatic responses, and many others. The same dosage given to different individuals or repeatedly to the same person can induce very different experiences.

Chemical changes in the organism obviously catalyze the experience, but are not, in and of themselves, capable of creating the intricate imagery and the rich philosophical and spiritual insights, let alone mediating access to accurate new information about various aspects of the universe. The administration of LSD and other similar substances can account for the emergence of deep unconscious material into consciousness, but cannot explain its nature and content. Understanding the phenomenology of psychedelic states necessitates a much more sophisticated approach than a simple reference to abnormal biochemical or biological processes in the body. It requires a comprehensive approach that has to include transpersonal psychology, mythology, philosophy, and comparative religion. The same is true in regard to psychospiritual crises.

The experiences that constitute psychospiritual crises clearly are not artificial products of aberrant pathophysiological processes in the brain, but manifestations of the deeper levels of the psyche. Naturally, to be able to see it this way, we have to transcend the narrow understanding of the psyche offered by mainstream psychiatry and use a vastly expanded conceptual framework. Examples of such enlarged models of the psyche are the cartography described in my own books and papers (Grof 1975, 2000, 2007 a), Ken Wilber's spectrum psychology (Wilber 1977), Roberto Assagioli's psychosynthesis (Assagioli 1976), and C. G. Jung's concept of the psyche as identical with the world soul *(anima mundi)* that includes the historical and archetypal collective unconscious (Jung 1981). Such large and comprehensive understandings of the psyche are also characteristic of the great Eastern philosophies and the mystical traditions of the world.

Since functional psychoses are not defined medically but psychologically, it is impossible to provide a rigorous differential diagnosis between psychospiritual crisis ("spiritual emergency") and psychosis in the way it is done in medical practice in relation to different forms of encephalitis, brain tumors, or dementias. Considering this fact, is it possible to make any diagnostic conclusions at all? How can we approach this problem and what can we offer in lieu of a clear and unambiguous differential diagnosis between psychospiritual crisis and mental disease?

A viable alternative is to define the criteria that would make it possible to determine which individual experiencing an intense spontaneous holotropic state of consciousness is likely to be a good candidate for a therapeutic strategy that validates and supports the process. And, conversely, we can attempt to determine under what circumstances using an alternative approach would not be appropriate and when the current practice of routine psychopharmacological suppression of symptoms would be preferable.

A necessary prerequisite for such an evaluation is a good medical examination that eliminates conditions, which are organic in nature and require biological treatment. Once this is accomplished, the next important guideline is the phenomenology of the holotropic state of consciousness in question. Psychospiritual crises involve a combination of biographical, perinatal, and transpersonal experiences that were described in another context, in the discussion of the extended cartography of the psyche (Grof 1975, 2000, 2007). Experiences of this kind can be induced in a group of randomly selected "normal" people not only by psychedelic substances, but also by such simple means as meditation, shamanic drumming, faster breathing, evocative music, bodywork, and variety of other nondrug techniques.

Those of us who work with Holotropic Breathwork see such experiences daily in our workshops and seminars and have the opportunity to appreciate their healing and transformative potential. In view of this fact, it is difficult to attribute similar experiences to some exotic and yet unknown pathology when they occur spontaneously in the middle of everyday life. It makes eminent sense to approach these experiences in the same way they are approached in holotropic and psychedelic sessions - to encourage people to surrender to the process and to support the emergence and full expression of the unconscious material that becomes available.

Another important indicator is the person's attitude to the process and his or her experiential style. It is generally very encouraging when people who have holotropic experiences recognize that what is happening to them is an inner process, are open to experiential work, and interested to try it. Transpersonal strategies are not appropriate for individuals who lack this elementary recognition, use predominantly the mechanism of projection, or suffer from persecutory delusions. The capacity to form a good working relationship with an adequate amount of trust is an absolutely essential prerequisite for psychotherapeutic work with people in spiritual crisis.

It is also very important to pay attention to the way clients talk about their experiences. The communication style, in and of itself, often distinguishes promising candidates from inappropriate or questionable ones. It is a very good prognostic indicator if the person describes the experiences in a coherent and articulate way, however extraordinary and strange their content might be. In a sense, this would be similar to hearing an account of a person who has just had a psychedelic session and intelligently describes what to an uninformed person might appear to be strange and extravagant experiences.

Varieties of Spiritual Crises

A question that is closely related to the problem of differential diagnosis of psychospiritual crises is their classification. Is it possible to distinguish and define among them certain specific types or categories in the way it is attempted in the Diagnostic and Statistical Manual of Mental Disorders (DSM V) and its predecessors, used by traditional psychiatrists? Before we address this question, it is necessary to emphasize that the attempts to classify psychiatric disorders, with the exception of those that are clearly organic in nature, have been generally unsuccessful.

There is general disagreement about diagnostic categories among individual psychiatrists and also among psychiatric societies of different countries. Although DSM has been revised and changed a number of times, clinicians complain that they have difficulty matching the symptoms of their clients with the official diagnostic categories. Spiritual crises are no exception; if anything, assigning people suffering from these conditions to well-defined diagnostic categories is particularly problematic because of the fact that their phenomenology is unusually rich and can have its source on all levels of the psyche.

The symptoms of psychospiritual crises represent a manifestation and exteriorization of the deep dynamics of the human psyche. The individual human psyche is a multidimensional and multilevel system with no internal divisions and boundaries. The elements from postnatal biography and from the Freudian individual unconscious form a continuum with the dynamics of the perinatal level and the transpersonal domain. We cannot, therefore, expect to find clearly defined and demarcated types of spiritual emergency.

And yet, our work with individuals in psychospiritual crises, exchanges with colleagues doing similar work, and study of pertinent literature have convinced us that it is possible and useful to outline certain major forms of psychospiritual crises, which have sufficiently characteristic features to be differentiated from others. Naturally, their boundaries are not clear and, in practice, there are some significant overlaps among them. I will first present a list of the most important varieties of psychospiritual crises as Christina and I have identified them and then briefly discuss each of them.

1. *Shamanic crisis*
2. *Awakening of Kundalini*
3. *Episodes of unitive consciousness (Maslow's "peak experiences")*
4. *Psychological renewal through return to the center (John Perry)*
5. *Crisis of psychic opening*
6. *Past-life experiences*
7. *Communication with spirit guides and "channeling"*
8. *Near-death experiences (NDEs)*
9. *Close encounters with UFOs and alien abduction experiences*
10. *Possession states*
11. *Alcoholism and drug addiction*

1. Shamanic Crisis

The career of many shamans - witch doctors or medicine men and women - in different cultures, begins with a dramatic involuntary visionary state that the anthropologists call "shamanic illness." During such episodes, future shamans usually withdraw psychologically or even physically from their everyday environment and have powerful holotropic experiences. They typically undergo a journey into the underworld, the realm of the dead, where they experience attacks by vicious demons and are exposed to horrendous tortures and ordeals.

This painful initiation culminates in experiences of death and dismemberment followed by rebirth and ascent or magical flight to celestial regions. This might involve transformation into a bird, such as an eagle, falcon, thunderbird, or condor, and flight to the realm of the cosmic sun. The novice shaman can also have an experience of being carried by such a bird into the solar region. In some cultures the motif of magical flight is replaced by that of reaching the celestial realms by climbing the world tree, a rainbow, a pole with many notches, or a ladder made of arrows.

In the course of these arduous visionary journeys novice shamans develop deep contact with the forces of nature and with animals, both in their natural form and their archetypal versions – "animal spirits" or "power animals." When these visionary journeys are successfully completed, they can be profoundly healing. In this process, novice shamans often heal themselves from emotional, psychosomatic, and even physical diseases. For this reason, shamans are frequently referred to as "wounded healers."

In many instances, the involuntary initiates attain deep insights in this experience into the energetic and metaphysical causes of diseases and learn how to heal not only themselves, but also others. Following the successful completion of the initiatory crisis, the individual becomes a shaman and returns to his or her people as a fully functioning and honored member of the community. He or she assumes the combined role of an honored priest, visionary, and healer.

In our workshops and professional training, modern Americans, Europeans, Australians, and Asians have often experienced in their Holotropic Breathwork sessions episodes that bore close resemblance to shamanic crises. Besides the elements of physical and emotional torture, death, and rebirth, such states involved experiences of connection with animals, plants, and elemental forces of nature. The individuals experiencing such crises also often showed spontaneous tendencies to create rituals that were similar to those practiced by shamans of various cultures. On occasion, mental health professionals with this history have been able to use the lessons from their journeys in their work and develop and practice modern versions of shamanic procedures.

The attitude of native cultures toward shamanic crises has often been explained by the lack of elementary psychiatric knowledge of the shaman's tribesmen and the resulting tendency to attribute every experience and behavior that these people do not understand to supernatural forces. However, nothing could be farther from truth. Shamanic cultures, which recognize shamans and show them great respect, have no difficulty differentiating them from individuals who are crazy or sick.

To be considered a shaman, the individual has to successfully complete the transformational journey and fully integrate the episodes of challenging holotropic states of consciousness. In addition, he or she has to be able to function at least as well as other members of the tribe. The way shamanic crises are approached and treated in these societies is an extremely useful and illustrative model of dealing with psychospiritual crises in general.

2. THE AWAKENING OF KUNDALINI

The manifestations of this form of psychospiritual crisis resemble the descriptions of the awakening of *Kundalini*, or the Serpent Power, found in ancient Indian literature (Woodroffe 1974, Mookerjee and Khanna 1977, Mookerjee 1982). According to the yogis, Kundalini is the generative cosmic energy, feminine in nature, that is responsible for the creation of the cosmos. In its latent form it resides at the base of the human spine in the subtle or energetic body, which is a field that pervades and permeates, as well as surrounds, the physical body. This latent energy

Vision of the Goddess Kundalini in a field of fire.

can become activated by meditation, specific exercises, the intervention of an accomplished spiritual teacher (*guru*), or for unknown reasons.

The activated Kundalini, called *shakti*, rises through the *nadis*, channels or conduits in the subtle body; the principal three nadis rising along the body's vertical axis are called Ida, Shushumna, and Pingala. As Kundalini ascends, it clears old traumatic imprints and opens the centers of psychic energy, called *chakras*, situated at the points where Ida and Pingala are crossing. This process, although highly valued and considered beneficial in the yogic tradition, is not without dangers and requires expert guidance by a guru whose Kundalini is fully awakened and stabilized. The most dramatic signs of Kundalini awakening are physical and psychological manifestations called *kriyas*.

The kriyas involve intense sensations of energy and heat streaming up the spine, usually associated with violent shaking, spasms, and twisting movements. Intense waves of seemingly unmotivated emotions, such as anxiety, anger, sadness, or joy and ecstatic rapture, can surface and temporarily dominate the psyche. This can be accompanied by visions of brilliant light or various archetypal beings and a variety of internally perceived sounds.

Many people involved in this process also have emotionally charged and convincing experiences of what seem to be memories from their past lives. Involuntary and often uncontrollable behaviors complete the picture: speaking in tongues, chanting unknown songs or sacred invocations (*mantras*), assuming yogic postures (*asanas*) and gestures (*mudras*), and making a variety of animal sounds and movements.

C. G. Jung and his co-workers dedicated a series of special seminars to this phenomenon (Jung 1999). Jung's perspective on Kundalini proved to be probably the most remarkable error of his entire career. He concluded that the awakening of Kundalini was an exclusively Eastern phenomenon and predicted that it would take at least a thousand years before this energy would be set into motion in the West as a result of depth psychology. In the last several decades, unmistakable signs of Kundalini awakening have been observed in thousands of Westerners. The credit for drawing attention to this condition belongs to Californian psychiatrist and ophtalmologist Lee Sannella, who studied single-handedly nearly one thousand of such cases and summarized his findings in his book *The Kundalini Experience: Psychosis or Transcendence?* (Sannella 1987).

3. Episodes of Unitive Consciousness ("Peak Experiences")

The American psychologist Abraham Maslow studied many hundreds of people who had unitive mystical experiences and coined the term *peak experiences* for these experiences (Maslow 1964). He sharply criticized Western psychiatry's tendency to confuse such mystical states with mental disease. According to him, these states should be considered supernormal rather than abnormal phenomena. If they are not interfered with and are allowed to run their natural course, they typically lead to better functioning in the world and to "self-actualization" or "self-realization" - the capacity to express more fully one's creative potential and to live a more rewarding and satisfying life.

Psychiatrist and consciousness researcher Walter Pahnke developed a list of basic characteristics of a typical peak experience, based on the work of Abraham Maslow and W. T. Stace. He used the following criteria to describe this state of mind (Pahnke and Richards 1966):

*An unretouched picture taken at Esalen using a Po-
laroid camera at the time when Christina's Kundalini
was very active. Her chakras appear to be lit.*

Unity (inner and outer)
Strong positive emotion
Transcendence of time and space
Sense of sacredness (numinosity)
Paradoxical nature
Objectivity and reality of the insights
Ineffability
Positive aftereffects

As this list indicates, when we have a peak experience, we have a
sense of overcoming the usual fragmentation of the mind and body and

feel that we have reached a state of unity and wholeness. We also transcend the ordinary distinction between subject and object and experience an ecstatic union with humanity, nature, the cosmos, and God. This is associated with intense feelings of joy, bliss, serenity, and inner peace. In a mystical experience of this type, we have a sense of leaving ordinary reality, where space has three dimensions and time is linear. We enter a metaphysical, transcendent realm where these categories no longer apply. In this state, infinity and eternity become experiential realities. The numinous quality of this state has nothing to do with previous religious beliefs; it reflects a direct apprehension of the divine nature of reality.

Descriptions of peak experiences are usually full of paradoxes. The experience can be described as "contentless, yet all-containing." It has no specific content, but seems to contain everything in a potential form. We can have a sense of being simultaneously everything and nothing. While our personal identity and the limited ego have disappeared, we feel that we have expanded to such an extent that our being encompasses the entire universe. Similarly, it is possible to perceive all forms as empty, or emptiness as being pregnant with forms. We can even reach a state in which we see that the world exists and does not exist at the same time.

The peak experience can convey what seems to be ultimate wisdom and knowledge in matters of cosmic relevance, which the Upanishads describe as "knowing That, the knowledge of which gives the knowledge of everything." What we have learned during this experience is ineffable; it cannot be described by words. The very nature and structure of our language seem to be inadequate for this purpose. Yet, the experience can profoundly influence our system of values and strategy of existence.

Because of the generally benign nature and positive potential of the peak experience, this is a category of spiritual crisis that should be least problematic. These experiences are by their nature transient and self-limited. There is absolutely no reason why they should have adverse consequences. And yet, due to the misconceptions of the psychiatric profession concerning spiritual matters, many people who experience such states end up hospitalized, receive pathological labels, and their condition is suppressed by psychopharmacological medication.

4. PSYCHOLOGICAL RENEWAL THROUGH RETURN TO THE CENTER

Another important type of transpersonal crisis was described by Californian psychiatrist and Jungian analyst John Weir Perry, who called it the "renewal process" (Perry 1974, 1976, 1998). Because of its depth and intensity, this is the type of psychospiritual crisis that is most likely diagnosed as serious mental disease. The experiences of people involved in the renewal process are so strange, extravagant, and far from everyday reality that it seems obvious that some serious pathological process must be affecting the functioning of their brains.

Individuals involved in this kind of crisis experience their psyche as a colossal battlefield where a cosmic combat is being played out between the forces of Good and Evil, or Light and Darkness. They are preoccupied with the theme of death — ritual killing, sacrifice, martyrdom, and the afterlife. The problem of opposites fascinates them, particularly issues related to the differences between sexes. They experience themselves as the center of fantastic events that have cosmic relevance and are important for the future of the world. Their visionary states tend to take them farther and farther back — through their own history and the history of humanity, all the way to the creation of the world and the original ideal state of paradise. In this process, they seem to strive for perfection, trying to correct things that went wrong in the past.

After a period of turmoil and confusion the experiences become more and more pleasant and start moving toward a resolution. The process often culminates in the experience of *hieros gamos*, or "sacred marriage," in which the individual is elevated to an illustrious or even divine status and experiences union with an equally distinguished partner. This indicates that the masculine and the feminine aspects of the personality are reaching a new balance. The sacred union can be experienced either with an imaginal archetypal figure, or is projected onto an idealized person from one's life, who then appears to be a karmic partner or a soul mate.

At this time, one can also have experiences involving what Jungian psychology interprets as symbols representing the Self, the transpersonal center that reflects our deepest and true nature and is related to, but not totally identical with, the Hindu concept of Atman-Brahman. In visionary states, it can appear in the form of a source of light of supernatural beauty, radiant spheres, precious stones and jewels, pearls, and other similar symbolic representations. Examples of this development from painful and challenging experiences to the discovery of one's divinity can be found in John Perry's books (Perry 1953, 1974, 1976) and in *The Stormy Search for the Self*, our own book on spiritual emergencies (Grof and Grof 1990).

At this stage of the process, these glorious experiences are interpreted as a personal apotheosis, a ritual celebration that raises one's experience of oneself to a highly exalted human status or to a state above the human condition altogether — a great leader, a world savior, or even the Lord of the Universe. This is often associated with a profound sense of spiritual rebirth that replaces the earlier preoccupation with death. At the time of completion and integration, one usually envisions an ideal future — a new world governed by love and justice, where all ills and evils have been overcome. As the intensity of the process subsides the person realizes that the entire drama was a psychological transformation that was limited to his or her inner world and did not involve external reality.

According to John Perry, the renewal process moves the individual in the direction of what Jung called "individuation" - a full realization and expression of one's deep potential. One aspect of Perry's research deserves special notice, since it produced what is probably the most convincing evidence against simplistic biological understanding of psychoses. He was able to show that the experiences involved in the renewal process exactly match the main themes of royal dramas that were enacted in many ancient cultures on New Year's Day.

These ritual dramas celebrating the advent of the new year were performed during what Perry calls "the archaic era of incarnated myth." This was the period in the history of these cultures when the rulers were considered to be incarnated gods and not ordinary human beings. Examples of such God/kings were the Egyptian pharaohs, the Peruvian Incas, the Hebrew and Hittite kings, or the Chinese and Japanese emperors (Perry 1991).

The positive potential of the renewal process and its deep connection with archetypal symbolism and with specific periods of human history represents a very compelling argument against the theory that these experiences are chaotic pathological products of diseased brains. They are clearly closely connected with the evolution of consciousness on the individual and collective level.

5. THE CRISIS OF PSYCHIC OPENING

An increase in intuitive abilities and the occurrence of psychic or paranormal phenomena are very common during psychospiritual crises of all kinds. However, in some instances, the influx of information from nonordinary sources, such as astral projection, precognition, telepathy, or clairvoyance, becomes so overwhelming and confusing that it dominates the picture and constitutes a major problem, in and of itself.

Among the most dramatic manifestations of psychic opening are out-of-body experiences. In the middle of everyday life, and often without any noticeable trigger, one's consciousness can detach from the body and witness what is happening in the surroundings or in various remote locations. The information attained during these episodes by extrasensory perception often proves to correspond to consensus reality. Out-of-body experiences occur with extraordinary frequency in near-

The Great Mother Goddess
Personification of divine feminine energy that is the source of all creation, depicting a Holotropic Breathwork experience in an Esalen month-long seminar.

death situations, where the accuracy of this "remote viewing" has been established by systematic studies (Ring 1982, 1985, Ring and Valarino 1998, Ring and Cooper 1999).

People experiencing intense psychic opening might be so much in touch with the inner processes of others that they exhibit remarkable telepathic abilities. They might indiscriminately verbalize accurate incisive insights into other people's minds concerning various issues that these individuals are trying to hide. This can frighten, irritate, and alienate others so severely that it often becomes a significant factor contributing to unnecessary hospitalization or punitive measures within the psychiatric facility. Similarly, accurate precognitions of future situations and clairvoyant perceptions, particularly if they occur repeatedly in impressive clusters, can seriously upset the persons in crisis, as well as alarm those around them, since they undermine their notion of the nature of reality.

In experiences that can be called "mediumistic," one has a sense of losing one's own identity and taking on the identity of another person. This can involve assuming the other person's body image, posture, gestures, facial expression, feelings, and even thought processes. Accomplished shamans, psychics, and spiritual healers can use such experiences in a controlled and productive way. Unlike the persons in psychospiritual crisis, they are capable of taking on the identity of others at will and also resuming their own separate identity after they accomplish the task of the session. During the crises of psychic opening, the sudden, unpredictable, and uncontrollable loss of one's ordinary identity can be very frightening.

People in spiritual crisis often experience uncanny coincidences that link the world of inner realities, such as dreams and visionary states, to happenings in everyday life. This phenomenon was first recognized and described by C. G. Jung, who gave it the name *synchronicity* and explored it in a special essay (Jung 1960). The study of synchronistic events helped Jung realize that archetypes were not principles limited to the intrapsychic domain. It became clear to him that they have what he called "psychoid" quality, which means that they govern not only the individual psyche, but also happenings in the world of consensus reality. I have explored this fascinating topic in my other writings (Grof 1987, 1998, and 2006a).

Any researcher who studies Jungian synchronicities seriously discovers that they are without any doubt authentic phenomena and cannot be ignored and discounted as accidental coincidences. They also cannot be indiscriminately dismissed as pathological distortions of reality – erroneous perception of meaningful relations where, in actuality, there are none. This is a common practice in contemporary psychiatry where any allusion to meaningful coincidences is automatically diagnosed as "delusion of reference."

In case of true synchronicities, any open-minded witnesses, who have access to all the relevant information, recognize that the coincidences involved are beyond any reasonable statistical probability. Extraordinary synchronicities accompany many forms of transpersonal crises and in crises of psychic opening they are particularly common.

6. PAST-LIFE EXPERIENCES

Among the most dramatic and colorful transpersonal phenomena occurring in holotropic states of consciousness are experiences that appear to be memories from previous incarnations. These are sequences that take place in other historical periods and often in other countries and are usually associated with powerful emotions and physical sensations. They often portray in great detail the persons, circumstances, and historical settings involved. Their most remarkable aspect is a convincing sense of remembering and reliving something that one has already

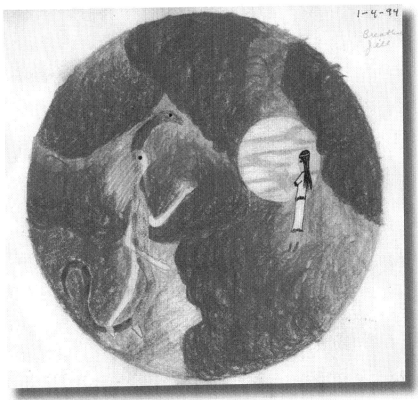

Snake Energy and White Buffalo Woman

*In the middle of chaos in the form of rising Snake Energy and clouds of rag-
ing, swirling colors appears White Buffalo Woman. She comes to teach the
artist to channel this energy and transmute it into her own power, enabling
her to pass through the dimensional doorway to a place of light, peace, and
self-knowledge. (Jan Vannatta)*

seen (déjà vu) or experienced (déjà vecu) at some time in the past. This
is clearly the same type of experience that in Asia and many other places
of the world inspired the belief in reincarnation and the law of karma.

The rich and accurate information that these "past-life memories"
provide, as well as their healing potential, impels us to take them seriously. When the content of a karmic experience fully emerges into
consciousness, it can suddenly provide an explanation for many otherwise incomprehensible aspects of one's daily life. Strange difficulties in
relationships with certain people, unsubstantiated fears, and peculiar
idiosyncrasies and attractions, as well as otherwise incomprehensible
emotional and psychosomatic symptoms suddenly seem to make sense

as karmic carry-overs from a previous lifetime. These problems typically disappear when the karmic pattern in question is consciously experienced and integrated.

Past-life experiences can complicate life in several different ways. Before their content emerges fully into consciousness and reveals itself, one can be haunted in everyday life by strange emotions, physical feelings, and visions without knowing where these are coming from or what they mean. Experienced out of context, these experiences naturally appear incomprehensible and irrational. Another kind of complication occurs when a particularly strong karmic experience starts emerging into consciousness in the middle of everyday life and interferes with normal functioning.

One might also feel compelled to act out some of the elements of the karmic pattern before it is fully experienced and understood or completed. For instance, it might suddenly seem that a certain person in one's present life played an important role in a previous incarnation, the memory of which is emerging into consciousness. When this happens, one may seek emotional contact with a person who now appears to be a "soul-mate" from one's karmic past or, conversely, confrontation and showdown with an adversary from another lifetime. This kind of activity can lead to unpleasant complications, since the alleged karmic partners usually have no basis in their own experiences for understanding this behavior.

Even if one manages to avoid the danger of embarrassing acting-out, the problems are not necessarily over. After a past-life memory has fully emerged into consciousness and its content and implications have been revealed to the experiencer, there remains one more challenge. One has to reconcile this experience with the traditional beliefs and values of the industrial civilization. Denial of the possibility of reincarnation represents a rare instance of complete agreement between the Christian Church and materialistic science. Therefore, in Western culture, acceptance and intellectual integration of a past-life memory is a difficult task for an atheist as well as a traditionally religious person.

Assimilation of past-life experiences into one's belief system can be a relatively easy task for someone who does not have a strong commitment to Christianity or the materialistic scientific worldview. The experiences are usually so convincing that one simply accepts their message and might even feel excited about this new discovery. However, fundamentalist Christians and those who have a strong investment in rationality and the traditional scientific perspective can be catapulted into a period of confusion when they are confronted with convincing personal past life experiences that seriously challenge their belief system.

7. Communication with Spirit Guides and "Channeling"

Occasionally, one can encounter a being in a holotropic state of consciousness who seems to show interest in a personal relationship and assumes the position of a teacher, guide, protector, or simply a convenient source of information. Such beings are usually perceived as discarnate humans, suprahuman entities, or deities existing on higher planes of consciousness and endowed with extraordinary wisdom. Sometimes they take on the form of a person; at other times they appear as radiant sources of light, or simply let their presence be sensed. Their messages are usually received in the form of direct thought transfer or through other extrasensory means. In some instances, communication can take the form of verbal messages.

A particularly interesting phenomenon in this category is *channeling*, which has received much attention from the public and mass media. A person who is "channeling" transmits to others messages received from a source that appears to be external to his or her consciousness. It occurs through speaking in a trance, using automatic writing, or recording of telepathically received thoughts. Channeling has played an important role in the history of humanity. Among the channeled spiritual teachings are many scriptures of enormous cultural influence, such as the ancient Indian Vedas, the Qur'an, and the Book of Mormon. A remarkable modern example of a channeled text is *A Course in Miracles*, recorded by psychologist Helen Schucman (Anonymous 1975, Grof 2006 a).

Experiences of channeling can precipitate a serious psychological and spiritual crisis. The individual involved can interpret the experience as an indication of beginning insanity. This is particularly likely if the channeling involves hearing voices, a well-known symptom of paranoid schizophrenia. The quality of the channeled material varies from trivial and questionable chatter to extraordinary information. On occasion, channeling can provide consistently accurate data about subjects to which the recipient was never exposed. This fact can then appear to be a particularly convincing proof of the involvement of supernatural realities and can lead to serious philosophical confusion for an atheistic layperson or a scientist with a materialistic worldview. Readers interested in this phenomenon will find much valuable information in special studies by Arthur Hastings and Jon Klimo (Hastings 1991, Klimo 1998).

Spirit guides are usually perceived as advanced spiritual beings on a high level of consciousness evolution who are endowed with superior intelligence and extraordinary moral integrity. This can lead to highly problematic ego inflation in the channeler, who might feel chosen for a special mission and see it as a proof of his or her own superiority.

8. NEAR-DEATH EXPERIENCES (NDEs)

World mythology, folklore, and spiritual literature abound in vivid accounts of the experiences associated with death and dying. Special sacred texts have been dedicated exclusively to descriptions and discussions of the posthumous journey of the soul, such as the *Tibetan Book of the Dead (Bardo Thödol)*, the *Egyptian Book of the Dead (Pert Em Hru)*, the Aztec *Codex Borgia*, the *Mayan Book of the Dead*, and their European counterpart, *Ars Moriendi (The Art of Dying)* (Grof 1994, 2006 b).

In the past this eschatological mythology was discounted by Western scholars as a product of fantasy and wishful thinking by primitive peoples who were unable to face the fact of impermanence and their own mortality. This situation changed dramatically after the publication of Raymond Moody's international best-seller Life After Life, which brought scientific confirmation of these accounts and showed that an encounter with death can be a fantastic adventure in consciousness. Moody's book was based on reports of 150 people who had experienced a close confrontation with death, or were actually pronounced clinically dead, but regained consciousness and lived to tell their stories (Moody 1975).

Moody reported that people who had near-death experiences (NDEs) frequently witnessed a review of their entire lives in the form of a colorful, incredibly condensed replay occurring within only seconds of clock time. Consciousness often detached from the body and floated freely above the scene, observing it with curiosity and detached amusement, or traveled to distant locations. Many people described passing through a dark tunnel or funnel toward a divine light of supernatural brilliance and beauty.

This light was not physical in nature, but had distinctly personal characteristics. It was a Being of Light, radiating infinite, all-embracing love, forgiveness, and acceptance. In a personal exchange, often perceived as an audience with God, these individuals received lessons regarding existence and universal laws and had the opportunity to evaluate their past by these new standards. Then they chose to return to ordinary reality and live their lives in a new way congruent with the principles they had learned. Since their publication, Moody's findings have been repeatedly confirmed by other researchers (Ring 1982, Ring 1985, Sabom 1982, Greyson and Flynn 1984).

Most survivors emerge from their near-death experiences profoundly changed. They have a universal and all-encompassing spiritual vision of reality, a new system of values, and a radically different general strategy of life. They have deep appreciation for being alive and feel kinship

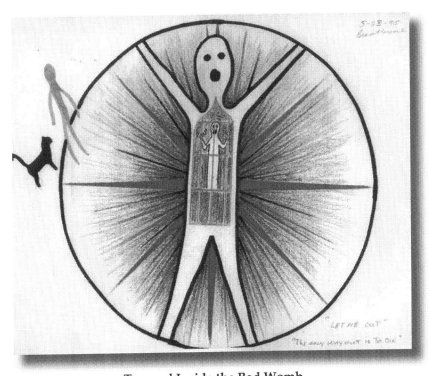

Trapped Inside the Bad Womb
The experience of being caught and squeezed in the black, tight womb of the Mother Dragon. "There is no way out, the only way out is to die."
(Jan Vannatta)

with all living beings and concern for the future of humanity and the planet. However, the fact that the encounter with death has a great positive potential does not mean that this transformation is always easy.

Near-death experiences very frequently lead to psychospiritual crises. A powerful NDE can radically undermine the worldview of the persons involved because it catapults them abruptly and without warning into a reality that is radically different from their everyday experience. A car accident in the middle of rush-hour traffic or a heart attack during morning jogging can launch someone within a matter of seconds into a fantastic visionary adventure that tears his or her ordinary reality asunder. Following an NDE, people might need special counseling and support to be able to integrate these extraordinary experiences into their everyday life.

Unfortunately, the approach of the personnel in most medical facilities to NDE survivors leaves much to be desired, in spite of the fact that in the last few decades this phenomenon has received much attention in the professional literature, as well as in the mass media. Few survivors of NDEs receive professional counseling that most of them sorely need. It is also not yet mandatory to include the reports of the patients' NDEs in the medical folders, although it is well known that these experiences can have profound impact on their emotional and psychosomatic condition. A comprehensive discussion of the problems related to NDEs can be found in my book The Ultimate Journey: Consciousness and the Mystery of Death (Grof 2006 b).

9. Close Encounters with UFOs and Alien Abduction Experiences

The experiences of encounters with extraterrestrial spacecrafts and of abduction by alien beings can often precipitate serious emotional and intellectual crises that have much in common with psychospiritual crises. This fact requires an explanation, since most people consider UFOs simply in terms of four alternatives: actual visitation of the earth by alien spacecraft, hoax, misperception of natural events and devices of terrestrial origin, and psychotic hallucinations. Alvin Lawson has also made an attempt to interpret UFO abduction experiences as misinterpretations of the memory of the trauma of birth, using my own clinical material (Lawson 1984).

Descriptions of UFO sightings typically refer to lights that have an uncanny, supernatural quality. These lights resemble those mentioned in many reports of visionary states. C. G. Jung, who dedicated a special study to the problem of "flying saucers," suggested that these phenomena might be archetypal visions originating in the collective unconscious of humanity, rather than psychotic hallucinations or visits by extraterrestrials from distant civilizations (Jung 1964 a). He supported his thesis by careful analysis of legends about flying discs that have been told throughout history and reports about various similar apparitions that have occasionally caused crises and mass panic.

It has also been pointed out that the extraterrestrial beings involved in these encounters have important parallels in world mythology and religion, systems that have their roots in the collective unconscious. The alien spacecrafts and cosmic flights depicted by those who were allegedly abducted or invited for a ride resemble certain phenomena described in spiritual literature, such as the chariot of the Vedic god Indra or Ezekiel's flaming machine described in the Bible. The fabulous landscapes and cities visited during these journeys resemble the visionary experiences of paradise, celestial realms, and cities of light.

The abductees often report that the aliens took them into a special laboratory and subjected them to painful examinations and frightening experiments using various exotic instruments. This involved probing the cavities of the body, examination of the sexual organs, and taking samples of sperm and ova. There are frequent references to genetic experiments with the goal of producing hybrid offspring. These interventions are typically very unpleasant and occasionally border on torture. This brings the experiences of the abductees close to the initiatory crises of the shamans and to the ordeals of the neophytes in aboriginal rites of passage, such as circumcision and subincision of the penis.

There is an additional reason why a UFO experience can precipitate a spiritual crisis. It is similar to the problem we have discussed earlier in relation to spirit guides and channeling. The alien visitors are usually seen as representatives of civilizations that are incomparably more advanced than ours, not only technologically but also intellectually, morally, and spiritually. Such contact often has very powerful mystical undertones and is associated with insights of cosmic relevance. It is thus easy for the recipients of such special attention to interpret it as an indication of their own uniqueness.

Abductees might feel that they have attracted the interest of superior beings from an advanced civilization because they themselves are in some way exceptional and particularly suited for a special purpose. In Jungian psychology, a situation in which the individual claims the luster of the archetypal world for his or her own person is referred to as "ego inflation." For all these reasons, experiences of "close encounters" can lead to serious transpersonal crises.

People who have experienced the strange world of UFO experiences and alien abduction need professional help from someone who has general knowledge of archetypal psychology and who is also familiar with the specific characteristics of the UFO phenomenon. Experienced researchers, such as Harvard psychiatrist John Mack, have brought ample evidence that the alien abduction experiences are phenomena *sui generis*, that represent a serious conceptual challenge for Western psychiatry and materialistic science in general. An aspect of the UFO phenomena that is particularly baffling is that they occasionally have definite psychoid features. This means that they are synchronistically linked with events in the material world. It has become clear that it is naive and indefensible to see them as manifestations of mental disease or dismiss all of them as misperceptions and misinterpretations of ordinary phenomena (Mack 1994, 1999).

Over the years, I have worked with many individuals who had experiences of alien abduction in their psychedelic or Holotropic Breathwork sessions and during spiritual emergencies. Almost without exception, these episodes were extremely intense and experientially convincing.

In view of my observations, I share the opinion of many serious UFO researchers that these experiences represent fascinating and authentic phenomena that deserve to be seriously studied. The position of traditional psychiatrists who see them as products of an unknown pathological process in the brain is clearly oversimplistic and highly implausible.

It is equally improbable that we are dealing with actual visits of extraterrestrial beings. A civilization capable of sending spaceships to our planet would have to have technical means that we cannot even imagine. We have enough information about the planets of the solar system to know that they are unlikely sources of such an alien expedition. The distance of the earth from the nearest celestial bodies outside of the solar system amounts to many light years.

Negotiating such distances would require velocities equaling or surpassing the speed of light or interdimensional travel through hyperspace. A civilization capable of such formidable achievements would very likely have technology that would make it impossible for us to differentiate between hallucinations and reality. Until more reliable information is available, it seems therefore most plausible to see the UFO experiences as manifestations of archetypal elements from the collective unconscious.

10. POSSESSION STATES

People experiencing this type of transpersonal crisis have a distinct feeling that their psyche and body have been invaded and that they are being controlled by an evil entity or energy with personal characteristics. They perceive it as coming from the outside of their own personality and as being hostile and disturbing. It can appear to be a confused discarnate entity, a demonic being, or the consciousness of a wicked person invading them by means of black magic and hexing procedures.

There are many different types and degrees of such conditions. In some instances, the true nature of this disorder remains hidden. The problem manifests as serious psychopathology, such as antisocial or even criminal behavior, suicidal depression, murderous aggression or self-destructive behavior, promiscuous and deviant sexual impulses and acting-out, or excessive use of alcohol and drugs. It is often not until such a person starts experiential psychotherapy that "possession" is identified as a condition underlying these problems.

In the middle of an experiential session, the face of a possessed person can become cramped and take the form of a "mask of evil," and the eyes can assume a wild expression. The hands and body might develop strange contortions, and the voice may become altered and take on an otherworldly quality. When this situation is allowed to develop, the session can bear a striking resemblance to exorcisms in the Catholic Church, or exorcist rituals in various aboriginal cultures.

The resolution often comes after dramatic episodes of choking, projectile vomiting, screaming, and frantic physical activity, or even temporary loss of control. Sequences of this kind can be unusually healing and transformative and often result in a deep spiritual conversion of the person involved. A detailed description of the most dramatic episode of this kind I have observed during my entire professional career can be found in my account of the case of Flora (Grof 2006 a).

At other times, the possessed person is aware of the presence of the "evil entity" in his or her body and spends much effort trying to fight it and control its influence. In the extreme version of the possession state, the problematic energy can spontaneously manifest and take over in the middle of everyday life. This situation resembles the one described earlier for experiential sessions, but the individual here lacks the support and protection provided by the therapeutic context. Under such circumstances, he or she can feel extremely frightened and desperately alone. Relatives, friends, and often even therapists tend to withdraw from the "possessed" individual and respond with a strange mixture of metaphysical fear and moral rejection. They often label the person as evil and refuse further contact.

This condition clearly belongs in the category of psychospiritual crises, in spite of the fact that it involves negative energies and is associated with many objectionable forms of behavior. The demonic archetype is by its very nature transpersonal, since it represents the negative mirror image of the divine. It also often appears to be a "gateway phenomenon," comparable to the terrifying guardians flanking the doors of Buddhist temples leading to radiant images of the Buddha. Encounter with an entity of this kind often immediately precedes a profound spiritual experience. With the help of someone who is not afraid of its uncanny nature and is able to encourage its full conscious manifestation, this energy can be dissipated, and remarkable healing occurs.

11. Alcoholism and Drug Addiction as Psychospiritual Crises

It makes good sense to describe addiction as a form of transpersonal crisis ("spiritual emergency"), in spite of the fact that it differs in its external manifestations from more obvious types of psychospiritual crises. In addiction, as in possession states, the spiritual dimension is obscured by the destructive and self-destructive nature of the disorder. While in other forms of spiritual crises people encounter problems because of their difficulty to cope with mystical experiences, in addiction the source of the problem is a strong spiritual longing combined with the fact that the contact with the mystical dimension has not been made.

There is ample evidence that behind the craving for drugs or alcohol is an unrecognized craving for transcendence or wholeness (Grof 1987). Many recovering people talk about their restless search for some unknown missing element or dimension in their lives and describe their unfulfilling and frustrating pursuit of substances, foods, relationships, possessions, or power that reflects an unrelenting but vain effort to satiate this craving (Grof, C. 1993).

The key to the understanding of addiction seems to be the fact that there exists a certain superficial similarity between mystical states and intoxication by alcohol or hard drugs. Both of these conditions share the feeling of dissolution of individual boundaries, dissipation of disturbing emotions, and transcendence of mundane problems. Although the intoxication with alcohol or drugs lacks many important characteristics of the mystical state, such as serenity, numinosity, and richness of philosophical insights, the experiential overlap is sufficient to seduce alcoholics and addicts into abuse.

William James was aware of this connection and wrote about it in Varieties of Religious Experience: "The sway of alcohol over mankind is unquestionably due to its power to stimulate the mystical faculties of human nature, usually crushed to earth by the cold facts and criticisms of the sober hour. Sobriety diminishes, discriminates, and says no; drunkenness expands, unites and says yes" (James 1961). James also saw the implications of this fact for therapy, which he expressed very succinctly in his famous statement: "The best treatment for dipsomania (an archaic term for alcoholism) is religiomania."

C. G. Jung's independent insight in this regard was instrumental in the development of the worldwide network of Twelve Step Programs. It is not generally known that Jung played a very important role in the history of Alcoholics Anonymous (AA). The information about this little-known aspect of Jung's work can be found in a letter that Bill Wilson, the co-founder of AA, wrote to Jung in 1961 (Wilson and Jung 1963).

Jung had a patient, Roland H., who came to him after having exhausted other means of recovery from alcoholism. Following a temporary improvement after a year's treatment with Jung, he suffered a relapse. Jung told him that his case was hopeless and suggested that his only chance was to join a religious community and hope for a profound spiritual experience. Roland H. joined the Oxford Group, an evangelical movement emphasizing self-survey, confession, and service.

There he experienced a religious conversion that freed him from alcoholism. He then returned to New York City and became very active in the Oxford Group there. He was able to help Bill Wilson's friend, Edwin

T., who in turn helped Bill Wilson in his personal crisis. In his powerful spiritual experience, Bill Wilson had a vision of a worldwide chain-style fellowship of alcoholics helping each other.

Years later, Wilson wrote Jung a letter in which he brought to his attention the important role that Jung played in the history of AA. In his answer, Jung wrote in reference to his patient: "His craving for alcohol was the equivalent, on a low level, of the spiritual thirst of our being for wholeness, expressed in medieval language: the union with God." Jung pointed out that in Latin, the term *spiritus* covers both meanings — alcohol and spirit. He then expressed very succinctly his belief that only a deep spiritual experience can save people from the ravages of alcohol. He suggested that the formula for treatment of alcoholism is "Spiritus contra spiritum," James's and Jung's insights have since been confirmed by the experiences of the Twelve Step Program and by clinical research with psychedelics (Grof 1980).

Treatment of Psychospiritual Crises

The psychotherapeutic strategy for individuals undergoing spiritual crises is based on the realization that these states are not manifestations of an unknown pathological process, but results of a spontaneous movement in the psyche that engages deep dynamics of the unconscious and has healing and transformative potential. Understanding and appropriate treatment of spiritual crises requires a vastly extended cartography of the psyche that includes the perinatal and transpersonal region. This new model has been described at some length elsewhere (Grof 1975, 2001).

The nature and degree of the therapeutic assistance that is necessary depends on the intensity of the psychospiritual process involved. In mild forms of spiritual crisis, the individual is usually able to function in everyday life and cope with the holotropic experiences as they emerge into consciousness. All that he or she needs is an opportunity to discuss the process with a transpersonally oriented therapist, who provides constructive supportive feedback, helps the client to integrate the experiences into everyday life, and suggests literature that contains useful information.

If the process is more active, it might require regular sessions of experiential therapy during which faster breathing, music, and bodywork are used to facilitate the emergence of the unconscious material and the full expression of emotions and blocked physical energies. The general strategy of this approach is identical with that used in Holotropic Breathwork sessions (Grof and Grof, 2010). Allowing full expression of the emerging unconscious material in the sessions specifically designated and scheduled for this purpose reduces the possibility that the material will surface unexpectedly and interfere with the client's life in the interim periods.

When the experiences are very intense, all we have to do during the work with the clients is to encourage them to close their eyes, surrender to the process, observe what is happening, and find expression for the emerging emotions and physical feelings. If we encounter psychological resistance, we might occasionally use releasing bodywork as in the termination periods of breathwork sessions. Holotropic Breathwork as such is indicated only if the natural unfolding of the process reaches an impasse. Therapeutic work with this category of clients has to be conducted in a residential facility where supervision is available twenty-four hours a day.

These intense experiential sessions can be complemented with Fritz Perls' Gestalt practice (Perls 1976), Dora Kalff's Jungian sandplay (Kalff and Kalff 2004), Francine Shapiro's Eye Movement Desensitization and Reprocessing (EMDR) (Shapiro 2001), or bodywork with a psychologically experienced practitioner. A variety of auxiliary techniques can also prove extremely useful under these circumstances. Among them are writing of a log, painting of mandalas, expressive dancing, and jogging, swimming, or other sport activities. If the client is able to concentrate on reading, transpersonally oriented books, particularly those focusing on the problem of psychospiritual crises or on some specific aspect of the client's inner experiences, can be extremely helpful.

People whose experiences are so intense and dramatic that they cannot be handled on an out-patient basis represent a serious problem. Practically no facilities exist which offer supervision twenty-four hours a day without the use of routine suppressive psychopharmacological intervention. Several experimental facilities of this kind that existed in the past in California, such as John Perry's Diabasis in San Francisco and Chrysalis in San Diego, or Barbara Findeisen's Pocket Ranch in Geyserville, were short-lived. The main reason for their lack of long term success was not a lack of interest in or need for such facilities, nor a lack of success with clients, but the fact that the insurance companies refused to pay for alternative therapy that had not been officially sanctioned and the individuals experiencing spiritual emergencies are almost never in a situation to be able to finance their treatment themselves. Solving the problem of financing such alternative centers is a necessary prerequisite for effective therapy of intense spiritual crises in the future.

In some places, helpers have tried to overcome this shortcoming by creating teams of trained assistants who took shifts in the client's home for the time of the duration of the episode. Management of intense acute forms of spiritual crises requires some extraordinary measures, whether conducted in a special facility or in a private home. Extended episodes of this kind can last days or weeks and can be associated with a lot of physical activity, intense emotions, loss of appetite, and insomnia.

There is a danger of dehydration, vitamin and mineral deficiency, and physical exhaustion. An insufficient intake of food can lead to hypoglycemia that is known to weaken psychological defenses and bring additional material from the unconscious. This can lead to a vicious circle that perpetuates the acute condition. Tea with honey, bananas, or another form of food containing glucose can be of help in grounding the process.

A person in intense psychospiritual crisis is usually so deeply involved in his or her experience that they forget about food, drink, and elementary hygiene. It is thus up to the helpers to take care of the client's basic needs. Since the care for people undergoing the most acute forms of spiritual crises is unusually demanding, the helpers have to take shifts of reasonable duration to protect their own mental and physical health. To guarantee comprehensive and integrated care under these circumstances, it is necessary to keep a log and carefully record the client's intake of food, liquids, and vitamins.

Sleep deprivation has similar effects as fasting; it tends to weaken the defenses and facilitate the influx of unconscious material into consciousness. This can also lead to a vicious circle that needs to be interrupted. It might, therefore, be necessary to occasionally administer a minor tranquilizer or a hypnotic. In this context, tranquilizing medication is not considered therapy, as it is the case in traditional psychiatric facilities. It is given solely for the purpose of securing the client's sleep. The administration of minor tranquilizers or hypnotics interrupts the vicious circle and gives the client the necessary rest and the energy to continue the following day with the uncovering process.

In later stages of spiritual crises, when the intensity of the process subsides, the person no longer requires constant supervision. He or she gradually returns to everyday activities and resumes the responsibility concerning basic care. The overall duration of the stay in a protected environment depends on the rate of stabilization and integration of the process. If necessary, we might schedule occasional experiential sessions and recommend the use of selected complementary and auxiliary techniques described earlier. Regular discussions about the experiences and insights from the time of the episode can be of great help in integrating the episode.

The treatment of alcoholism and drug addiction presents some specific problems and has to be discussed separately from therapy of other psychospiritual crises. In particular the element of physiological addiction and the progressive nature of the disorder require special measures. Before dealing with the psychological problems underlying addiction, it is imperative to break the chemical cycle that perpetuates the use of substances. The individual has to go through a period of withdrawal and detoxification in a special residential facility.

Once this is accomplished, the focus can turn to the psychospiritual roots of the problem. As we have seen, alcoholism and drug addiction represent a misguided search for transcendence. For this reason, to be successful, the therapeutic program has to include as an integral part strong emphasis on the spiritual dimension of the problem. Historically, the programs of Alcoholics Anonymous (AA) and Narcotics Anonymous (NA), fellowships offering a comprehensive approach based on the Twelve Step philosophy outlined by Bill Wilson, have been most successful in combating addiction.

Following the program step by step, the alcoholic or addict recognizes and admits that they have lost control over their lives and have become powerless. They are encouraged to surrender and let a higher power of their own definition take over. A painful review of their personal history produces an inventory of their wrongdoings. This provides the basis for making amends to all the people whom they have hurt by their addiction. Those who have reached sobriety and are in recovery are then asked to carry the message to other addicts and to help them to overcome their habit.

The Twelve Step Programs are invaluable in providing support and guidance for alcoholics and addicts from the beginning of treatment throughout the years of sobriety and recovery. Since the focus of this book is the healing potential of holotropic states, we will now explore whether and in what way these states can be useful in the treatment of addiction. This question is closely related to the Eleventh Step that emphasizes the need "to improve through prayer and meditation our conscious contact with God as we understand God." Since holotropic states can facilitate mystical experiences, they clearly fit into this category.

Over the years, I have had extensive experience with the use of holotropic states in the treatment of alcoholics and addicts and also in the work with recovering people who used them to improve the quality of their sobriety. I participated in a team at the Maryland Psychiatric Research Center in Baltimore that conducted large, controlled studies of psychedelic therapy in alcoholics and hard drug addicts (Grof 1980). My wife Christina and I have also had the opportunity to witness the effect of serial Holotropic Breathwork sessions on many recovering people in the context of our training. I will first share my own observations and experiences from this work and then discuss the problems involved in the larger context of the Twelve Step movement.

In my experience, it is highly unlikely that either Holotropic Breathwork or psychedelic therapy can help alcoholics and addicts at the time when they are actively using. Even deep and meaningful experiences do not seem to have the power to break the chemical cycle involved. Therapeutic work with holotropic states should be introduced only after alcoholics and addicts have undergone detoxification, overcome the withdrawal symptoms, and reached sobriety. Only then can they benefit from holotropic experiences and do some deep work on the psychological problems underlying their addiction. At this point, holotropic states can be extremely useful in helping them to confront traumatic memories, process difficult emotions associated with them, and obtain valuable insights into the psychological roots of their abuse.

Holotropic experiences can also mediate the process of psychospiritual death and rebirth that is known as "hitting bottom" and represents a critical turning point in the life of many alcoholics and addicts. The experience of ego death happens here in a protected situation where it does not involve the physical, psychological, interpersonal, and social risks it would have if it happened spontaneously in the client's natural surroundings. And finally, holotropic states can mediate experiential access to profound spiritual experiences, the true object of the alcoholic's or addict's craving, and make it thus less likely that they will seek unfortunate surrogates in alcohol or narcotics.

The programs of psychedelic therapy for alcoholics and addicts conducted at the Maryland Psychiatric Research Center were very successful, in spite of the fact that the protocol limited the number of psychedelic sessions to a maximum of three. At a six-month follow-up, over one half of chronic alcoholics and one-third of hard-core narcotic drug addicts participating in these programs were still sober and were considered "essentially rehabilitated" by an independent evaluation team (Pahnke et al. 1970, Savage and McCabe 1971, Grof 1980). Recovering people in our training and workshops, almost without exception, see Holotropic Breathwork as a way of improving the quality of their sobriety and facilitating their psychospiritual growth.

In spite of the evidence of its beneficial effects, the use of holotropic states in recovering people meets strong opposition among some conservative members of the Twelve Step movement. These people assert that alcoholics and addicts seeking any form of a "high" are experiencing a "relapse." They pass this judgment not only when the holotropic state involves the use of psychedelic substances, but extend it also to experiential forms of psychotherapy and even to meditation, an approach explicitly mentioned in the description of the Eleventh Step.

It is likely that this extremist attitude has its roots in the history of Alcoholics Anonymous. Shortly before the second international AA convention Bill Wilson, the co-founder of AA, discovered the psychedelic LSD after twenty years of sobriety. He took it for the first time in 1956 and continued experimenting with it with a coterie of friends and acquaintances, including clergymen and psychiatrists. He was quite enthusiastic about it and believed that this substance had the ability to remove barriers which keep us from directly experiencing God. The AA board was shocked by his suggestion that LSD sessions should be introduced into AA program. This caused a major turmoil in the movement and was eventually rejected.

We are confronted here with two conflicting perspectives on the relationship between holotropic states and addiction. One of them sees any effort to depart from the ordinary state of consciousness as unacceptable for an addicted person and considers it a relapse. The contrary view is based on the idea that seeking a spiritual experience is a legitimate and natural tendency of every human being and that striving for transcendence is the most powerful motivating force in the psyche (Weil 1972). Addiction then is a misguided and distorted form of this effort and the most effective remedy for it is facilitating access to a genuine spiritual experience.

The future will decide which of these two approaches will be adopted by professionals and by the recovering community. In my opinion, the most promising development in the treatment of alcoholism and drug abuse would be a marriage of the Twelve Step Program, the most effective strategy for treating alcoholism and addiction, with transpersonal psychology that can provide a solid theoretical background for spiritually grounded therapy. Responsible use of holotropic therapy would be a very logical integral part of such a comprehensive treatment.

My wife Christina and I organized two meetings of the International Transpersonal Association (ITA) in the 1980s in Eugene, Oregon, and Atlanta, Georgia, that demonstrated the feasibility and usefulness of bringing together the Twelve Step Programs and transpersonal psychology. The empirical and theoretical justification for such merging was discussed in several publications (Grof 1987, Grof, C. 1993, Sparks 1993).

The concept of "spiritual emergency" is new and will undoubtedly be complemented and refined in the future. However, we have repeatedly seen that even in its present form, as defined by Christina and myself, it has been of great help to many individuals in crises of transformation. We have observed that when these conditions are treated with respect and receive appropriate support they can result in remarkable healing, deep positive transformation, and a higher level of functioning in everyday life. This has often happened in spite of the fact that the conditions for treating people in psychospiritual crises are currently far from ideal.

In the future the success of this endeavor could increase considerably if people capable of assisting individuals in spiritual emergencies had at their disposal a network of twenty-four-hour centers for those whose experiences are so intense that they cannot be treated on an outpatient basis. At present the absence of such facilities and lack of support from the insurance companies for unconventional approaches to treatment represent the most serious obstacles to effective application of the new therapeutic strategies.

Roots of Human Violence and Greed:
Psychospiritual Perspective

Greed

Personification of insatiable greed, a driving force of human life and history, from a Holotropic Breathwork session. (Anne Høivik)

Roots of Human Violence and Greed: Psychospiritual Perspective

The study of holotropic states of consciousness has amassed a rich array of observations that have revolutionized our understanding of the human psyche in health and disease. The importance of many of these findings transcends the framework of individual psychology; they seem to offer deep insights into dimensions of the current global crisis which have so far been neglected and suggest strategies that might be useful for its alleviation. In this chapter, I will explore these new perspectives with special emphasis on two elemental forces that have driven human history since time immemorial to the present time - the proclivities to unbridled violence and to insatiable greed. Because of their expression through the development of weapons of mass destruction, relentless population explosion, escalating plundering of natural resources, and increasing of industrial pollution, these two scourges now threaten survival of the human species and the other forms of life on this planet.

Violence and Greed in Human History

The number and degree of atrocities that have been committed throughout the ages in various countries of the world, many of them in the name of God, are truly unimaginable and indescribable. Millions of soldiers and civilians have been killed in wars and revolutions of all times or in other forms of atrocities. During his unparalleled military campaign, Alexander the Great destroyed the Persian empire and conquered all the countries between Macedonia and India. Secular and religious ambitions - from the expansion of the Roman Empire to the spread of Islam and the Christian Crusades - found their expression in the merciless use of sword and fire. In ancient Rome, countless Christians and other prisoners were sacrificed in the arenas to provide a highly sought-after spectacle for the masses.

Hundreds of thousands of innocent victims were tortured, killed, or burned alive in the autos-da-fe by the medieval Inquisition. In Mesoamerica, countless soldiers of the tribes defeated by the Aztecs, who had not died in the battle, were slaughtered on sacrificial altars. The Aztec cruelty found its match in the bloody ventures of the Spanish conquistadors. Genghis Khan's and Tamerlan's Mongolian hordes swept through Asia killing, pillaging, and burning towns and villages. The colonialism of Great Britain and other European countries and the Napoleonic wars were additional examples of violence and relentless greed.

This trend continued in an unmitigated fashion in the twentieth century. The loss of life in World War I was estimated at ten million soldiers and twenty million civilians. Additional millions died from war-spread epidemics and famine. In World War II, approximately twice as many lives were lost. The century saw the expansionism of Nazi Germany and the horrors of the Holocaust, Stalin's reckless domination of Eastern Europe and his Gulag Archipelago, and the civil terror in Communist China. We can add to it the victims of South American dictatorships, the atrocities and genocide committed by the Chinese in Tibet, and the cruelties of South African Apartheid. The wars in Korea and Vietnam, the wars in the Middle East, and the slaughter in Yugoslavia and Rwanda are more examples of the senseless bloodshed we have witnessed during the last hundred years. The twenty-first century has raised human violence to another level by bringing global terrorism, suicide missions of Islamic fundamentalists, unprovoked invasion of Iraq, and threat of "sacred war" between Islam, Judaism, and Christianity.

The human greed has also found new, less violent forms of expression in the philosophy and strategy of capitalist economies emphasizing increase of the gross national product, unlimited growth, conspicuous consumption, and planned obsolescence, resulting in reckless plundering of nonrenewable natural resources and industrial pollution. Moreover, much of this wasteful economic policy and its disastrous ecological consequences has been driven by the arms race, producing weapons of increasing destructive power and thereby raising the risk of global disaster.

Doomsday Scenarios Threatening Life on Our Planet

In the past, violence and greed had tragic consequences for the individuals involved in the internecine encounters and for their immediate families. However, they did not threaten the evolution of the human species as a whole and certainly did not represent a danger for the ecosystem and for the biosphere of the planet. Even after the most violent wars, nature was able to recycle all the aftermath and completely recover within a few decades. This situation changed radically in the course of the twentieth century. Rapid technological progress, exponential growth of industrial production, massive population explosion, and particularly the discovery of atomic energy have forever changed the equations involved.

Economic crisis as descent into the Maelstrom.

Military intervention in Lebanon portrayed as entry into the underworld.

In the course of the twentieth century, we witnessed more major scientific and technological breakthroughs within a single decade, or even a single year, than people in earlier historical periods experienced in an entire century. However, these astonishing intellectual successes have brought modern humanity to the brink of a global catastrophe, since they were not matched by a comparable growth of emotional and moral maturity. We have the dubious privilege of being the first species in natural history that has achieved the capacity to eradicate itself and destroy in the process all life on this planet.

The intellectual history of humanity is one of incredible triumphs. We have been able to learn the secrets of nuclear energy, send spaceships to the moon and all the planets of the solar system, transmit sound and color pictures all around the globe and across cosmic space, crack the DNA code, and begin experimenting with cloning and genetic engineering. At the same time, these superior technologies are being used in the service of primitive emotions and instinctual impulses that are not very different from those that drove the behavior of the people in the Stone Age.

Unimaginable sums of money have been wasted in the insanity of the arms race, and the use of even a miniscule fraction of the existing arsenal of atomic weapons would destroy all life on earth. Tens of millions of people have been killed in the two world wars and in countless other violent confrontations occurring for ideological, racial, religious, or economic reasons. Hundreds of thousands have been bestially tortured by the secret police of various totalitarian systems. Insatiable greed is driving people to hectic pursuit of profit and acquisition of personal property beyond any reasonable limits. This strategy has resulted in a situation where, besides the specter of a nuclear war, humanity is threatened by several less spectacular, but insidious and more predictable doomsday scenarios.

Among these are industrial pollution of soil, water, and air; the threat of nuclear waste and accidents; destruction of the ozone layer; the greenhouse effect and global warming; possible loss of planetary oxygen through reckless deforestation and poisoning of the ocean plankton; and the dangers of toxic additives in our food and drinks. To this we can add a number of developments that are of less apocalyptic nature, but equally disturbing, such as species extinction proceeding at an astronomical rate, homelessness and starvation of a significant percentage of the world's population, deterioration of family and crisis of parenthood, disappearance of spiritual values, absence of hope and positive perspective, loss of meaningful connection with nature, and general alienation. As a result of all the above factors, humanity now lives in chronic anguish on the verge of a nuclear and ecological catastrophe, while in possession of fabulous technology approaching the world of science fiction.

Modern science has developed effective means that could solve most of the urgent problems in today's world - combat the majority of diseases, eliminate hunger and poverty, reduce the amount of industrial waste, and replace destructive fossil fuels by renewable sources of clean energy. The problems that stand in the way are not of economic or technological nature; their deepest sources lie inside the human personality. Because of them, unimaginable resources have been wasted in the absurdity of the arms race, power struggle, and pursuit of "unlimited growth." They also prevent a more appropriate distribution of wealth among individuals and nations, as well as a reorientation from purely economic and political concerns to ecological priorities that are critical for survival of life on this planet.

Psychospiritual Roots of the Global Crisis.

Diplomatic negotiations, administrative and legal measures, economic and social sanctions, military interventions, and other similar efforts have had very little success; as a matter of fact, they have often produced more problems than they solved. It is becoming increasingly clear why they had to fail. The strategies used to alleviate this crisis are rooted in the same ideology that created it in the first place. In the last analysis, the current global crisis is basically a psychospiritual crisis; it reflects the level of consciousness evolution of the human species. It is, therefore, hard to imagine that it could be resolved without a radical inner transformation of humanity on a large scale and its rise to a higher level of emotional maturity and spiritual awareness. As Albert Einstein pointed out, "Problems cannot be solved at the same level of awareness that created them."

The task of imbuing humanity with an entirely different set of values and goals might appear too unrealistic and utopian to offer any real hope. Considering the paramount role of violence and greed in human history, the possibility of transforming modern humanity into a species of individuals capable of peaceful coexistence with their fellow men and women regardless of race, color, and religious or political conviction, let alone with other species, certainly does not seem very plausible. We are facing the necessity to instill humanity with profound ethical values, sensitivity to the needs of others, acceptance of voluntary simplicity, and a sharp awareness of ecological imperatives. At first glance, such a task appears too fantastic even for a science fiction movie.

However, although serious and critical, the situation might not be as hopeless as it appears. After more than fifty years of intensive study of holotropic states of consciousness, I have come to the conclusion that the theoretical concepts and practical approaches developed by transpersonal psychology, a discipline that is trying to integrate spirituality with the new paradigm emerging in Western science, could help alleviate the crisis we are all facing. These observations suggest that radical psychospiritual transformation of humanity is not only possible, but is already underway. The question is only whether it can be sufficiently fast and extensive to reverse the current self-destructive trend of modern humanity.

The Three Poisons from the Perspective of Tibetan Buddhism

Let us take a look at the theoretical insights from the research of holotropic states and their practical implications for our everyday life. Can the new knowledge be used in a way that would make our life more fulfilling and rewarding? How could systematic self-exploration using holotropic states improve our emotional and physical well-being and bring about positive personality transformation and beneficial changes of the worldview and system of values? And, more specifically, how could this strategy contribute to alleviation of the global crisis and survival of life on this planet?

Spiritual teachers of all ages seem to agree that pursuit of material goals, in and of itself, cannot bring us fulfillment, happiness, and inner peace. The rapidly escalating global crisis, moral deterioration, and growing discontent accompanying the increase of material affluence in the industrial societies bear witness to this ancient truth. There seems to be general agreement in the mystical literature that the remedy for the existential malaise that besets humanity is to turn inside, look for the answers in our own psyche, and undergo a deep psychospiritual transformation.

It is not difficult to understand that an important prerequisite for successful existence is general intelligence - the ability to learn and recall, think and reason, and adequately respond to our material environment. More recent research emphasizes the importance of "emotional intelligence," the capacity to adequately respond to our human environment and skillfully handle our interpersonal relationships (Goleman 1996). Observations from the study of holotropic states confirm the basic tenet of perennial philosophy that the quality of our life ultimately depends on what can be called "spiritual intelligence."

Spiritual intelligence is the capacity to conduct our life in such a way that it reflects deep philosophical and metaphysical understanding of reality and of ourselves. This, of course, brings questions about the nature of the psychospiritual transformation that is necessary to achieve

Tibetan Buddhist thangka depicting the Wheel of Life.

this form of intelligence, the direction of the changes that we have to undergo, and the means that can facilitate such development. A very clear and specific answer to these questions can be found in different schools of Mahayana Buddhism.

We can use the famous Tibetan screen painting (*thangka*) portraying the cycle of life, death, and reincarnation as the basis for our discussion. It depicts the Wheel of Life held in the grip of the horrifying Lord of Death. The wheel is divided into six segments representing the different *lokas*, or realms into which we can be reborn. The celestial domain of gods (*devaloka*) is shown as being challenged from the adjacent segment (*asuraloka*) by the jealous warrior gods. The region of hungry ghosts (*pretaloka*) is inhabited by pitiful creatures representing insatiable greed. They have giant bellies, enormous appetites, and mouths the size of a pinhole. The remaining sections of the wheel depict the world of human beings (manakaloka), the realm of the wild beasts (tiryakaloka), and hell (narakaloka). Inside the wheel are two concentric circles. The outer one shows the ascending and descending paths along which souls travel. The innermost circle contains three animals - a pig, a snake, and a rooster.

The animals in the center of the wheel represent the "three poisons" or forces that, according to the Buddhist teachings, perpetuate the cycles of birth and death and are responsible for all the suffering in our life. The pig symbolizes *ignorance* concerning the nature of reality and our own nature, the snake stands for *anger and aggression,* and the rooster depicts *desire and lust* leading to attachment. The quality of our life and our ability to cope with the challenges of existence depend critically on the degree to which we are able to eliminate or transform these forces that run the world of sentient beings. Let us now look at the process of systematic self - exploration involving holotropic states of consciousness from this perspective.

Practical Knowledge and Transcendental Wisdom.

The most obvious benefit that we can obtain from deep experiential work is access to extraordinary knowledge about ourselves, other people, nature, and the cosmos. In holotropic states we can reach a deep understanding of the unconscious dynamics of our psyche. We can discover how our perception of ourselves and of the world is influenced by forgotten or repressed memories from childhood, infancy, birth, and prenatal existence. In addition, in transpersonal experiences we can identify with other people, various animals, plants, and elements of the inorganic world. Experiences of this kind represent an extremely rich source of unique insights about the world we live in and can radically transform our worldview.

In recent years, many authors have pointed out that a significant factor in the development of the global crisis has been the Newtonian-Cartesian paradigm and monistic materialism that have dominated Western science for the last three hundred years. This way of thinking involves a sharp dichotomy between mind and nature and portrays the universe as a giant, fully deterministic supermachine governed by mechanical laws. The image of the cosmos as a mechanical system has led to the erroneous belief that it can be adequately understood by dissecting it and studying all its parts. This has been a serious obstacle for viewing problems in terms of their complex interactions and from a holistic perspective.

In addition, by elevating matter to the most important principle in the cosmos, Western science reduces life, consciousness, and intelligence to accidental by-products of material processes. In this context, humans appear to be nothing more than highly developed animals. This led to the acceptance of antagonism, competition, and the Darwinian "survival of the fittest" as the leading principles of human society. In addition, the description of nature as unconscious provided the justification for its exploitation by humans, following the program very eloquently formulated by Francis Bacon (Bacon 1870).

Psychoanalysis has painted a pessimistic picture of human beings as creatures whose primary motivating forces are bestial instincts. According to Freud, if we were not afraid of societal repercussions and controlled by the superego (internalized parental prohibitions and injunctions), we would kill and steal indiscriminately, commit incest, and be involved in unbridled promiscuous sex (Freud 1955). This image of human nature relegated such concepts as complementarity, synergy, mutual respect, and peaceful cooperation into the domain of temporary opportunistic strategies or naive utopian fantasies. It is not difficult to see how these concepts and the system of values associated with them have helped to create the crisis we are facing.

Insights from holotropic states have brought convincing support for a radically different understanding of the cosmos, nature, and human beings. They brought experiential confirmation for the concepts formulated by pioneers of information theory and the theory of systems, which have shown that our planet and the entire cosmos represent a unified and interconnected web of which each of us is an integral part (Bateson 1979, Capra 1996). In holotropic states, we can gain deep experiential knowledge of various aspects of material reality, of its interconnectedness, and of the unity underlying the world of seeming separation. However, the ignorance symbolized in the Tibetan thangkas by the pig is not the absence or lack of knowledge in the ordinary sense. It does not mean simply inadequate information about various aspects of the material world, but ignorance of a much deeper and more fundamental kind.

The form of ignorance that is meant here (*avidya*) is a fundamental misunderstanding and confusion concerning the nature of reality and our own nature. The only remedy for this kind of ignorance is transcendental wisdom (*prajña paramita*). From this point of view, it is essential that the inner work involving holotropic states offers more than just increase, deepening, and correction of our knowledge concerning the material universe. It is also a unique way of gaining insights about issues of transcendental relevance.

In the light of this evidence, consciousness is not a product of the physiological processes in the brain, but a primary attribute of existence. The deepest nature of humanity is not bestial, but divine. The universe is imbued with creative intelligence and consciousness is inextricably woven into its fabric. Our identification with the separate body-ego is an illusion and our true identity is the totality of existence. This understanding provides a natural basis for reverence for life, cooperation and synergy, concerns for humanity and the planet as a whole, and deep ecological awareness.

Anatomy of Human Destructiveness

Let us now look from the same perspective at the second "poison," human propensity to aggression. Modern study of aggressive behavior started with Charles Darwin's epoch-making discoveries in the field of evolution in the middle of the nineteenth century (Darwin 1952). The attempts to explain human aggression from our animal origin generated such theoretical concepts as Desmond Morris's image of the "naked ape" (Morris 1967), Robert Ardrey's idea of the "territorial imperative" (Ardrey 1961), Paul MacLean's "triune brain" (MacLean 1973), and Richard Dawkins's sociobiological explanations interpreting aggression in terms of genetic strategies of the "selfish genes" (Dawkins 1976). More refined models of behavior developed by pioneers in ethology, such as Konrad Lorenz, Nikolaas Tinbergen, and others, complemented mechanical emphasis on instincts by the study of ritualistic and motivational elements (Lorenz 1963, Tinbergen 1965).

Any theories suggesting that the human tendency to violence simply reflects our animal origin are inadequate and unconvincing. With rare exceptions, such as the occasional violent group raids of the chimpanzees against neighboring groups (Wrangham and Peterson 1996), animals do not prey on their own kind. They exhibit aggression when they are hungry, defend their territory, or compete for sex. The nature and scope of human violence - Erich Fromm's "malignant aggression" - has no parallels in the animal kingdom (Fromm 1973). The realization that human aggression cannot be adequately explained as a result of phylogenetic evolution led to the formulation of psychodynamic and psychosocial theories that consider a significant part of human aggression to be learned phenomena. This trend began in the late 1930s and was initiated by the work of Dollard and Miller (Dollard et al. 1939).

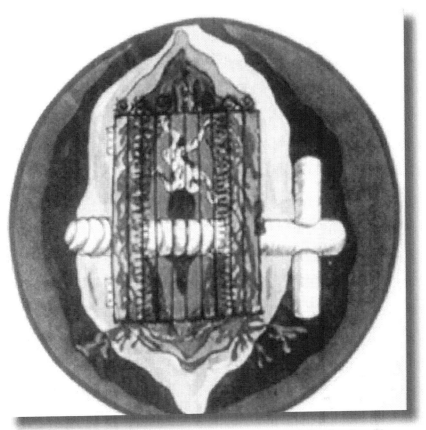

*Painting from a perinatal LSD session; it portrays the delivering female ge-
netilia as a combination of a prison, a torture chamber, and a giant press.*

Biographical Sources of Aggression

Psychodynamic theories attempt to explain the specifically human
aggression as a reaction to frustration, abuse, and lack of love in infancy
and childhood. However, explanations of this kind fall painfully short of
accounting for extreme forms of individual violence, such as serial murders of the Boston Strangler and Geoffrey Dahmer or the indiscriminate
multiple killing of the "running amok" type. Current psychodynamic
and psychosocial theories are even less convincing when it comes to bestial acts committed by entire groups, like the Sharon Tate murders or
atrocities that occur during prison uprisings. They fail completely when
it comes to mass societal phenomena that involve entire nations, such as
Nazism, Communism, bloody wars, revolutions, genocide, and concentration camps.

In the last several decades, psychedelic research and deep experiential psychotherapies have been able to throw much light on the problem of human aggression. This work has revealed that the roots of this problematic and dangerous aspect of human nature are much deeper and more formidable than traditional psychology ever imagined. However, this work has also discovered extremely effective approaches that have the potential to neutralize and transform these violent elements in human personality. In addition, these observations indicate that malignant aggression does not reflect true human nature. It is connected with a domain of unconscious dynamics that separates us from our deeper identity. When we reach the transpersonal realms that lie beyond this screen, we realize that our true nature is divine rather than bestial.

Perinatal Roots of Violence

There is no doubt that a part of "malignant aggression" is connected with traumas and frustrations in childhood and infancy. However, modern consciousness research has revealed additional significant roots of violence in deep recesses of the psyche that lie beyond postnatal biography and are related to the trauma of biological birth. The vital emergency, pain, and suffocation experienced for many hours during biological delivery generate enormous amounts of anxiety and murderous aggression that remain stored in the organism. The reliving of birth in various forms of experiential psychotherapy involves not only concrete replay of the original emotions and sensations, but is also typically associated with a variety of experiences from the collective unconscious portraying scenes of unimaginable violence. Among these are often powerful sequences depicting wars, revolutions, racial riots, concentration camps, totalitarianism, and genocide.

The spontaneous emergence of this imagery during the reliving of birth is often associated with convincing insights concerning perinatal origin of such extreme forms of human violence. Naturally, wars and revolutions are extremely complex phenomena that have historical, economic, political, religious, and other dimensions. The intention here is not to offer a reductionistic explanation replacing all the other causes, but to add some new insights concerning the psychological and spiritual dimensions of these forms of social psychopathology that have been neglected or received only superficial treatment in earlier theories.

The images of violent sociopolitical events accompanying the reliving of biological birth tend to appear in very specific connection with the four basic perinatal matrices (BPMs), which is my name for complex experiential patterns associated with the consecutive stages of the birth process. While reliving episodes of undisturbed intrauterine existence

(BPM I), we typically experience images from human societies with an ideal social structure, from cultures that live in complete harmony with nature, or from future utopian societies where all major conflicts have been resolved. Disturbing intrauterine memories, such as those of a toxic womb, imminent miscarriage, or attempted abortion, are accompanied by images of human groups living in industrial areas where nature is polluted and spoiled, or in societies with an insidious social order and all-pervading paranoia.

Regressive experiences related to the first clinical stage of birth (BPM II), during which the uterus periodically contracts but the cervix is not yet open, present a diametrically different picture. They portray oppressive and abusive totalitarian societies with closed borders, victimizing their populations, and "choking" personal freedom, such as Czarist or Communist Russia, Hitler's Third Reich, Eastern European Soviet satellites, South American dictatorships, and the African Apartheid, or bring specific images of the inmates in Nazi concentration camps and Stalin's Gulag Archipelago. While experiencing these scenes of living hell, we identify exclusively with the victims and feel deep sympathy for the down-trodden and the underdog.

The experiences accompanying reliving of the second clinical stage of delivery (BPM III), when the cervix is dilated and continued contractions propel the fetus through the narrow passage of the birth canal, feature a rich panoply of violent scenes -- bloody wars and revolutions, human or animal slaughter, mutilation, sexual abuse, and murder. These scenes often contain demonic elements and repulsive scatological motifs. Additional frequent concomitants of BPM III are visions of burning cities, launching of rockets, and explosions of nuclear bombs. Here we are not limited to the role of victims, but can participate in three roles - that of the victim, of the aggressor, and of an emotionally involved observer.

The events characterizing the third clinical stage of delivery (BPM IV), the actual moment of birth and the separation from the mother, are typically associated with images of victory in wars and revolutions, liberation of prisoners, and success of collective efforts, such as patriotic or nationalistic movements. At this point, we can also experience visions of triumphant celebrations and parades or of exciting postwar reconstruction.

In 1975, I described these observations, linking sociopolitical upheavals to stages of biological birth, in my book *Realms of the Human Unconscious* (Grof 1975). Shortly after its publication, I received an enthusiastic letter from Lloyd de Mause, a New York psychoanalyst and journalist. De Mause is one of the founders of psychohistory, a discipline that applies the findings of depth psychology to the study of history

Political cartoon identifying a nuclear bomb with a pregnant belly.

and political science. Psychohistorians explore such issues as the relationship between the childhood of political leaders and their system of values and process of decision-making, or the influence of child-rearing practices on the nature of revolutions of that particular historical period. Lloyd de Mause was very interested in my findings concerning the trauma of birth and its possible sociopolitical implications because they provided independent support for his own research.

For some time, de Mause had been studying the psychodynamics of the periods immediately preceding wars and revolutions. It interested him how military leaders succeed in mobilizing masses of peaceful civilians and transforming them practically overnight into killing machines. His approach to this problem was very original and creative. In addition to analysis of traditional historical sources, he drew data of great psychological importance from caricatures, jokes, dreams, personal imagery, slips of the tongue, side comments of speakers, and even doodles and scribbles on the edge of the rough drafts of political documents. By the time he contacted me, he had used this approach to analyze seventeen situations preceding the outbreak of wars and revolutionary upheavals, spanning many centuries since antiquity to most recent times (de Mause 1975).

He was struck by the extraordinary abundance of figures of speech, metaphors, and images related to biological birth that he found in this material. Military leaders and politicians of all ages describing a critical situation or declaring war typically used terms that equally applied to perinatal distress. They accused the enemy of choking and strangling their people, squeezing the last breath out of their lungs, or constricting them, and not giving them enough space to live (Hitler's "Lebensraum").

Equally frequent were allusions to dark caves, tunnels, and confusing labyrinths, dangerous abysses into which one might be pushed, and the threat of engulfment by treacherous quicksand or a terrifying whirlpool. Similarly, the offer of the resolution of the crisis had the form of perinatal images. The leader promised to rescue his nation from an ominous labyrinth, to lead it to the light on the other side of the tunnel, and to create a situation where the dangerous aggressor and oppressor will be overcome and everybody will again breathe freely.

Lloyd de Mause's historical examples at the time included such famous personages as Alexander the Great, Napoleon, Samuel Adams, Kaiser Wilhelm II., Hitler, Khrushchev, and Kennedy. Samuel Adams talking about the American Revolution referred to "the child of Independence now struggling for birth." In 1914, Kaiser Wilhelm stated that "the Monarchy has been seized by the throat and forced to choose between letting itself be strangled and making a last ditch effort to defend itself against attack."

Even more explicit was the coded message used by Japanese ambassador Kurusu when he phoned Tokyo to signal that negotiations with Roosevelt had broken down and that it was all right to go ahead with the bombing of Pearl Harbor. He announced that the "birth of the child was imminent" and asked how things were in Japan: "Does it seem as if the child might be born?" The reply was: "Yes, the birth of the child seems imminent." Interestingly, the American intelligence listening in recognized the meaning of the "war-as-birth" code. During the Cuban missile crisis Krushchev wrote to Kennedy, pleading that the two nations not "come to a clash, like blind moles battling to death in a tunnel." More recent examples can be found in Osama bin Laden's videotape, where he threatens to turn the United States into a "choking hell" and in the speech of US State Secretary Condoleezza Rice, who described the acute crisis in Lebanon as the "birth pangs of a New Middle East."

Particularly chilling was the use of perinatal language in connection with the explosion of the atomic bomb in Hiroshima. The airplane was given the name of the pilot's mother, Enola Gay, the atomic bomb itself carried a painted nickname "The Little Boy," and the agreed-upon message sent to Washington as a signal of successful detonation was "The baby was born." It would not be too far-fetched to see the image of a newborn also behind the nickname of the Nagasaki bomb, Fat Man. Since the time of our correspondence, Lloyd de Mause has collected many additional historical examples and refined his thesis that the memory of the birth trauma plays an important role as a source of motivation for violent social activity.

The relationship between nuclear warfare and birth is of such relevance that I would like to explore it further using the material from a paper by Carol Cohn entitled "Sex and Death in the Rational World of the Defense Intellectuals" (Cohn 1987). The defense intellectuals (DIs) are civilians who move in and out of government, working sometimes as administrative officials or consultants, sometimes at universities and think tanks. They create the theory that informs and legitimates U.S. nuclear strategic practice - where to place the rockets with nuclear warheads, how to manage the arms race, how to deter the use of nuclear weapons, how to fight a nuclear war if the deterrence fails, and how to explain why it is not safe to live without nuclear weapons.

Carol Cohn had attended a two-week summer seminar on nuclear weapons, nuclear strategic doctrine, and arms control. She was so fascinated by what had transpired there that she spent the following year immersed in the almost entirely male world of defense intellectuals (except for secretaries). She collected some extremely interesting facts confirming the perinatal dimension in nuclear warfare. In her own terminology, this material confirms the importance of the motif of "male birth" and "male creation" as important psychological forces underlying the psychology of nuclear warfare. She uses the following historical examples to illustrate her point of view:

In 1942, Ernest Lawrence sent a telegram to a Chicago group of physicists developing the nuclear bomb that read: "Congratulations to the new parents. Can hardly wait to see the new arrival." At Los Alamos, the atom bomb was referred to as "Oppenheimer's baby." Richard Feynman wrote in his article "Los Alamos from Below" that when he was temporarily on leave after his wife's death, he received a telegram that read: "The baby is expected" on such and such a day.

At Lawrence Livermore laboratories, the hydrogen bomb was referred to as "Teller's baby," although those who wanted to disparage Edward Teller's contribution claimed he was not the bomb's father, but its mother. They claimed that Stanislaw Ulam was the real father, who had all the important ideas and "conceived it;" Teller only "carried it" after that. Terms related to motherhood were also used to the provision of "nurturance" -- the maintenance of the missiles.

General Grove sent a triumphant coded cable to Secretary of War Henry Stimson at the Potsdam conference reporting the success of the first atomic test: "Doctor has just returned most enthusiastic and confident that the little boy is as husky as his big brother. The light in his eyes discernible from here to Highhold (Stimson's country home) and I could have heard his screams from here to my farm." Stimson, in turn, informed Churchill by writing him a note that read: "Babies satisfactorily born."

William L. Laurence witnessed the test of the first atomic bomb and wrote: "The big boom came about a hundred seconds after the great flash -- the first cry of a new-born world." Edward Teller's exultant telegram to Los Alamos, announcing the successful test of the hydrogen bomb "Mike" at the Eniwetok atoll in Marshall Islands read "It's a boy." The Enola Gay, "Little Boy," and "The baby was born" symbolism of the Hiroshima bomb, and the "Fat Man" symbolism of the Nagasaki bomb were already mentioned earlier. According to Carol Cohn, "male scientists gave birth to a progeny with the ultimate power of domination over female Nature."

Carol Cohn also mentions in her paper an abundance of overtly sexual symbolism in the language of defense intellectuals. The nature of this material, linking sex to aggression, domination, and scatology shows a deep similarity to the imagery occurring in the context of birth experiences (BPM III). Cohn used the following examples: American dependence on nuclear weapons was explained as irresistible, because "you get more bang for the buck." A professor's explanation of why the MX missiles should be placed in the silos of the newest Minuteman missiles instead of replacing the older, less accurate ones: "You are not going to take the nicest missile you have and put it into a crummy hole." At one point, there was a serious concern that "we have to harden our missiles, because the Russians are a little harder than we are." One military adviser to the National Security Council referred to "releasing 70 to 80 percent of our megatonnage in one orgasmic whump."

Lectures were filled with terms like vertical erector launchers, thrust-to-weight ratios, soft lay-downs, deep penetration, and the comparative advantages of protracted versus spasm attacks. Another example was the popular and widespread custom of patting the missiles, practiced by the visitors to nuclear submarines, which Carol Cohn saw as an expression of phallic supremacy and also homoerotic tendencies. In view of this material, it is quite appropriate for feminist critics of nuclear policies to refer to "missile envy" and "phallic worship."

Further support for the pivotal role of the perinatal domain of the unconscious in war psychology can be found in Sam Keen's excellent book *The Faces of the Enemy* (Keen 1988). Keen brought together an outstanding collection of war posters, propaganda cartoons, and caricatures from many historical periods and countries. He demonstrated that the way the enemy is described and portrayed during a war or revolution is a stereotype that shows only minimal variations and has very little to do with the actual characteristics of the country and its inhabitants. This material also typically disregards the diversity and heterogeneity characterizing the population of each country and makes blatant generalization: "This is what the Germans, Americans, Japanese, Russians, etc. are like!"

Keen was able to divide these images into several archetypal categories according to the prevailing characteristics (e.g., Stranger, Aggressor, Worthy Opponent, Faceless, Enemy of God, Barbarian, Greedy, Criminal, Torturer, Rapist, Death). According to him, the alleged images of the enemy are essentially projections of the repressed and unacknowledged shadow aspects of our own unconscious. Although we would certainly find in human history instances of just wars, those who initiate war activities are typically substituting external targets for elements in their own psyches that should be properly faced in personal self-exploration.

Sam Keen's theoretical framework does not specifically include the perinatal domain of the unconscious. However, the analysis of his picture material reveals a preponderance of symbolic images that are characteristic of BPM II and BPM III. The enemy is typically depicted as a dangerous octopus, a vicious dragon, a multiheaded hydra, a giant venomous tarantula, or an engulfing Leviathan. Other frequently used symbols include vicious predatory felines or birds, monstrous sharks, and ominous snakes, particularly vipers and boa constrictors. Scenes depicting strangulation or crushing, ominous whirlpools, and treacherous quicksands also abound in pictures from the time of wars, revolutions, and political crises. Juxtaposition of pictures from holotropic states of consciousness that focus on reliving of birth with the historical pictorial documentation collected by Lloyd de Mause and Sam Keen represents strong evidence for the perinatal roots of human violence.

According to the new insights, provided jointly by observations from consciousness research and by the findings of psychohistory, we all carry in our deep unconscious powerful energies and emotions associated with the trauma of birth that we have not adequately processed and assimilated. For some of us, this aspect of our psyche can be completely unconscious until and unless we embark on some in-depth self-exploration with the use of psychedelics or some powerful experiential techniques of psychotherapy, such as the Holotropic Breathwork or re-

LSD session experience of strangulation by an octopus in the womb.

In holotropic states the giant octopus symbolizes the contracting and stran-gling uterus. It is also a popular image in political posters and cartoons. Here as Slobodan Milosevic.

birthing. Others can have varying degrees of awareness of the emotions and physical sensations stored on the perinatal level of the unconscious.

Activation of this material can lead to serious individual psychopathology, including unmotivated violence. Lloyd de Mause suggests that, for unknown reasons, the awareness of the perinatal elements can increase simultaneously in a large number of people. This creates an atmosphere of general tension, anxiety, and anticipation. The leader is an individual who is under a stronger influence of the perinatal energies than the average person. He also has the ability to disown his unacceptable feelings (the Shadow in Jung's terminology) and to project them on the external situation. The collective discomfort is blamed on the enemy and a military intervention is offered as a solution. Richard Tarnas' extraordinary book Cosmos and Psyche added an interesting dimension to de Mause's thesis. In this meticulously researched study, Tarnas was able to show that throughout history the times of wars and revolutions have been correlated with specific astrological transits (Tarnas 2006) suggesting participation of archetypal forces in these phenomena.

War and revolution provide an opportunity to disregard the psychological defenses that ordinarily keep the dangerous perinatal forces in check. Freud's superego, a psychological force that demands restraint and civilized behavior, is replaced by the "war superego." We receive praise and medals for murder, indiscriminate destruction, and pillaging, the same behaviors that in peacetime are unacceptable and would land us in prison or worse. Similarly, sexual violence has been a common practice during wartime and has been generally tolerated. As a matter of fact, military leaders have often promised their soldiers unlimited access to women in the conquered territory to motivate them for battle.

Once the war erupts, the destructive and self-destructive perinatal impulses are freely acted out. The themes that we normally encounter in a certain stage of the process of inner exploration and transformation (BPM II and III) now become parts of our everyday life, either directly or in the form of TV news. Various no exit situations, sadomasochistic orgies, sexual violence, bestial and demonic behavior, unleashing of enormous explosive energies, and scatology, which belong to standard perinatal imagery, are all enacted in wars and revolutions with extraordinary vividness and power.

Witnessing scenes of destruction and acting out of violent unconscious impulses, whether it occurs on the individual scale or collectively in wars and revolutions, does not result in healing and transformation as would an inner confrontation with these elements in a therapeutic context. The experience is not generated by our own unconscious, lacks the element of deep introspection, and does not lead to insights. The situation is fully externalized and the connection with the deep dynamics of the psyche is missing. And, naturally, there is no therapeutic intention and motivation for change and transformation. Thus the goal of the underlying birth fantasy, which represents the deepest driving force of such violent events, is not achieved, even if the war or revolution has been brought to a successful closure. The most triumphant external victory does not deliver what was expected and hoped for - an inner sense of emotional liberation and psychospiritual rebirth.

After the initial intoxicating feelings of triumph comes at first a sober awakening and later bitter disappointment. And it usually does not take long until a facsimile of the old oppressive system starts emerging from the ruins of the dead dream, since the same unconscious forces continue to operate in the deep unconscious of everybody involved. This happens again and again in human history, whether the event involved is the French Revolution, the Bolshevik Revolution in Russia, the Communist revolution in China, or any of the other violent upheavals associated with great hopes and expectations.

Since I conducted deep experiential work for many years in Prague at the time when Czechoslovakia had a Marxist regime, I was able to collect some fascinating material concerning the psychological dynamics of Communism. The issues related to Communist ideology typically emerged in the treatment of my clients at the time when these were struggling with perinatal energies and emotions. It soon became obvious that the passion the revolutionaries feel toward the oppressors and their regimes receives a powerful reinforcement from their revolt against the inner prison of their perinatal memories. And, conversely, the need to coerce and dominate others is an external displacement of the need to overcome the fear of being overwhelmed by one's own unconscious. The murderous entanglement of the oppressor and the revolutionary is thus an externalized replica of the situation experienced in the birth canal.

The Communist vision contains an element of psychological truth that has made it appealing to large numbers of people. The basic notion that a violent experience of a revolutionary nature is necessary to terminate suffering and oppression and institute a situation of greater harmony is correct when understood as related to the process of inner transformation. However, it is dangerously false when it is projected onto the external world as a political ideology of violent revolutions. The fallacy lies in the fact that what on a deeper level is essentially an archetypal pattern of spiritual death and rebirth takes the form of an atheistic and antispiritual program. Paradoxically, Communism has many features in common with organized religion in that it exploits people's spiritual needs, while not only failing to satisfy them, but actively suppressing any genuine spiritual search. The parallel of Communism with organized religion goes so far that Stalin, at the height of his power, was declared infallible even though he was expressing authoritative opinions in disciplines in which he had no actual knowledge.

Communist revolutions have been extremely successful in their destructive phase but, instead of the promised brotherhood and harmony, their victories have bred regimes where oppression, cruelty, and injustice ruled supreme. Today, when the economically ruined and politically corrupt Soviet Union has collapsed and the Communist world has fallen apart, it is obvious to all people with sane judgment that this gigantic historical experiment, conducted at the cost of tens of millions of human lives and unimaginable human suffering, has been a colossal failure. If the above observations are correct, no external interventions have a chance to create a better world, unless they are associated with a profound transformation of human consciousness.

The observations from the study of holotropic states also throw some important light on the psychology of concentration camps. Over a number of years, professor Bastiaans in Leyden, Holland, conducted LSD therapy with people suffering from the "concentration camp syndrome," a condition that develops in former inmates of these camps many years after the incarceration. Bastiaans has also worked with former kapos (concentration camp prisoners given authority over other prisoners by the SS) on their issues of profound guilt. An artistic description of this work can be found in the book *Shivitti* written by a former inmate, Ka-Tzetnik 135633, who underwent a series of therapeutic sessions with Bastiaans (Ka-Tzetnik 135633 1989).

Bastiaans himself wrote a paper describing his work, entitled "Man in the Concentration Camp and Concentration Camp in Man." There he pointed out, without specifying it, that the concentration camps are a projection of a certain domain which exists in the human unconscious: "Before there was a man in the concentration camp, there was a concentration camp in man" (Bastiaans 1955). Study of holotropic states of consciousness makes it possible to identify the realm of the psyche Bastiaans was talking about. Closer examination of the general and specific conditions in the Nazi concentration camps reveals that they were a diabolical and realistic enactment of the nightmarish atmosphere that characterizes the reliving of biological birth.

The barbed-wire barriers, high-voltage fences, watch towers with submachine guns, minefields, and packs of trained dogs certainly created a hellish and almost archetypal image of an utterly hopeless and oppressive no exit situation that is so characteristic of the first clinical

Self-portrait of the Swiss fantastic realist Hansruedi Giger, reflecting his awarenss of the influence that the memory of biological birth had on his art. (H.R. Giger, with permission, www.hrgiger.com)

stage of birth (BPM II). At the same time, the elements of violence, bestiality, scatology, and sexual abuse of women and men, including rape and sadistic practices, all belong to the phenomenology of the second stage of delivery (BPM III), familiar to people who have relived their birth. In the concentration camps, the sexual abuse existed on a random individual level, as well as in the context of the "houses of dolls," institutions providing "entertainment" for the officers. The only escape out of this hell was death - by a bullet, by hunger, disease, or suffocation in the gas chambers. The books by Ka-Tzetnik 135633, *House of Dolls* and *Sunrise Over Hell* (Ka-Tzetnik 1955 and 1977), offer a shattering description of the life in concentration camps.

The bestiality of the SS seemed to have been focused particularly on pregnant women and little children, which brings further support for the perinatal hypothesis. The most powerful passage from Terrence des Près's book *The Survivor* is, without any doubt, the description of a truck full of babies dumped into fire, followed by a scene in which pregnant women are beaten with clubs and whips, torn by dogs, dragged around by the hair, kicked in the stomach, and then thrown into the crematorium while still alive (des Près 1976).

The perinatal nature of the irrational impulses manifesting in the camps is evident also in the scatological behavior of the kapos. Throwing eating bowls into the latrines and asking the inmates for their retrieval and forcing the inmates to urinate into each other's mouths were practices that besides their bestiality brought the danger of epidemics. Had the concentration camps been simply institutions providing isolation of political enemies and cheap slave labor, maintenance of hygienic rules would have been a primary concern of the organizers, as is the case in any facility accommodating large numbers of people. In Buchenwald alone, as a result of these perverted practices, twenty-seven inmates drowned in feces in the course of a single month.

The intensity, depth, and convincing nature of all the experiences of collective violence associated with the perinatal process suggests that they are not individually fabricated from such sources as adventure books, movies, and TV shows, but originate in the deep unconscious. When our experiential self-exploration reaches the memory of the birth trauma we also connect to an immense pool of painful memories of the human species and gain access to experiences of other people who once were in a similar predicament. It is not hard to imagine that the perinatal level of our unconscious that "knows" so intimately the history of human violence is actually partially responsible for wars, revolutions, and similar atrocities.

The intensity and quantity of the perinatal experiences portraying various brutalities of human history is truly astonishing. Christopher Bache, after having carefully analyzed various aspects of this phenomenon, made an interesting conclusion. He suggested that the memories of the violence perpetrated throughout the ages in human history contaminated the collective unconscious in the same way in which the traumas from our infancy and childhood polluted our individual unconscious. According to Bache, it might then be possible that when we start experiencing these collective memories, our inner process transcends the framework of personal therapy and we participate in the healing of the field of species consciousness (Bache 2000).

The role of the birth trauma as a source of violence and self-destructive tendencies has been confirmed by clinical studies. For example, there seems to be an important correlation between difficult birth and criminality (Litt 1974, Kandel and Mednick 1991, Raine, Brennan, and Mednick 1995). In a similar way, aggression directed inward, particularly suicide, seems to be psychogenetically linked to difficult birth (Appleby 1998). The Scandinavian researcher Bertil Jacobson found a close correlation between specific forms of self-destructive behavior and the nature of birth. Suicides involving asphyxiation were associated with suffocation at birth, violent suicides with mechanical birth trauma, and drug addiction leading to suicide with opiate and/or barbiturate administration during labor (Jacobson et al. 1987).

The circumstances of birth play an important role in creating a disposition to violence and self-destructive tendencies or, conversely, to loving behavior and healthy interpersonal relationships. French obstetrician Michel Odent has shown how the hormones involved in the birth process and in nursing and maternal behavior participate in this imprinting. The catecholamines (adrenaline and noradrenaline) play an important role in evolution as mediators of the aggressive/protective instinct of the mother at the time when birth was occurring in unprotected natural environments. Oxytocine, prolactine, and endorphins are known to induce maternal behavior in animals and foster dependency and attachment. The busy, noisy, and chaotic milieu of many hospitals induces anxiety, unnecessarily engages the adrenaline system, and imprints the picture of a world that is potentially dangerous and requires aggressive responses. This interferes with the hormones that mediate bonding between the mother and child as well as positive interpersonal imprinting. It is, therefore, essential to provide a quiet, safe, and private environment for birthing (Odent 1995).

Transpersonal Origins of Violence

The above material shows that a conceptual framework limited to postnatal biography and the Freudian unconscious does not adequately explain extreme forms of human aggression on the individual or collective scale. However, it seems that the roots of human violence reach even deeper than to the perinatal level of the psyche. Consciousness research has revealed significant additional sources of aggression in the transpersonal domain, such as archetypal figures of demons and wrathful deities, complex destructive mythological themes, and past-life memories of physical and emotional abuse.

C. G. Jung believed that the archetypes of the collective unconscious have a powerful influence not only on the behavior of individuals but also on the events of human history. From this point of view, entire nations and cultural groups might be enacting important mythological themes. In the decade preceding the outbreak of World War II, Jung found many elements related to the Nordic god Wotan and the myth of Ragnarok - the twilight of the gods - in the dreams of his German patients. On the basis of these observations, he concluded that this archetype was emerging in the collective psyche of the German nation and that it would lead to a major catastrophe, which would ultimately turn out to be self-destructive (Jung 1957). In his brilliant book A Terrible Love of War James Hillman amassed convincing evidence that war is a powerful archetypal force that has almost irresistible power over individuals and nations (Hillman 2004).

In many instances, leaders of nations specifically use not only perinatal but also archetypal images and spiritual symbolism to achieve their political goals. The medieval crusaders were asked to sacrifice their lives for Jesus in a war that would recover the Holy Land from the Mohammedans. Adolf Hitler exploited the mythological motifs of the supremacy of the Nordic race and of the millennial empire, as well as the ancient Vedic symbols of the swastika and the solar eagle. Ayatollah Khomeini and Osama bin Laden ignited the imagination of their Moslem followers by references to *jihad,* the holy war against the infidels. American presidents Ronald Reagan referred to the Soviet Union as the Evil Empire and George W. Bush used references to the Axis of Evil and Armaggedon in his political speeches.

In her paper, Carol Cohn discussed not only the perinatal but also the spiritual symbolism associated with the language used in relation to nuclear weaponry and doctrine. The authors of the strategic doctrine referred to members of their community as the "nuclear priesthood." The first atomic test was called Trinity -- the unity of Father, Son, and

Holy Ghost, the male forces of creation. From her feminist perspective, Cohn saw this as an effort of male scientists to appropriate and claim ultimate creative power (Cohn 1987). The scientists who worked on the atomic bomb and witnessed the test described it in the following way: "It was as though we stood at the first day of creation." And Robert Oppenheimer thought of Krishna's words to Arjuna in the Bhagavad Gita: "I am become Death, the Shatterer of Worlds."

Biographical Determinants of Insatiable Greed

This brings us to the third poison as defined by Tibetan Buddhism, a powerful psychospiritual force that combines the qualities of lust, desire, and insatiable greed. Together with "malignant aggression," these qualities are certainly responsible for some of the darkest chapters in human history. Western psychologists link various aspects of this force to the libidinal drives described by Sigmund Freud. Psychoanalytic interpretation of the insatiable human need to achieve, to possess, and to become more than one is, attributes this psychological force to sublimation of lower instincts.

According to Freud, "What appears as . . . an untiring impulse toward further perfection can easily be understood as a result of the instinctual repression upon which is based all that is most precious in human civilization. The repressed instinct never ceases to strive for complete satisfaction, which would consist in the repetition of a primary experience of satisfaction. No substitutive or reactive formations and no sublimations will suffice to remove the repressed instinct's persisting tension" (Freud 1955).

More specifically, Freud saw greed as a phenomenon related to problems during the nursing period. According to him, frustration or overindulgence during the oral phase of libidinal development can reinforce the primitive infantile need to incorporate objects to such an extent that it is in adulthood transferred in a sublimated form to a variety of other objects and situations. When the acquisitive drive focuses on money, psychoanalysts attribute it to fixation on the anal stage of libidinal development. Insatiable sexual appetite is then considered to be the result of phallic fixation. Many other unrelenting human pursuits are then interpreted in terms of sublimation of such phallic instinctual urges. Modern consciousness research has found these interpretations to be superficial and inadequate. It has discovered significant additional sources of acquisitiveness and greed on the perinatal and transpersonal levels of the unconscious.

Perinatal Sources of Insatiable Greed

In the course of biographically oriented psychotherapy, many people discover that their life has been inauthentic in certain specific sectors of interpersonal relations. For example, problems with parental authority can lead to specific patterns of difficulties with authority figures, repeated dysfunctional patterns in sexual relationships can be traced to parents as models for sexual behavior, sibling issues can color and distort future peer relationships, and so on.

When the process of experiential self-exploration reaches the perinatal level, we typically discover that our life up to that point has been largely inauthentic in its totality, not just in certain partial segments. We find to our surprise and astonishment that our entire life strategy has been misdirected and therefore incapable of providing genuine satisfaction. The reason for this is that we were primarily motivated in our choices and behavior by our fear of death and by unconscious forces associated with biological birth which we had not adequately processed and integrated. In other words, during biological birth we completed the process anatomically but not emotionally.

When our field of consciousness is strongly influenced by the underlying memory of the struggle in the birth canal, it leads to a feeling of discomfort and dissatisfaction with the present situation. This discontent can focus on a large spectrum of issues - unsatisfactory physical appearance, inadequate resources and material possessions, low social position and influence, insufficient amount of power and fame, and many others. Like the child stuck in the birth canal, we feel a strong need to get to a better situation that lies somewhere in the future.

Whatever the reality of the present circumstances is, we do not find it satisfactory. Our fantasy keeps creating images of a future situation that appears more fulfilling than the present one. It seems that, until we reach it, life will be only preparation for a better future, not yet "the real thing." This results in a life pattern that people involved in experiential self-exploration have described as a "treadmill" or "rat-race" type of existence. The existentialists talk about "auto-projecting" into the future. This strategy is a basic fallacy of human life. It is essentially a loser strategy, whether or not we achieve the goals that we have set for ourselves, since it does not deliver the satisfaction that is expected from it.

When the goal is not reached, the continuing dissatisfaction is attributed to the fact that we have failed to reach the corrective measures. When we succeed in reaching the goal of our aspirations, it typically does not have much influence on our basic life feelings. The continuing dissatisfaction is then blamed either on the fact that the choice of the goal was not correct or that it was not ambitious enough. The result is either substitution of the old goal with a different one or amplification of the same type of ambitions. We cannot get enough of what we really do not want or need.

In any case, the failure is not correctly diagnosed as being an inevitable result of a fundamentally wrong strategy, which is in principle incapable of providing satisfaction. This fallacious pattern applied on a large scale is responsible for reckless irrational pursuit of various grandiose goals that results in much suffering and many problems in the world. It can be played out on any level of importance and affluence, since it never brings true satisfaction. The only strategy that can significantly reduce this irrational drive is full conscious reliving and integration of the trauma of birth in systematic inner self-exploration.

Transpersonal Causes of Insatiable Greed

Modern consciousness research and experiential psychotherapy have discovered that the deepest source of our dissatisfaction and striving for perfection lies even beyond the perinatal domain. This insatiable craving that drives human life is ultimately transpersonal in nature. In Dante Alighieri's words, "The desire for perfection is that desire which always makes every pleasure appear incomplete, for there is no joy or pleasure so great in this life that it can quench the thirst in our soul" (Dante 1990).

In the most general sense, the deepest transpersonal roots of insatiable greed can best be understood in terms of Ken Wilber's concept of the Atman Project (Wilber 1980). Our true nature is divine - God, Cosmic Christ, Allah, Buddha, Brahma, the Tao - and, although the process of incarnation separates and alienates us from our source, the awareness of this fact is never completely lost. The deepest motivating force in the psyche on all the levels of consciousness evolution is to return to the experience of our divinity. However, the constraining conditions of the consecutive stages of development stand in the way of this experience.

Real transcendence requires death of the separate self, dying to the exclusive subject. Because of the fear of annihilation and because of grasping onto the ego, the individual has to settle for Atman substitutes or surrogates, which are specific for each particular stage. For the fetus and the newborn, this means the satisfaction experienced in the good womb or on the good breast. For an infant, this is satisfaction of age-specific physiological needs. For the adult the range of possible Atman projects is large; it includes besides food and sex also money, fame, power, appearance, knowledge, and many others.

Because of our deep sense that our true identity is the totality of cosmic creation and the creative principle itself, substitutes of any degree and scope - the Atman Projects - will always remain unsatisfactory. Only the experience of one's divinity in a holotropic state of consciousness can ever fulfill our deepest needs. Thus the ultimate solution for the insatiable greed is in the inner world, not in secular pursuits of any kind and scope. The great thirteenth century Persian mystic and poet Rumi made it very clear:

> *All the hopes, desires, loves, and affections that people have for different things - fathers, mothers, friends, heavens, the earth, palaces, sciences, works, food, drink - the saint knows that these are desires for God and all those things are veils. When men leave this world and see the King without these veils, then they will know that all were veils and coverings, that the object of their desire was in reality that One Thing (quoted in Hines 1996).*

Technologies of the Sacred and Human Survival

The finding that the roots of human violence and insatiable greed reach far deeper than academic psychiatry ever suspected and that their reservoirs in the psyche are truly enormous could in and of itself be very discouraging. However, it is balanced by the exciting discovery of new therapeutic mechanisms and transformative potentials that become available in holotropic states on the perinatal and transpersonal levels of the psyche.

I have seen profound emotional and psychosomatic healing over the years, as well as radical personality transformation in many people who were involved in a serious and systematic inner quest. Some of them were meditators and had regular spiritual practice, others had supervised psychedelic sessions or participated in various forms of experiential psychotherapy and self-exploration. I have also witnessed profound positive changes in many people who received adequate support during spontaneous episodes of psychospiritual crises.

As the content of the perinatal level of the unconscious emerged into consciousness and was integrated, these individuals underwent radical personality changes. The level of aggression typically decreased considerably and they became more peaceful, more comfortable with themselves, and more tolerant of others. The experience of psychospiritual death and rebirth and conscious connection with positive postnatal or prenatal memories reduced irrational drives and ambitions. It caused a shift of focus from the past and future to the present moment and enhanced the ability to enjoy simple circumstances of life, such as everyday activities, food, love-making, nature, and music. Another important result of this process was the emergence of spirituality of a universal and

Wisdom Eye

An experience from the end of a Holotropic Breathwork session. The artist said: "Wholeness has been restored. The life power (Kundalini/chi) is content and is resting in peace above the 'Eye of Wisdom.' Heaven and Earth and Masculine and Feminine are in balance." (Anne Høivik)

mystical nature that was authentic and convincing because it was based on deep personal experience.

The process of spiritual opening and transformation typically deepened further as a result of transpersonal experiences, such as identification with other people, entire human groups, animals, plants, and even inorganic materials and processes in nature. Other experiences provided conscious access to events occurring in other countries, cultures, and historical periods and even to the mythological realms and archetypal beings of the collective unconscious. Experiences of cosmic unity and one's own divinity led to increasing identification with all of creation and brought the sense of wonder, love, compassion, and inner peace.

What had begun as psychological probing of the unconscious psyche automatically became a philosophical quest for the meaning of life and a journey of spiritual discovery. People who connected to the transpersonal domain of their psyche tended to develop a new appreciation for existence and reverence for all life. One of the most striking consequences of various forms of transpersonal experiences was spontaneous emergence and development of deep humanitarian and ecological concerns and need to get involved in service for some common purpose. This was based on an almost cellular awareness that the boundaries in the universe are arbitrary and that each of us is ultimately identical with the entire web of existence.

It was suddenly clear that we can not do anything to nature without simultaneously doing it to ourselves. Differences among people appeared to be interesting and enriching rather than threatening, whether they were related to sex, race, color, language, political conviction, or religious belief. It is obvious that a transformation of this kind would increase our chances for survival if it could occur on a sufficiently large scale.

Lessons from Holotropic States for the Psychology of Survival

Some of the insights of people experiencing holotropic states of consciousness are directly related to the current global crisis and its relationship with consciousness evolution. They show that we have exteriorized in the modern world many of the essential themes of the perinatal process that a person involved in spiritual quest and deep personal transformation has to face internally. The same elements that we would encounter in the process of psychological death and rebirth in our visionary experiences make up our evening news. This is particularly true in regard to the phenomena that characterize BPM III.

We certainly see the enormous unleashing of the aggressive impulse in the many wars and revolutionary upheavals in the world, in the rising criminality, escalating terrorism, and racial riots. Equally dramatic and striking is the lifting of sexual repression and freeing of the sexual impulse in both healthy and problematic ways. Sexual experiences and behaviors are taking unprecedented forms, as manifested in the sexual freedom of youngsters, gay liberation, general promiscuity, open marriages, high divorce rate, overtly sexual books, plays and movies, sadomasochistic experimentation, and many others.

The demonic element is also becoming increasingly manifest in the modern world. Renaissance of satanic cults and the misuse of witchcraft, popularity of books and horror movies with occult themes, and crimes with satanic motivations attest to that fact. The acts of Nazis, Communists, and terrorists, including suicide bombers, resulting in deaths of thousands of innocent civilians certainly qualify for satanic behavior. The scatological dimension is evident in the progressive industrial pollution, accumulation of waste products on a global scale, and rapidly deteriorating hygienic conditions in large cities. A more abstract form of the same trend is the escalating corruption and degradation in political and economic circles.

Many of the people with whom we have worked have seen humanity at a critical crossroad facing either collective annihilation or an evolutionary jump in consciousness of unprecedented proportions. Terence McKenna put it very succinctly: "The history of the silly monkey is over, one way or another" (McKenna 1992). It seems that we all are collectively involved in a process that parallels the psychological death and rebirth process that so many people have experienced internally in holotropic states of consciousness. If we continue to act out the problematic destructive and self-destructive tendencies originating in the depth of the unconscious, we will undoubtedly destroy ourselves and possibly life on this planet. However, if we succeed in internalizing this process on a large enough scale, it might result in evolutionary progress of unprecedented proportions. As utopian as the possibility of such a development might seem, it may be our only real hope for the future.

Let us now explore how the concepts that have emerged from consciousness research, from transpersonal psychology, and from the new paradigm in science could be put into action in the world. Although revolutionary advances in many disciplines have laid foundations of a new scientific worldview, the new ideas still form a disjointed mosaic rather than a complete and comprehensive new vision of the universe. Much work has to be done in terms of accumulating more data, formulating new theories, and achieving a creative synthesis. In addition, the existing information has to reach much larger audiences before a significant impact on the world situation can be expected.

But even a radical intellectual shift to a new paradigm on a large scale would not be sufficient to alleviate the global crisis and reverse the destructive course we are on. This would require a deep emotional and spiritual transformation of humanity. Using the existing evidence, it is possible to suggest certain strategies that might facilitate and support such a process. Efforts to change humanity would have to start with psychological prevention at an early age. The data from prenatal and perinatal psychology indicate that much could be achieved by changing the conditions of pregnancy, delivery, and postnatal care. This would include improving the emotional preparation of the mother during pregnancy, practicing natural childbirth, creating a psychospiritually informed birth environment, and cultivating emotionally nourishing contact between the mother and the child in the postpartum period.

Much has been written about the importance of child rearing, as well as disastrous emotional consequences of traumatic conditions in infancy and childhood. Certainly this is an area where continued education and guidance is necessary. However, to apply the theoretically known principles, parents themselves must reach sufficient emotional stability and maturity. It is well known that emotional problems are passed like a curse from generation to generation; it is not unlike the well-known problem of the chicken and the egg.

Humanistic and transpersonal psychologies have developed effective experiential methods of self-exploration, healing, and personality transformation. Some of these come from Western therapeutic traditions, others represent modern adaptations of ancient and native spiritual practices. Besides offering emotional healing, these approaches have the potential to return genuine experiential spirituality into Western culture and remedy the alienation of modern humanity. There exist approaches with a very favorable ratio between professional helpers and clients and others that can be practiced in the context of self-help groups. Systematic work with them could return spiritual values into the industrial civilization and facilitate a transformation of humanity that is sorely needed for survival of our species. For this to succeed, it would be essential to involve mass media and spread the information about these possibilities to get enough people personally interested in pursuing them.

We seem to be involved in a dramatic race for time that has no precedent in the entire history of humanity. What is at stake is nothing less than the future of life on this planet. If we continue the old strategies, which in their consequences are clearly extremely destructive and self-destructive, it is unlikely that the human species will survive. However, if a sufficient number of people could undergo a process of deep inner transformation, we might reach a level of consciousness evolution where we would deserve the name we have so proudly given to our species: *Homo sapiens sapiens.*

Psychedelic Research:
Past, Present, and Future

Stan Grof sharing private time with Albert Hofmann during one of his visits at the Hofmann residence in Berg, Switzerland.

Psychedelic Research: Past, Present, and Future.

The use of psychedelic substances can be traced back for millennia to the dawn of human history. Since time immemorial, plant materials containing powerful consciousness-expanding compounds were used in many different parts of the world in various ritual and spiritual contexts to induce non-ordinary states of consciousness or, more specifically, an important subgroup of them, which I call "holotropic" (Grof 2000). These plants have played an important role in shamanic practice, aboriginal healing ceremonies, rites of passage, mysteries of death and rebirth, and various other spiritual traditions. The ancient and native cultures using psychedelic materials held them in great esteem and considered them to be sacraments, "flesh of the gods" (Schultes, Hofmann, and Rätsch 2001).

Human groups which had at their disposal psychedelic plants took advantage of their entheogenic effects (entheogenic means literally "awakening the divine within") and made them the principal vehicles of their ritual and spiritual life. The preparations made from these plants mediated for these people experiential contact with the archetypal dimensions of reality - deities, mythological realms, power animals, and numinous forces and aspects of nature. Another important area where states induced by psychedelics played a crucial role was diagnosing and healing of various disorders. Anthropological literature also contains many reports indicating that native cultures have used psychedelics for enhancement of intuition and extrasensory perception for a variety of divinatory, as well as practical purposes, such as finding lost persons and objects, obtaining information about people in remote locations, and following the movement of the game that these people hunted. In addition, psychedelic experiences served as important sources of artistic inspiration, providing ideas for rituals, paintings, sculptures, and songs.

In the history of Chinese medicine, reports about psychedelic substances can be traced back about 3,000 years. The legendary divine potion referred to as *haoma* in the ancient Persian *Zend Avesta* and as *soma* in the Indian *Vedas* was used by the Indo-Iranian tribes millennia ago. The mystical states of consciousness induced by soma were very likely the principal source of the Vedic and Hindu religions. Preparations from different varieties of hemp have been smoked and ingested under various names - *hashish, charas, bhang, ganja, kif, and marijuana* - in Asia, in Africa, and in the Caribbean area for recreation, pleasure, and during religious ceremonies. They represented an important sacrament for such diverse groups as the Indian Brahmans, certain orders of Sufis, ancient Scythians, and the Jamaican Rastafarians.

Ceremonial use of various psychedelic substances also has a long history in Central America. Highly effective mind-altering plants were well known in several Pre-Columbian Indian cultures - among them the Aztecs, Mayans, and Olmecs. The most famous of these are the Mexican cactus peyote (*Anhalonium Lewinii*), the sacred mushroom *teonanacatl* (*Psilocybe mexicana*) and *ololiuqui,* or morning glory seeds (*Rivea corymbosa*). These materials have been used as sacraments until this day by several Mexican Indian tribes (Huichols, Mazatecs, Cora people, and others), and by the Native American Church.

The famous South American yajé or ayahuasca is a decoction from a jungle liana (*Banisteriopsis caapi*) with other plant additives. The Amazonian area is also known for a variety of psychedelic snuffs (*Virola callophylla, Piptadenia peregrina*). Preparations from the bark of the shrub iboga (*Tabernanthe iboga*) have been used by African tribes in lower dosage as a stimulant during lion hunts and long canoe trips and in higher doses as a ritual sacrament. The above list represents only a small fraction of psychedelic compounds that have been used over many centuries in various countries of the world. The impact that the experiences encountered in these states had on the spiritual and cultural life of preindustrial societies has been enormous.

The long history of ritual use of psychedelic plants contrasts sharply with a relatively short history of scientific efforts to identify their psychoactive alkaloids, prepare them in a pure form, and to study their effects. The first psychedelic substance that was synthesized in a chemically pure form and systematically explored under laboratory conditions was mescaline, the active alkaloid from the peyote cactus. Clinical experiments conducted with this substance in the first three decades of the twentieth century focused on the phenomenology of the mescaline experience and its interesting effects on artistic perception and creative expression (Vondráček 1935, Nevole 1947, 1949). Surprisingly, they did not reveal the therapeutic, heuristic, and entheogenic potential of this substance. Kurt Beringer, author of the influential book *Der Meskalinrausch* (Mescaline Inebriation) published in 1927, concluded that mescaline induced a toxic psychosis (Beringer 1927).

After these pioneering clinical experiments with mescaline, very little research was done in this fascinating problem area until Albert Hofmann's 1942 epoch-making accidental intoxication and serendipitous discovery of the psychedelic properties of LSD-25, or diethylamid of lysergic acid. After the publication of the first clinical paper on LSD by Werner A. Stoll in the late 1940's (Stoll 1947), this new semisynthetic ergot derivative, active in incredibly minute quantities of micrograms or gammas (millionths of a gram) became a sensation practically overnight in the world of science.

The discovery of powerful psychoactive effects of miniscule dosages of LSD started what has been called a "golden era of psychopharmacology." During a relatively short period of time, the joint efforts of biochemists, pharmacologists, neurophysiologists, psychiatrists, and psychologists succeeded in laying the foundations of a new scientific discipline that can be referred to as the "pharmacology of consciousness." The active substances from several remaining psychedelic plants were chemically identified and prepared in chemically pure form. Following the discovery of the psychedelic effects of LSD-25, Albert Hofmann identified the active principles of the Mexican magic mushrooms (*Psilocybe mexicana*), psilocybin and psilocin, and that of ololiuqui, or morning glory seeds (*Ipomoea violacea*), which turned out to be monoethylamid of lysergic acid (LAE-32), closely related to LSD-25.

The armamentarium of psychedelic substances was further enriched by psychoactive derivatives of tryptamine - DMT (dimethyltryptamine), DET (diethyl-tryptamine), and DPT (dipropyltryptamine) - synthesized and studied by the Budapest group of chemists, headed by Stephen Szara, The active principle from the African shrub *Tabernanthe iboga*, ibogaine, and the pure alkaloid from ayahuasca's main ingredient *Banisteriopsis caapi*, known under the names harmaline, yageine, and telepathine had already been isolated and chemically identified earlier in the twentieth century. In the 1950s, a wide range of psychedelic alkaloids in pure form was available to researchers. It was now possible to study their properties in the laboratory and explore the phenomenology of their clinical effects and their therapeutic potential. The revolution triggered by Albert Hofmann's serendipitous discovery of LSD was underway.

During this exciting era, LSD remained the center of attention of researchers. Never before had a single substance held so much promise in such a wide variety of fields of interest. For psychopharmacologists and neurophysiologists, the discovery of LSD meant the beginning of a golden era of research that could solve many puzzles concerning neuroreceptors, synaptic transmitters, chemical antagonisms, and the intricate biochemical interactions underlying cerebral processes.

Experimental psychiatrists saw LSD as a unique means for creating a laboratory model for naturally occurring functional, or endogenous, psychoses. They hoped that the "experimental psychosis," induced by miniscule dosages of this substance, could provide unparalleled insights into the nature of these mysterious disorders and open new avenues for their treatment. It was suddenly conceivable that the brain or other parts of the body could under certain circumstances produce small quantities of a substance with effects similar to LSD. This meant that disorders like schizophrenia would not be mental diseases, but metabolic aberrations that could be counteracted by specific chemical intervention. The promise of this research was nothing less than the fulfillment of the dream of biologically oriented clinicians, the Holy Grail of psychiatry – a test-tube cure for schizophrenia.

LSD was also highly recommended as an extraordinary unconventional teaching device that would make it possible for clinical psychiatrists, psychologists, medical students, and nurses to spend a few hours in a world similar to that of their patients and as a result of it to understand them better, be able to communicate with them more effectively, and hopefully be more successful in treating them. Thousands of mental health professionals took advantage of this unique opportunity. These experiments brought surprising and astonishing results. They not only provided deep insights into the world of psychiatric patients, but also revolutionized the understanding of the nature and dimensions of the human psyche and consciousness.

Many professionals involved in these experiments discovered that the current model, limiting the psyche to postnatal biography and the Freudian individual unconscious, was superficial and inadequate. My own new map of the psyche that emerged out of this research added two large transbiographical domains – the perinatal level, closely related to the memory of biological birth, and the transpersonal level, harboring the historical and archetypal domains of the collective unconscious as envisioned by C. G. Jung (Grof 1975, Jung 1981). Early experiments with LSD also showed that the sources of emotional and psychosomatic disorders were not limited to traumatic memories from childhood and infancy, as traditional psychiatrists assumed, but that their roots reached much deeper into the psyche, into the perinatal and transpersonal regions (Grof 2000). This surprising revelation was accompanied by the discovery of new powerful therapeutic mechanisms operating on these deep levels of the psyche.

Using LSD as a catalyst, it became possible to extend the range of applicability of psychotherapy to categories of patients that previously had been difficult to reach – sexual deviants, alcoholics, narcotic drug addicts, and criminal recidivists (Grof 2001). Particularly valuable and promising were the early efforts to use LSD psychotherapy in work with

Through Suffering to the Black Sun
Painting from an LSD session in which the Black Sun symbolizes the innermost core of the human being, the Divine Self. The red vertical stripes represent the suffering one must endure to connect with one's true nature.

terminal cancer patients. Research on this population showed that LSD was able to relieve severe pain, often even in those patients who had not responded to medication with narcotics. In a large percentage of these patients, it was also possible to ease or even eliminate difficult emotional and psychosomatic symptoms, such as depression, general tension, and insomnia, alleviate the fear of death, increase the quality of their life during the remaining days, and positively transform the experience of dying (Cohen 1965, Kast and Collins 1966, Grof 2006 b).

For historians and critics of art, the LSD experiments provided extraordinary new insights into the psychology and psychopathology of art, particularly paintings and sculptures of various native, so-called "primitive" cultures and psychiatric patients, as well as various modern movements, such as abstractionism, impressionism, cubism, surrealism and fantastic realism (Roubíček 1961). For professional painters, who participated in LSD research, the psychedelic session often marked a radical change in their artistic expression. Their imagination became much richer, their colors more vivid, and their style considerably freer. They could also often reach into deep recesses of their unconscious psyche and tap archetypal sources of inspiration. On occasion, people who had never painted before were able to produce extraordinary pieces of art.

LSD experimentation also brought fascinating observations of great interest to spiritual teachers and scholars of comparative religion. The mystical experiences frequently observed in LSD sessions offered a radically new understanding of a wide variety of phenomena from the spiritual domain, including shamanism, the rites of passage, the ancient mysteries of death and rebirth, the Eastern religions and philosophies, and the mystical traditions of the world (Forte 1997, Roberts 2001, Grof 1998).

The fact that LSD and other psychedelic substances were able to trigger a broad range of spiritual experiences became the subject of heated scientific discussions. They revolved around the fascinating problem concerning the nature and value of this "instant" or "chemical" mysticism" (Grof 1998). As Walter Pahnke demonstrated in his famous Good Friday experiment, mystical experiences induced by psychedelics are indistinguishable from those described in mystical literature (Pahnke 1963). This finding that was recently confirmed by a meticulous study by researchers at Johns Hopkins University (Griffiths et al. 2006) has important theoretical and legal implications.

Psychedelic research involving LSD, psilocybine, mescaline, and the tryptamine derivatives seemed to be well on its way to fulfill all the above promises and expectations when it was suddenly interrupted by the unsupervised mass experimentation of the young generation in the USA and other Western countries. In the infamous Harvard affair, psychology professors Timothy Leary and Richard Alpert lost their academic posts and had to leave the school after their overeager proselytizing of LSD's promises. The ensuing administrative, legal, and political repressive measures had very little effect on street use of LSD and other psychedelics but effectively ended legitimate clinical research. Although the problems associated with uncontrolled experimentation were blown out of proportion by sensation-hunting journalists, the possible risks were not the only reason why LSD and other psychedelics were rejected by the Euro-American mainstream culture. An important contributing factor was also the attitude of technological societies toward holotropic states of consciousness.

As I mentioned earlier, all ancient and pre-industrial societies held these states in high esteem, whether they were induced by psychedelic plants or some of the many powerful non-drug "technologies of the sacred" – fasting, sleep deprivation, social and sensory isolation, dancing, chanting, music, drumming, or physical pain. Members of these social groups had the opportunity to repeatedly experience holotropic states of consciousness during their lifetime in a variety of sacred contexts. By comparison, the industrial civilization has pathologized holotropic states, rejected or even outlawed the contexts and tools that can facilitate them, and developed effective means of suppressing them when they occur spontaneously. Because of the resulting naiveté and ignorance concerning holotropic states, Western culture was unprepared to accept and incorporate the extraordinary mind-altering properties and power of LSD and other psychedelics.

The sudden emergence of the Dionysian element from the depths of the unconscious and the heights of the superconscious was too threatening for Euro-American society. In addition, the irrational and transrational nature of psychedelic experiences seriously challenged the very foundations of the materialistic worldview of Western science. The existence and nature of these experiences could not be explained in the context of mainstream theories and seriously undermined the metaphysical assumptions concerning priority of matter over consciousness on which Western culture is built. It also threatened the leading myth of the industrial world by showing that true fulfillment does not come from achievement of material goals but from a profound mystical experience.

It was not just the culture at large that was unprepared for the psychedelic experience; this was also true for the helping professions. For most psychiatrists and psychologists, psychotherapy meant disciplined face-to-face discussions or free-associating on the couch. The intense emotions and dramatic physical manifestations in psychedelic sessions appeared to them to be too close to what they were used to associate with psychopathology. It was hard for them to imagine that such states could be healing and transformative. As a result, they did not trust the reports about the extraordinary power of psychedelic psychotherapy coming from colleagues who had had enough courage to take their chances and do psychedelic therapy, or from their clients.

To complicate the situation even further, many of the phenomena occurring in psychedelic sessions could not be understood within the context of theories dominating academic thinking. The possibility of re-living birth or episodes from embryonic life, obtaining accurate information about world history and mythology from the collective unconscious, experiencing archetypal realities and karmic memories, or perceiving remote events in out-of-body states, were simply too fantastic to be believable for an average professional. Yet those of us who had the chance to work with LSD and were willing to radically change our theoretical understanding of the psyche and practical strategy of therapy were able to see and appreciate the enormous potential of psychedelics, both as therapeutic tools and as substances of extraordinary heuristic value.

In one of my early books, I suggested that the potential significance of LSD and other psychedelics for psychiatry and psychology was comparable to the value the microscope has for biology and medicine or the telescope has for astronomy. My later experience with psychedelics only confirmed this initial impression. These substances function as unspecific amplifiers that increase the cathexis (energetic charge) associated with the deep unconscious contents of the psyche and make them available for conscious processing. This unique property of psychedelics makes it possible to study psychological undercurrents that govern our experiences and behaviors to a depth that cannot be matched by any other method or tool available in modern mainstream psychiatry and psychology. In addition, it offers unique opportunities for healing of emotional and psychosomatic disorders, for positive personality transformation, and consciousness evolution.

Naturally, tools with this power carry with them greater risks than more conservative and far less effective tools currently accepted and used by mainstream psychiatry, such as verbal psychotherapy or tranquillizing medication. Clinical research has shown that these risks can be minimized by responsible use and careful control of the set and setting. The safety of psychedelic therapy when conducted in a clinical setting was demonstrated by Sidney Cohen's study based on information drawn from more than 25,000 psychedelic sessions. According to Cohen,

LSD therapy appeared to be much safer than many other procedures that had been at one time or another routinely used in psychiatric treatment, such as electroshock therapy, insulin coma therapy, and psychosurgery (Cohen 1960). However, legislators responding to unsupervised mass use of psychedelics did not get their information from scientific publications, but from the stories of sensation-hunting journalists. The legal and administrative sanctions against psychedelics did not deter lay experimentation, but they all but terminated legitimate scientific research of these substances.

For those of us who had the privilege to explore and experience the extraordinary potential of psychedelics, this was a tragic loss for psychiatry, psychology, and psychotherapy. We felt that these unfortunate developments wasted what was probably the single most important opportunity in the history of these disciplines. Had it been possible to avoid the unnecessary mass hysteria and continue responsible research of psychedelics, they could have undoubtedly radically transformed the theory and practice of psychiatry. I believe that the observations from this research have the potential to initiate a revolution in the understanding of the human psyche and of consciousness comparable to the conceptual cataclysm that modern physicists experienced in the first three decades in relation to their theories concerning matter. This new knowledge could become an integral part of a comprehensive new scientific paradigm of the twenty-first century.

At present, when more than four decades have elapsed since official research with psychedelics was effectively terminated, I can attempt to evaluate the past history of these substances and glimpse into their future. After having personally conducted over the last fifty years more than four thousand psychedelic sessions, I have developed great awe and respect for these compounds and their enormous positive, as well as negative potential. They are powerful tools and like any tool they can be used skillfully, ineptly, or destructively. The result will be critically dependent on the set and setting.

The question of whether LSD is a phenomenal medicine or a devil's drug makes as little sense as a similar question asked about the positive or negative potential of a knife. Naturally, we will get a very different report from a surgeon who bases his or her judgment on successful operations and from the police chief who investigates murders committed with knives in the back alleys of New York City. A housewife would see the knife primarily as a useful kitchen tool and an artist would employ it in carving wooden sculptures. It would make little sense to judge the usefulness and dangers of a knife by watching children who play with it without adequate maturity and skill. Similarly, the image of LSD will vary whether we focus on the results of responsible clinical or spiritual use, naive and careless mass self-experimentation of the younger generation, or deliberately destructive experiments of the military or secret police.

Until it is clearly understood that the results of the administration of psychedelics are critically influenced by the factors of set and setting, there is no hope for rational decisions in regard to psychedelic drug policies. I firmly believe that psychedelics can be used in such a way that the benefits far outweigh the risks. This has been amply proven by millennia of safe ritual and spiritual use of psychedelics by generations of shamans, individual healers, and entire aboriginal cultures. However, the Western industrial civilization has so far abused nearly all its discoveries and there is not much hope that psychedelics will be an exception, unless we rise as a group to a higher level of consciousness and emotional maturity.

Whether or not psychedelics will return to psychiatry and will again become part of the therapeutic armamentarium is a complex problem and its solution will probably be determined not only by the results of scientific research, but also by a variety of political, legal, economic, and mass psychological factors. However, I believe that Western society is at present much better equipped to accept and assimilate psychedelics than it was in the 1950s. At the time when psychiatrists and psychologists started to experiment with LSD, psychotherapy was limited to verbal exchanges between therapists and clients. Intense emotions and active behavior were referred to as "acting-out" and were seen as violations of basic therapeutic rules. Psychedelic sessions were on the other side of the spectrum, evoking dramatic emotions, psychomotor excitement, and vivid perceptual changes. They thus seemed to be more like states that psychiatrists considered pathological and tried to suppress by all means than conditions to which one would attribute therapeutic potential. This was reflected in the terms "hallucinogens," "delirogens," "psychotomimetics," and "experimental psychoses," used initially for psychedelics and the states induced by them. In any case, psychedelic sessions more closely resembled scenes from anthropological movies about healing rituals of "primitive" cultures and other aboriginal ceremonies than those expected in a psychiatrist's or psychotherapist's office.

In addition, many of the experiences and observations from psychedelic sessions seemed to seriously challenge the image of the human psyche and of the universe developed by Newtonian-Cartesian science and considered to be accurate and definitive descriptions of "objective reality." Psychedelic subjects reported experiential identification with

Paintings of the clock tower in the research institute where the author had one of his early LSD experiences. The first painting shows the tower as perceived in the ordinary state of consciousness. The remaining paintings depict the illusive optical transformations of the same object in the terminal stage of the session.

other people, animals, and various aspects of nature, during which they gained access to new information in areas about which they previously had no intellectual knowledge. The same was true about experiential excursions into the lives of their human and animal ancestors, as well as racial, collective, and karmic memories.

On occasion, this new information was drawn from experiences involving reliving of biological birth and memories of prenatal life, encounters with archetypal beings, and visits to mythological realms of different cultures of the world. In out-of-body experiences, experimental subjects were able to witness and accurately describe remote events occurring in locations that were outside of the range of their senses. None of these happenings were considered possible in the context of traditional materialistic science, and yet, in psychedelic sessions, they were observed frequently. This naturally caused deep conceptual turmoil and confusion in the minds of conventionally trained experimenters. Under these circumstances, many professionals chose to shy away from this area in order to preserve their respectable scientific world-view and professional reputation and to protect their common sense and sanity.

The last several decades have brought many revolutionary changes that have profoundly influenced the climate in the world of psychotherapy. Humanistic and transpersonal psychology have developed powerful experiential techniques that emphasize deep regression, direct expression of intense emotions, and bodywork leading to release of physical energies. Among these new approaches to self-exploration are Gestalt practice, bioenergetics and other neo-Reichian methods, primal therapy, rebirthing, and Holotropic Breathwork. The inner experiences and outer manifestations in these therapies, as well as their therapeutic strategies, bear a great similarity to those observed in psychedelic sessions. These non-drug therapeutic strategies involve not only a similar spectrum of experiences, but also comparable conceptual challenges. As a result, for therapists practicing along these lines, the introduction of psychedelics would represent the next logical step rather than a dramatic change in their practice.

Moreover, the Newtonian-Cartesian thinking in science, which in the 1960s enjoyed great authority and popularity, has been progressively undermined by astonishing developments in a variety of disciplines. This has happened to such an extent that an increasing number of scientists feel an urgent need for an entirely different world-view, a new scientific paradigm. Salient examples of this development are philosophical implications of quantum-relativistic physics (Capra 1975, Goswami 1995), David Bohm's theory of holomovement (Bohm 1980), Karl Pribram's holographic theory of the brain (Pribram 1971), Ilya Prigogine's theory of dissipative structures (Prigogine 1980), Rupert Sheldrake's theory of morphogenetic fields (Sheldrake 1981), Gregory Bateson's brilliant synthesis of systems and information theory, cybernetics, anthropology, and psychology (Bateson 1979), and particularly Ervin Laszlo's concept of the PSI field (akashic field), his connectivity hypothesis, and his "integral theory of everything" (Laszlo 1993, 2004). It is very encouraging to see that all these new developments that are in irreconcilable conflict with traditional science seem to be compatible with the findings of psychedelic research and with transpersonal psychology. This list would not be complete without mentioning the remarkable efforts of Ken Wilber to create a comprehensive synthesis of a variety of scientific disciplines and perennial philosophy (Wilber 2000 a).

Even more encouraging than the changes in the scientific worldview, that in the past was a serious obstacle in accepting the findings of psychedelic research, is the relaxation of the administrative and legal constraints that in the past stood in the way of experimentation with psychedelics. At present, we can see not only a significant renaissance of interest in psychedelic substances in academic circles, but also the worldwide emergence of many new clinical and laboratory research programs exploring the effects of these remarkable substances. This development engenders hope that in the future psychedelics will return into the hands of responsible therapists and experimenters.

Stanislav Grof's Foreword to a Book About Albert Hofmann's Life and Work

Stanislav Grof, Albert Hofmann, Christina Grof, and Anita Hofmann in the Hofmann garden in Berg, Switzerland.

Stanislav Grof's Foreword to a Book About Albert Hofmann's Life and Work

This chapter is the English version of the German foreword to the book:
Hagenbach, Dieter and Werthmueller, Lucius. 2011. *Albert Hofmann und sein LSD: Ein bewegtes Leben und eine bedeutende Entdeckung (Albert Hofmann and his LSD: An Exciting Life and An Important Discovery)*. Baden, Germany: AT-Verlag.

It is an extraordinary privilege and pleasure for me to write a foreword for the book honoring the life and work of Albert Hofmann, a brilliant researcher and scientist in the best sense of the word, whom I consider my spiritual father. Words can hardly describe the deep gratitude I feel to him for everything that his discoveries brought into my personal and professional life and the lives of countless other people who used the substances he had synthesized responsibly and with the respect that these extraordinary tools deserve.

I first heard Albert's name in 1954 when I worked as a medical student volunteer at the Psychiatric Department of the School of Medicine of Charles University in Prague. My preceptor, Docent George Roubíček, had a good working relationship with the Sandoz Pharmaceutical Company in Basel and regularly received complimentary samples of new products from this firm as they were coming to the market. As part of this cooperation, he received a supply of diethylamid of lysergic acid, or LSD-25, a new experimental substance with unprecedented psychoactive power. The package arrived with a letter describing the discovery of LSD – Albert's accidental intoxication during the synthesis of this substance, his subsequent self-experiment, and Werner Stoll's pilot study with a group of normal volunteers and psychiatric patients.

Werner Stoll's paper "LSD, ein Phantastikum aus der Mutterkorngruppe" (LSD: An Amazing Wonder from the Ergot Group) (Stoll 1947) became an overnight sensation in the scientific world. His pilot study showed that miniscule dosages of this new substance (in the range of millionths of a gram – micrograms or gammas) were able to induce a state in experimental subjects that resembled in many ways naturally occurring psychoses; Stoll also mentioned in his paper that

LSD might have interesting therapeutic potential. Sandoz sent samples of the new substance to psychiatric research institutes, university departments, and individual therapists asking them if they would be interested in experimenting with LSD and exploring whether this substance had any legitimate uses in psychiatry and psychology. The letter gave two suggestions for possible use of LSD: as an agent inducing "experimental psychosis" that might provide insights into biochemical causes of schizophrenia and as an unconventional therapeutic tool that would make it possible for mental health professionals to spend a few hours in a state resembling the experiential world of psychotic patients.

Docent Roubíček was very interested in conducting research with LSD but his busy schedule did not allow him to spend six to eight hours in the sessions of experimental subjects. He asked me and a few other students to be guides for these people, observe them, and keep records about their experiences. This gave me a unique opportunity to be present in psychedelic sessions of many volunteers, including psychiatrists, psychologists, and artists. I was fascinated by what I saw and heard and was eager to volunteer for a session myself. Unfortunately, to my great dismay, the faculty board decided that students should not be used as experimental subjects.

I could not wait to experience LSD personally and as soon as I graduated from the medical school I volunteered for a session. One of docent Roubíček's main research interests was electroencephalography and, more specifically, a process called "driving" or "entraining" the brainwaves. He exposed his subjects to a powerful stroboscopic light and studied the effect of various frequencies on the brainwaves in their suboccipital cortex. He was curious how this process would be influenced by administration of LSD; participation in this research was thus a necessary prerequisite for having an LSD session under his aegis.

The combined effect of LSD and the stroboscopic light triggered in me an experience of cosmic consciousness of extraordinary power (Grof 2006 a). Although it lasted only several hours - and its most significant part only about ten minutes - it resulted in a profound personal transformation and spiritual awakening and sent me on a radically different course professionally than the one for which I had been trained and prepared. I have, in fact, been following that trajectory with great determination until this very day. The research of non-ordinary states of consciousness has been my passion, vocation, and profession ever since.

Now, more than fifty years later, I look at this experience as an initiation similar to that of participants in ancient mysteries of death and rebirth. I could not agree more with Albert, who saw a deep similarity between LSD and the sacramental drink kykeon used in the Eleusinian mysteries (Wasson, Hofmann, Ruck 1978) and hoped that responsible ritual use of LSD would one day be integrated into Western civilization. He believed that this New Eleusis would bring spiritual and cultural benefits to modern humanity similar to those that its ancient antecedent bestowed on ancient Greece and her neighboring countries.

After my first LSD session, I became deeply involved in psychedelic research and in the study of all related literature. Albert Hofmann's "wonder child" engendered an unprecedented wave of scientific enthusiasm and optimism and spawned a new discipline – the science of consciousness. Never before in the history of science had a single substance held so much promise in such a wide variety of fields. For neuropharmacologists and neurophysiologists, the discovery of LSD meant the beginning of a golden era of research that could potentially lead to major advances concerning neuroreceptors, synaptic transmitters, chemical antagonisms, the role of serotonin in the brain, and the intricate biochemical interactions underlying cerebral processes.

Experimental psychiatrists saw LSD as a unique means for creating a laboratory model for naturally occurring functional, or endogenous, psychoses. They hoped that the "experimental psychosis," induced by miniscule dosages of this substance, could provide unparalleled insights into the nature of these mysterious disorders and open up new avenues for their treatment. It was suddenly conceivable that the brain or other parts of the body could under certain circumstances produce small quantities of a substance with effects similar to those of LSD. This meant that disorders like schizophrenia would not be mental diseases, but metabolic aberrations that could be counteracted and neutralized by specific chemical intervention. The potential of this research was nothing less that the fulfillment of the dream of biologically oriented clinicians, the Holy Grail of psychiatry – a test-tube cure for schizophrenia.

LSD was also highly recommended as an extraordinary unconventional teaching device that would make it possible for clinical psychiatrists, psychologists, medical students, and nurses to spend a few hours in a world resembling that of their patients and as a result be able to understand them better, communicate with them more effectively, and be more successful in their treatment. Thousands of mental health professionals took advantage of this unique opportunity. These experiments brought surprising and astonishing results. They not only provided deep insights into the inner world of psychiatric patients, but also revolutionized the understanding of the nature of consciousness and the dimensions of the human psyche.

As a result of their experiences, many professionals found that the current model, limiting the psyche to postnatal biography and the Freudian individual unconscious, was superficial and inadequate. The new map of the psyche that emerged out of this research added two large transbiographical domains – the perinatal level, closely related to the memory of biological birth, and the transpersonal level, harboring among others the historical and archetypal domains of the collective unconscious as envisioned by C. G. Jung. Early experiments with LSD showed that the roots of emotional and psychosomatic disorders were not limited to traumatic memories from childhood and infancy, as traditional psychiatrists assumed, but reached much deeper into the psyche, into the perinatal and transpersonal regions.

Reports from psychedelic psychotherapists revealed LSD's unique potential as a powerful tool that could deepen and accelerate the psychotherapeutic process. With LSD as a catalyst, psychotherapy could now be useful with categories of patients that previously had been difficult to reach – sexual deviants, alcoholics, narcotic drug addicts, and criminal recidivists. Particularly valuable and promising were the early efforts to use LSD psychotherapy in the work with terminal cancer patients. With this population, administration of LSD could relieve severe pain, often even for patients who had not responded to medication with narcotics. In a large percentage of these patients, it was also possible to ease or even eliminate difficult emotional and psychosomatic symptoms, including depression, general tension, insomnia, and the fear of death. With this kind of relief for patients, the quality of their lives was significantly increased during their remaining days and their experience of dying was positively transformed.

For historians and art critics, the LSD experiments provided extraordinary new insights into the psychology and psychopathology of art, particularly various modern movements, such as abstractionism, cubism, surrealism, fantastic realism, and into paintings and sculptures of various native, so-called "primitive" cultures. Professional painters who participated in LSD research often found that their psychedelic sessions marked a radical change in their artistic expression. Their imagination became much richer, their colors more vivid, and their style considerably freer. They could also often reach into deep recesses of their unconscious psyche and tap archetypal sources of inspiration. On occasion, people who had never painted before were able to produce extraordinary works of art.

LSD experimentation brought also fascinating observations of great interest to spiritual teachers and scholars of comparative religion. The mystical experiences frequently observed in LSD sessions offered a radically new understanding of a wide variety of phenomena from the world of religion, including shamanism, the rites of passage, the ancient mysteries of death and rebirth, the Eastern spiritual philosophies, and the mystical traditions of the world. The fact that LSD and other psychedelic substances could trigger a broad range of spiritual experiences became the subject of heated scientific discussions revolving around the fascinating problem concerning the nature and value of this "instant" or "chemical mysticism,"

LSD research seemed to be well on its way to fulfill all these promises and expectations when it was suddenly interrupted by the infamous Harvard affair, as a result of which Timothy Leary and Richard Alpert lost their academic posts, and the subsequent unsupervised mass experimentation of the young generation. In addition, the problems associated with this development were blown out of proportion by sensation-hunting journalists. The ensuing repressive measures of an administrative, legal, and political nature had very little effect on street use of LSD and other psychedelics, but they drastically terminated legitimate clinical research.

Those of us privileged to have personal experiences with psychedelics and to have used them in our work saw the great promise that they represented not only for psychiatry, psychology, and psychotherapy, but also for modern society in general. We were deeply saddened by the mass hysteria that pervaded not only the lay population, but also the clinical and academic circles. It tragically compromised and criminalized tools with extraordinary therapeutic potential that properly understood and used had the power to counteract the destructive and self-destructive tendencies of industrial civilization.

It was particularly heart-breaking to see the reaction of Albert Hofmann, the father of LSD and other psychedelics, as he watched his prodigious "wonder child" turn into a "problem child" (Hofmann 2005), I had the great privilege and pleasure to know Albert personally and meet him repeatedly on various occasions. Over the years, I developed great affection and deep admiration for him, not only as an outstanding and genuine scientist, but also as an extraordinary human being radiating astonishing vitality, curiosity, and love for all creation. I would like to briefly describe several of our meetings that have made a particularly deep impression on me.

I first met Albert in the late 1960s when he visited the newly built Maryland Psychiatric Research Center where we were conducting extensive research of psychedelic therapy. After spending some time with the members of our staff, Albert expressed an interest to go sightseeing in Washington, D.C. and I offered to be his guide. We visited the Capitol, the Washington and Lincoln Monuments, the Reflecting Pool, and the tomb of J. F. Kennedy at Arlington Cemetery. It was April, the time of the National Cherry Blossom festival, and Albert, a passionate lover of nature, enjoyed the beauty of the blossoming trees immensely.

Before we returned to Baltimore, he expressed the desire to see the White House. At that time, pedestrians and cars were still permitted in the immediate proximity of the White House. I pulled to the curb and stopped the car. Albert rolled down the window, laid his hands on the edge of the glass panel, and looked for a while at the majestic building towering over the flower-decorated lawn. Then he turned to me and said with an almost child-like expression in his face: "So this is the great White House where important people like Richard Nixon and Spiro Agnew make the decisions that change the course of the world!"

Albert's comment and his humility astonished me. Nixon certainly was not one of the most admirable American presidents and Spiro Agnew, Nixon's Vice-President, was a third-rate politician who was later forced to resign because of charges of extortion, tax fraud, bribery, and conspiracy. I said to Albert: "Do you realize what impact you have had on the world as compared to Spiro Agnew?" In his modesty, Albert clearly did not realize and appreciate how his own discoveries had affected the lives of millions of people.

In 1988, my wife Christina and I had the chance to invite Albert to be the keynote speaker for the Tenth International Transpersonal Conference in Santa Rosa, CA, entitled The Transpersonal Vision: Past, Present, and Future. There is hardly any part of the world where Albert was and still is appreciated more than in California. A large number of Californians have experimented with LSD and other psychedelics as part of their spiritual journey and feel deeply grateful for the profound contribution it has made in their lives. Albert received an enthusiastic welcome from conference participants and had the status of a rock star throughout this meeting.

Another of my memorable meetings with Albert occurred in the late years of his life when I was teaching an advanced training module for practitioners of Holotropic Breathwork entitled Fantastic Art. It was held in the H. R. Giger Museum in Gruyères, Switzerland, and we had invited Albert to come and spend a day with our group as the guest of honor. After lunch, Hansruedi Giger - extraordinary fantastic realist painter, sculptor, and interior architect who had received an Academy Award in 1980 for the otherworldly creatures and environments he had created for the movie Alien - took us for a guided tour through his remarkable museum. We were all curious to see how Albert, a man of fine discriminating esthetic taste, would respond to Hansruedi's large-scale biomechanoid paintings abounding with brutally realistic images of biological birth, explicit sexual imagery, and dark satanic and scatological motifs (Giger 1977). Albert's reaction was unequivocal - not only did he admire Hansruedi's artistic genius, but also the extraordinary

Albert Hofmann around the time he discovered LSD.

power and authenticity with which his art portrayed the dark recesses of the human psyche that could be revealed during our inner journeys in the depth of the unconscious.

After his tour of the museum, Albert sat down with our group for a lecture and panel discussion. One of the most striking aspects of his personality was his passionate love of nature. As a child, Albert had a powerful mystical experience while walking in a meadow and his favorite pastime was spending time in nature, including his beautiful garden. During his professional life, his main interest was the chemistry of plants and animals. He conducted important research regarding the chemical structure of *chitin*, the main component of the cell walls of fungi and the exoskeletons of arthropods such as crustaceans (crabs, lobsters, and shrimp) and insects, for which in 1930 he received his doctorate. Later he studied the Mediterranean medicinal plant squill (*Scilla glycosides*) and elucidated the chemical structure of its common nucleus as part of a program to purify and synthesize active constituents of plants for use as pharmaceuticals. And, of course, he became world-famous for his research of ergot and lysergic acid derivatives that led to the discovery of LSD and for the chemical identification of the active alkaloids of Psilocybin mushrooms (*teonanacatl*) and morning glory seeds (*ololiuqui*).

Albert talked about LSD in a way that was reminiscent of native cultures where psychedelic plants are seen as having certain characteristics of conscious beings. He shared with us his conviction that his discovery of the psychedelic effects of LSD-25 was not an accident or even "serendipity" as he used to call it in his public lectures. In 1938, when he first synthesized LSD, he found it difficult to accept the conclusion of the pharmacological department of Sandoz that this substance did not have any properties warranting further research. As he continued to synthesize additional derivatives of lysergic acid, he could not get LSD-25 off his mind; he had a strong sense that the pharmacologists must have overlooked something when they were testing this particular substance.

By April 1943, this feeling became so compelling that he decided to synthesize another sample of LSD-25. This was very unusual - as a rule, experimental substances were definitely eliminated from the research program if they were found to be of no pharmacological interest. While working on this synthesis, Albert experienced the non-ordinary state of consciousness ("accidental intoxication") that led him to his famous self-experiment with 250 mcg of LSD (Hofmann 2005). His strong conviction that there was something special about LSD, finally culminating in the urge to synthesize another sample for deeper investigation, was difficult to explain rationally. Describing this sequence of events, Albert said: "I did not discover LSD; LSD found and called me."

Albert's presentation to our group in Gruyères turned into a passionate apotheosis of the beauty and mystery of nature and creation in general. He spoke about the miraculous chemistry that gives rise to the pigments responsible for the gorgeous colors of flowers and butterfly wings. He saw the intricacy of the chemical formulas responsible for the colors in nature as unmistakable proof that the universe had a master blueprint and was created by superior cosmic intelligence. Studying this remarkable alchemy of nature, he could sense the thoughts and the hand of the Creator. According to him, those who believe that atoms can do such things all by themselves do not know what they are talking about.

Albert also spoke at some length about the gratitude he felt for being alive and participating in the miracle of consciousness. He emphasized the need to embrace creation in its totality - including its shadow side - because without polarity the universe we live in could not have been

Albert and Stan saying goodbye after the Gruyères module (see text).

created. When he left, we all felt that we just had attended a darshan with a spiritual teacher. It was clear that Albert had joined the group of great scientists -- like Albert Einstein and Isaac Newton — for whom rigorous pursuit of their discipline had brought recognition of the miraculous divine order underlying the world of matter and natural phenomena.

Several months after the Gruyères event, I returned to Switzerland to celebrate Albert's hundredth birthday. The morning celebration, in the Museum of Natural History in Basel, was a very official event, attended by many people from the psychedelic world, public figures, and Albert's friends. Swiss Bundespresident Moritz Leuenberger wrote a special letter for this occasion; he called Albert "a great figure in the exploration of human consciousness." In the evening, I was invited, along with my two friends and colleagues, Sonia and Juraj Styk, to a very different kind of celebration of Albert's birthday, held in an old inn in Berg, a small village on the Swiss-French border, where the Hofmanns lived. Children brought Albert flowers, recited poems, and sang songs. In this moving ceremony we did not hear LSD mentioned once; we were not sure if the villagers in Berg even knew what Albert had contributed to the world. They were just celebrating a wonderful neighbor who had reached the very respectable age of one hundred years.

The last time I had the chance to spend some time with Albert was two years later during the World Psychedelic Forum in Basel. His name was among the presenters, but he felt too weak to come and give a lecture. Hansruedi and Carmen Giger, their assistant Stephan Stucki, and I were invited to visit Albert in his home in Berg. Although Albert's intellect was still very clear, his physical condition was rapidly deteriorating. We spent several precious hours with Albert revisiting old memories and listening to him as he was sharing with us his most recent philosophical and metaphysical ideas. I was very moved to hear that he had been reading daily passages from my book The Ultimate Journey: Consciousness and the Mystery of Death (Grof 2006 b), which he kept on his bedside table. As we watched a beautiful sunset from the living room window, we were all very much aware that this was our last meeting and the end of an era. In view of Albert's long and productive life, we were experiencing very mixed feelings – deep sadness in anticipation of Albert's impending passing as well as celebration of a full and blessed life well spent. Albert died peacefully of a heart attack four weeks later.

However harsh and irrational the administrative and legal measures were against the personal and professional use of psychedelics, Albert never lost his faith in their therapeutic and spiritual potential and always hoped that scientific evidence would eventually prevail over mass hysteria. He continued to believe that one day these valuable tools would be used again with great benefit to human society. Thanks to his extraordinary vitality and longevity along with the determination and persistence of Rick Doblin and the Multidisciplinary Association for Psychedelic Research (MAPS), toward the end of his life Albert was able to see the beginning of a remarkable global renaissance of academic interest in psychedelic substances that included the resumption of LSD-assisted psychotherapy research.

In USA, several major universities have returned to psychedelic research – Harvard University, University of California Los Angeles (UCLA), Johns Hopkins University, New York University, University of California San Francisco (UCSF), University of Chicago, and University of Arizona Tucson. In Charleston, South Carolina, Dr. Michael Mithoefer and his wife Annie have reported positive results with the use of the entheogen MDMA (Ecstasy) in the treatment of post-traumatic stress disorder (PTSD) (Mithoefer et al. 2010). Their work could have important implications for solving the formidable problem of emotional disturbances (PTSD) in war veterans. And important psychedelic research is currently being conducted in Switzerland, Germany, Spain, England, Holland, Israel, Brazil, Peru, and many other countries of the world. The Seventeenth International Transpersonal Conference that took place in June 2010 in Moscow included a special track featuring the presentations of a new generation of psychedelic researchers.

While the renaissance of psychedelic research is very exciting, most of the new studies repeat the studies that had already been done in the past, including Walter Pahnke's Good Friday experiment that showed the entheogenic effects of psilocybin (Pahnke 1963), psychedelic therapy with cancer patients (Grof 2006 b), and administration of psychedelics to neurotic and alcoholic patients (Pahnke et al. 1970.) but now using more rigorous scientific methodology. Among the notable exceptions are the use of the new imaging techniques in basic research exploring the effects of psychedelics on the brain and the pioneering and groundbreaking work with individuals suffering from PTSD (Mithoefer et al. 2010).

The promising results in the last category have the best chance to inspire clinicians worldwide and make this therapy mainstream. The problems with American soldiers returning from the Korean War, Vietnam War, Persian Gulf War, Afghanistan War, and Iraq War, have been truly formidable: insomnia, terrifying nightmares, depression, a high suicide rate, and outbursts of violence. Traditional therapies have proven to be painfully ineffective for these recalcitrant disorders. The difficulties that PTSD has posed for the Russian and Soviet armies have been equally challenging.

If the therapeutic effects of LSD and other psychedelics withstand the test of these new studies, the research will hopefully move into areas presently lacking scientific data but abounding with anecdotal evidence. The capacity of psychedelics to facilitate creativity is one of the most promising areas of investigation. In the 1960s, Willis Harman, Robert McKim, Robert Mogar, James Fadiman, and Myron Stolaroff conducted a pilot study of the effects of psychedelics on the creative process. They administered LSD-25 and mescaline to a group of highly talented individuals and studied the effects of these substances on inspiration and problem-solving (Harman et al. 1966). In their book Higher Creativity: Liberating the Unconscious for Breakthrough Insights, Willis Harman and Howard Rheingold gave scores of examples of scientific and artistic breakthroughs that were facilitated by non-ordinary states of consciousness (Harman and Rheingold 1984). A program offering supervised psychedelic sessions to prominent researchers facing an impasse in their work on important projects and to prominent artists could significantly advance scientific progress and foster unique contributions to our cultural life.

Already LSD has facilitated discoveries that subsequently received the highest scientific awards. In 1993, molecular biologist and DNA chemist Kary Mullis received a Nobel Prize for his development of the Polymerase Chain Reaction (PCR), a central technique in biochemistry and molecular biology that allows the amplification of specific DNA sequences. During a symposium in Basel celebrating Albert Hofmann's 100th anniversary, Albert revealed that Kary Mullis attributed his accomplishment to insights from his experience with LSD. Francis Crick, the father of modern genetics, was under the influence of LSD when he discovered the double-helix structure of DNA. He told a fellow scientist that he often used small doses of LSD to boost his power of thought. He said it was LSD that helped him to unravel the structure of DNA, the discovery that won him the Nobel Prize.

In his non-fiction book What the Dormouse Said: How the Sixties Counterculture Shaped the Personal Computer Industry, John Markoff described the history of the personal computer (Markoff 2005). He showed the direct connection between the use of psychedelics in the American counterculture of the 1950s and 1960s and the development of the computer industry. Steve Jobs said that taking LSD was "among the two or three most important things he had done in his life." He noted that people in his staff who did not share his countercultural roots could not fully relate to his thinking. Douglas Engelbart, who invented the computer mouse, also explored and experimented with psychedelic drugs. Kevin Herbert, who worked for Cisco Systems in the early days, once said: "When I'm on LSD and hearing something that's pure rhythm, it takes me to another world and into another brain state where I've stopped thinking and started knowing." Mark Pesce, the co-inventor of virtual reality's coding language, VRML, agreed that there is a definite relationship between chemical mind expansion and advances in computer technology: "To a man and a woman, the people behind virtual reality were acidheads."

Albert Hofmann's "wonder child" thus helped other scientists solve challenging problems and even receive the highest award in science - the Nobel Prize. Those scientists who are not blinded by the stormy cultural controversy surrounding LSD-25, have no doubt that Albert Hofmann himself deserved the Nobel Prize for his brilliant and important discoveries. Unfortunately the sad irony – if not blunder – in the history of science is that the only Nobel Prize of relevance for psychiatry was awarded in 1949 to the Portuguese neurologist Antonio Edgar Moniz for the development of prefrontal lobotomy - a massive mutilating surgical intervention of questionable value and with serious side effects. This procedure was used especially during the period from the early 1940s to the mid-1950s for a wide range of conditions – psychosis, obsessive-compulsive disorder, depression, criminality, and aggressive behavior. The most infamous example of the use of lobotomy was Rosemary Kennedy, sister to John, Robert, and Edward Kennedy, who was given a lobotomy when her father complained to doctors about the mildly retarded girl's "embarrassing new interest in boys." Even in its greatly mitigated form (prefrontal or "icepick" lobotomy), this procedure was abandoned within a decade by the psychiatric profession.

Because of the unfortunate historical developments during the second half of the 20th century, mainstream academic circles have not recognized and acknowledged the importance of Albert's extraordinary and influential discoveries. And instead of honors and praise from his employer for his extraordinary achievements, he was blamed because the controversy associated with his discoveries had tarnished the reputation of Sandoz Pharmaceutical Company.

Human history features many great individuals – ground-breaking pioneers of various eras - who were not appreciated by their contemporaries, both the lay population and the scientific authorities of their time. Just to give a salient example: the heliocentric system of Nicolas Copernicus was not generally accepted until one hundred years after his epoch-making discovery. It is my firm belief that future generations will see Albert Hofmann as one the most influential scientists of the twentieth century, a Promethean visionary whose discoveries helped to chart a new trajectory not only for psychiatry, psychology, and neuroscience, but also for the evolution of the human species.

VISION 97

Award Ceremony of the Dagmar and

Václav Havel Foundation

Honoring
Dr. Stanislav Grof

Prague
Crossroads Spiritual Center
October 5, 2007

Václav Havel, Stanislav Grof and Paul Grof at the Vision 97 presentation.

President Václav Havel's Speech

Ladies and gentlemen, dear friends,

In the name of our Foundation Vision 97, I welcome you and thank you for coming. With your permission, I would like to say a few words – or a few sentences – concerning three themes. The first theme – our Foundation. The second theme – the Award that is being granted. The third theme – the laureate.

Our Foundation is involved in many things; it has its educational, social, and other projects. One of its cultural projects has been, for example, the reconstruction, maintenance, and ongoing use of this temple. However, the Foundation also tries – in the spirit of its name - to orient itself in the direction of what in a certain way points to the future, what is – I would say – farsighted, what transcends the horizon of momentary attractive opportunities, but may not be appreciated and validated until some years pass. What is in a certain way visionary and pioneering. And the Award that our Foundation grants every year at this time is in full consonance with this mission.

This prize is awarded to personalities, thinkers, who emerged from the paradigm of modern, contemporary, rational science, but who, in some way transcended its traditional boundaries, who paid attention to previously unknown, not anticipated, hard to explain connections between phenomena that they themselves saw, found, and explored within the field of science. It is a prize that aims to give validation to those who have transcended their own original profession.

It is a risky endeavor, because it usually has two groups of opponents. Perhaps not directly opponents, but two groups of dangerous people. One group consists of the hard scientistic traditionalists, who are unable to imagine that modern science could transcend its own boundaries and traditional paradigms; they engage in a great determined fight against that which eludes their grasp. It is interesting that their fight undertaken in the name of rationality often reaches fanatic proportions; they tend to have a peculiar obsessive gleam in their eyes.

The other group that is dangerous, even though probably less, consists of a wide range of madmen, sectarians, and members of various strange fringe groups wanting to attach themselves, by their little claws, to this kind of scientific exploration, so that they could test and validate their various, more or less interesting, delusions.

And now, in conclusion, a few words about today's laureate. I have always, all my life, thought that once something has happened, it cannot un-happen, that the entire history of the cosmos, of our solar system, of the Earth, and of humanity, are by some means recorded. That existence itself has some kind of memory. I had no inkling where this memory resides, what it is based on, and if it actually exists. I did not know anything about it, but something kept telling me that something of this kind exists.

Obviously I thought, as do all others who have a similar feeling, that everything flows into this memory of existence only in one direction. And the body of work of professor Grof has all of a sudden shown me that, here and there, something is able to return, by a special pathway, from this memory back to our time and place, into our consciousness. To our great surprise, we all of a sudden experience, identify with, or for a moment see something that happened many years ago, in remote places, and what we absolutely could not have previously known by any ordinary means. However, it is often possible to verify that it actually had happened.

This is by no means the only thing that professor Grof teaches and researches. Nevertheless, for me personally, this - let us say - almost metaphysical dimension of his teaching speaks to me and continues to captivate me. I keep thinking about it, fully convinced that I am not a madman, who just believes in a delusion.

Thank you.

Dr. Miloš Vojtěchovský's LAUDATIO

Stanislav Grof is a highly proficient and world-renowned psychiatrist and philosopher, whose first half of life was formed by Prague, the Faculty of Medicine of the Charles University, by the psychiatric practice at the treatment facilities in Kosmonosy and Bohnice, and significantly also by the creative environment of Prague's Research Institute of Psychiatry. His personality was deeply influenced by psychoanalytic training and a series of personal LSD experiences in 1956-1967. At the age of 29, Grof was awarded the specialist certification in psychiatry and, at the age of 34, he successfully defended his Ph.D. thesis entitled "Use of LSD in Clinical Practice."

Up until his leaving for a scholarship stay in the United States, in the spring of 1967, he had been highly engaged in psychotherapeutically-focused lectures and, together with MUDr. Milan Hausner, presented his new views of the treatment of numerous psychical disorders resistant to therapy available at that time. In the 1960's, Czechoslovakia was one of the major centers of research into psychedelic substances. The easing of international relations thus opened the path to presenting substantial and often revolutionary discoveries in uncovered mechanisms of human unconscious at world expert meetings. So much, in brief, for Grof's professional career in our country.

Stanislav Grof's American epoch in the second half of his life is marked by nearly a lightning-fast growth in his career of scientific research on the new ways of discovering the realm of the human unconscious. For several years, Grof led a research project on the therapeutic use of psychedelics at the Maryland Psychiatric Research Center, Baltimore. Later, he came to California's Esalen Institute and became an important member of an interdisciplinary team of top U.S. intellectuals, forming the foundations of a new discipline – Transpersonal Psychology. In 1974, he co-founded the International Transpersonal Association (ITA) and became its first President. Similarly to Czechoslovakia, the legal conditions for use of psychedelic drugs in the U.S. became significantly tightened, and consequently Stanislav Grof and his wife Christina tried to find other non-pharmacological approaches to researching the human unconscious.

They found them in the modification of ancient practices of the East – and formed a non-pharmacological method of self-exploration and therapy that they called "Holotropic Breathwork." Stanislav Grof summarized the expertise from his own experiences, and from the experiences of many hundreds of clients – healthy volunteers, professionals, somatically ill patients and patients with mental disorders, with more than 4,000 psychedelic journeys into the unconscious, in hundreds of magazine stories and published it in numerous monographs, eight of which have been translated into Czech. Since 1991, our professionals as well as the general public have had several opportunities to gain an insight into the theory and practice of Grof's transpersonal psychology at multiple events in Prague, of which the 1992 ITA conference was the official scientific and social return of his teaching to his native Prague.

The life of every individual is limited by two milestones: birth and death. We mostly remember nothing from the period of a few years after birth, while we do not even wish to think of the last phase of our lives. Using psychedelics, Grof could go as far as the very roots of the ontogenetic development of human lives as well as the complexities of perimortal psychology. When Sigmund Freud slightly uncovered the laws of the development of child sexuality more than 100 years ago, and pointed to their importance for future mental health, the cultural world was shocked and most of that time's neuro-psychiatrists cast doubt on Freud's conclusions. Later, when two Vienna psychoanalysts (Wilhelm Reich and Otto Rank) came up with a proposition that future human mental life may be traumatized from as early as the experiences from the progress of the fetus through the birth canal, even Sigmund Freud himself was shocked, reprimanded his colleagues, and even expelled one of them from the Psychoanalytic Association.

Grof not only confirmed the observations and ideas of Freud, but also those of Reich and Rank. He integrated these concepts with the traumatic experiences of the fetus passing through the consecutive stages of birth, with a symbolically experienced state of death and re-birth, and showed that they played an important role in the genesis of numerous psychiatric disorders of adults. These of Grof's postulates are even today impugned by not only orthodox psychoanalysts, but also by neurophysiologists, who assert that the fetal brain lacks the matrices for the permanent storage of early perceptions in memory. However, Grof goes even further: during the continuing psychedelic therapy, he encountered other unusual experiences of his clients, which exceed the boundaries of understanding the human psyche and which have a significant therapeutic potential if they are lived.

Grof seeks support in the interpretation of these transcendental experiences in other fields: in Jung's teaching about archetypes and the collective unconscious, in the mystic experiences of Eastern religions, in the concept of cosmic consciousness of current astrophysicists, in trances and ceremonials, in rituals of Afro-Asian nations and in the episodes of religious, art and scientific inspirations. He assumes that the spirituality included in the modern scientific paradigms will play an important role in the philosophies of the 21st century. He formulates a new psychological hypothesis of "holotropic" (expanded) states of consciousness.

However, Grof's concept of transpersonal psychology is confronted with criticism, with misunderstanding from current psychiatry, psychology, anthropology, as well as the other sciences, and also with a reticent approach or even rejection by skeptically oriented natural scientists and representatives of contemporary churches. Some postulates of Grof's studies are hard to believe if we have not experienced non-ordinary states of consciousness induced by psychedelic drugs ourselves. Bear in mind that psychedelics in Grof's concept are pharmacologic catalysts for releasing the mental processes that have been hidden so far and cannot be otherwise examined under normal states of consciousness. These substances aid a psychiatrist just as a telescope aids an astronomer or a microscope aids a scientist. The scientific conference on the occasion of the 100th birthday of Albert Hofmann, the discoverer of LSD and psilocybin, which was held in January 2006 in Basel, let us know again that the era of more than 60 years of clinical use of psychedelics involves a significant treatment potential, which has not been utilized enough so far. This substance, if used by a responsible physician and researcher such as Stanislav Grof and his like, brings new possibilities of experimental psychiatry, psychology and psychotherapy, and can reduce the risks of the hazardous and uncontrolled misuse we can see today across the globe.

Stanislav Grof presenting his Acceptance Speech at the Vision 97 event.

Dr. Stanislav Grof's Acceptance Speech

Dear Mrs. Havel, dear President Havel, ladies and gentlemen,

It is a great pleasure for me to return to Prague, where I was born, spent my childhood, grew up, and received my basic training. An even greater source of pleasure than my visit to this city that I love so much are the extraordinary circumstances that brought me to Prague this time. I would like to thank President Havel, Mrs. Havel, and the board of consultants of the Dagmar and Václav Havel Foundation wholeheartedly for granting me the prestigious Award Vision 97 for my work in the area of consciousness research and the human psyche. It is for me an immense honor and also a great surprise after fifty years of struggle with the "public anonym" in science, described in such an articulate way by professor Vopěnka in his 2004 acceptance speech, after he himself received the Award Vision 97.

An important reason why the Award Vision 97 means so much to me is my profound admiration and respect for President Havel as an artist, a philosopher, a statesman with a broad spiritual vision, and as a man of extraordinary personal values. My admiration is shared by many of my American friends, who have repeatedly expressed to me their wish to have in the present difficult situation a president with the intellectual, moral, and spiritual qualities of Václav Havel. And during my journeys to different countries, I often had the opportunity to find out that similar feelings are shared by many people all over the world. I cannot imagine another appreciation of my work that would be for me personally more meaningful. Today's ceremony falls on President Havel's birthday and I would like to use this opportunity to congratulate him on this important anniversary and wish him much happiness, inner peace, personal satisfaction, and good health in the years to come.

It seems to be my destiny – or karma if you wish – to be involved in research of areas that are subjects of great controversy in science and society. My unconventional professional career started here in Prague more than fifty years ago when I volunteered as a beginning psychiatrist for a session with LSD-25, diethylamid of lysergic acid. My preceptor, Docent Roubíček, received this fascinating experimental substance from the Swiss pharmaceutical company Sandoz. The incredibly powerful psychedelic effects of this ergot alkaloid had been discovered by Dr. Albert Hofmann, who accidentally intoxicated himself while working on its synthesis.

The research project of Docent Roubíček required a combination of the pharmacological effect of LSD with exposure to a powerful stroboscopic light oscillating at various frequencies. This combination evoked in me a powerful mystical experience that has radically changed my personal and professional life. It had such a profound effect on me that research of the heuristic, therapeutic, transformative, and evolutionary potential of non-ordinary states of consciousness has become my profession, vocation, and personal passion for the rest of my life.

During approximately half of this period, my interest focused on clinical research of psychedelic substances, first at the Psychiatric Research Institute in Prague-Bohnice and later at the Maryland Psychiatric Research Center in Baltimore, MD, where I headed for several years the last surviving official psychedelic research in the United States. During the second half of this period my wife Christina and I jointly developed the method of Holotropic Breathwork, which induces deep non-ordinary states of consciousness with the use of very simple means: accelerated breathing, evocative music, and a certain kind of bodywork. Over the years we have also worked with many people undergoing spontaneous episodes of non-ordinary states of consciousness – psychospiritual crises or "spiritual emergencies" as we call them.

Research of non-ordinary states of consciousness (or their important subgroup, for which I coined the term "holotropic") has been for me a source of countless surprises and conceptual shocks, requiring radical changes in understanding consciousness, the human psyche, and the nature of reality. After many years of daily encounters with "anomalous phenomena," which contemporary science was unable to explain and the existence of which was in conflict with its fundamental metaphysical assumptions, I came to the conclusion that careful study of holotropic states and various phenomena, which are associated with them, such as statistically highly improbable meaningful coincidences (Jung's "synchronicities") shows the inevitability of a radical revision of thinking in psychology and psychiatry.

Conceptual changes required in these disciplines would in their nature, depth, and scope resemble the revolution which the physicists experienced in the first three decades of the twentieth century when they had to move from Newtonian mechanics to theories of relativity and later to quantum physics. It is even possible to say that – in a certain sense – this conceptual revolution would be a logical completion of the radical changes which began in physics many years ago.

The changes in the understanding of consciousness and of the human psyche in health and disease that naturally follow from the research of holotropic states fall into several categories. This research has shown the necessity to expand the traditional model of the psyche, limited to postnatal biography and the Freudian individual unconscious, by two vast areas – perinatal (which has a close connection with the memories of biological birth) and transpersonal (mediating experiences of identification with other people, animals, and the botanical realm and with human and animal ancestors, as well as experiences of the historical and archetypal collective unconscious, as described by C. G. Jung). Traditional psychiatry sees the beginnings of "psychogenic" disorders – those that do not have any demonstrable biological causes – in infancy and childhood. The work with holotropic states shows clearly that these disorders have additional deep roots in the perinatal and transpersonal realms of the unconscious. This finding might seem – in and of itself – very pessimistic, but it is outweighed by the discovery of new effective therapeutic mechanisms which operate on these deep levels of the unconscious.

The goal in traditional psychotherapies is to reach intellectual understanding of how the human psyche functions, what its basic motivating forces are, why symptoms develop, and what those symptoms mean. This understanding then forms the basis for the development of techniques that psychotherapists use for the treatment of their clients. A serious problem associated with this strategy is striking lack of agreement among psychologists and psychiatrists concerning the most fundamental theoretical problems and, consequently, an astonishing number of competing schools of psychotherapy. The work with holotropic states offers a surprising radical alternative – mobilization of the deep inner healing intelligence of the clients themselves that we now know is capable of governing the process of healing and transformation.

Materialistic science does not have a place for any form of spirituality and considers it to be essentially incompatible with the scientific worldview. It perceives any form of spirituality as an indication of lack of education, superstition, gullibility, primitive magical thinking or a serious psychopathological condition. Modern consciousness research shows that spirituality is a natural and legitimate dimension of the human psyche and of the universal order of things. However, it is important to emphasize that this statement refers to direct authentic spirituality based on personal experience and not to the ideology and dogmas of organized religions.

New observations show that consciousness is not an epiphenomenon of matter – a product of complex neurophysiological processes in the brain – but a fundamental primary attribute of existence, as it is described in the great spiritual philosophies of the East. As suggested by the Swiss psychiatrist C. G. Jung, the psyche is not enclosed in the human skull and brain, but permeates all of existence (as anima mundi). The individual human psyche is an integral part of this cosmic matrix and can under certain circumstances experientially identify with its various aspects.

This new understanding of the human psyche has important sociopolitical implications. Medical anthropologists have shown that the striking physical differences between various human groups disappear when the scientific research of homo sapiens penetrates the thin layers of the epidermis; the basic anatomical, physiological, and biochemical characteristics are shared by all of humanity. Modern consciousness research complements this observation by similar findings related to the human psyche. On the postnatal biographical level there are large individual and cultural differences; the conditions of life differ radically from person to person from family to family, and from culture to culture. However, these differences begin to disappear as soon as experiential self-exploration in holotropic states of consciousness reaches the perinatal level. All members of the human species share the experiences of prenatal life and birth; the differences in this area are interindividual rather than specific for various racial groups. And when the process of deep experiential probing reaches the transpersonal level, all differences disappear.

Our observations have shown that people from all the human groups with which Christina and I have worked in various parts of the world – in Europe, India, Japan, Taiwan, Australia, South, Central, and North America, Australia, and Polynesia – had access to the entire collective unconscious as described by C. G. Jung in their holotropic experiences, both the historical and archetypal-mythological realms, without regard to their own racial, national, and cultural background. These experiences have frequently even bridged gender differences – many karmic, ancestral, and racial experiences contained convincing identification with members of the opposite sex. Equally frequent were identifications with representatives of various animal species. Observations of this kind provide strong evidence for something that traditional materialistic scientists would consider impossible and utterly absurd – that the entire history of humanity and life on this planet are permanently recorded in an immaterial field to which each of us has under certain circumstances experiential access. Hungarian/Italian system theorist Ervin Laszlo has been able to define such a field scientifically and has given it the name the "psi field." More recently, he renamed it the "akashic field" by linking it explicitly to spiritual traditions.

Perinatal and transpersonal experiences have profound psychological implications. When the content of the perinatal level of the unconscious surfaces into consciousness and is adequately processed and integrated it results in a radical personality change. The individual experiences a considerable decrease of aggressive tendencies and becomes more tolerant and compassionate toward others. The experience of psychospiritual death and rebirth and conscious connection with positive postnatal and prenatal memories reduces irrational ambitions and urges and increase élan vital and joie de vivre – the ability to enjoy life and draw satisfaction from simple situations such as everyday activity, eating, love-making, nature, and music.

The process of spiritual opening and transformation typically deepens further as a result of transpersonal experiences. Feelings of oneness with the universe and its creative principle lead to identification with all sentient beings and bring a sense of awe, wonder, love, compassion, and inner peace. Spirituality that results from this process is universal, all-encompassing, transcending all organized religions; it resembles the attitude to the Cosmos found in the mystics of all ages. It is extremely authentic and convincing because it is based on deep personal experience. It is therefore capable of competing successfully with the dogmas of organized religions as well as the worldview of monistic-materialistic Western science.

People who are experientially connected with the transpersonal dimensions have a tendency to appreciate existence and feel reverence for all creation. One of the most remarkable consequences of various forms of transpersonal experiences is spontaneous emergence and development of genuine humanitarian and ecological interests and a need to take part in activities aimed at peaceful coexistence and the well-being of humanity. This is based on an almost cellular understanding that any boundaries in the Cosmos are relative and arbitrary and that each of us is, in the last analysis, identical and commensurable with the entire fabric of existence. As a result of these experiences, individuals tend to develop feelings that they are planetary citizens and members of the human family before belonging to a particular country or a specific racial, social, ideological, political, or religious group. It seems obvious that transformation of this kind could significantly increase our chances of survival if it could occur on a sufficiently large scale.

It seems that we are involved in a dramatic race for time, which has no parallel in human history. What is at stake is nothing less than the future of humanity and the fate of life on our planet. If we continue using the old strategies that have caused the current global crisis, which are destructive and self-destructive, they may lead to the annihilation of modern civilization and possibly even the human species. However, if a sufficient number of people undergo a process of inner psychospiritual transformation and attain a higher level of awareness, we may reach a situation in the future where we will deserve the name which we have so proudly given to our species: homo sapiens sapiens.

In closing I would like to express my deep gratitude to Christina, my wife, best friend, and co-worker for everything that she contributed over the years to the research, which has today received such an extraordinary appreciation.

Dagmar Havlová (wife of Václav Havel), Václav Havel, Stanislav Grof, and Christina Grof at the Vison 97 presentation event.

Notes:

History of the International Transpersonal Association (ITA)

Founding of the ITA

*Founding of the International Transpersonal Association at the 1977
transpersonal conference in Belo Horizonte in Brazil - organized by Pierre
Weil and Leo Matos - where the decision was made to start an international
transpersonal association. Participants voted unanimously for the foundation of the new association and suggested that
Stan and Christina take on the task of managing it.*

History of the International Transpersonal Association (ITA)

Since its inception in the late 1960's, the Association of Transpersonal Psychology (ATP) has held regular annual conferences in Asilomar, California. As the interest in the movement was growing and extending beyond the San Francisco Bay Area and outside of the United States, occasional international transpersonal meetings were organized in various parts of the world. The first two took place in Bifrost, Iceland, the third in Inari, Finland, and the fourth in Belo Horizonte, Brazil. By the time of the Brazilian meeting, these conferences were so popular and well attended that it was decided to formalize them by creating an institution that would organize them, the International Transpersonal Association (ITA). The ITA was launched by Stanislav Grof, who became its founding president, joined by Michael Murphy, and Richard Price; the latter two had in the early 1960s started the Esalen Institute in Big Sur, California, the first human potential center.

In comparison with the Association of Transpersonal Psychology, the ITA was explicitly international and interdisciplinary. By this time, the transpersonal orientation had appeared in many branches of science and other areas of human endeavor. So the program of the ITA conferences included not only psychologists, psychiatrists, and psychotherapists, but also physicists, biologists, physicians anthropologists, mythologists, philosophers, mathematicians, artists, spiritual teachers, educators, politicians, economists, and many others. The ITA has held its conferences in Boston, Massachusetts; Melbourne, Australia; Bombay, India; Davos, Switzerland; Kyoto, Japan; Santa Rosa, California; Eugene, Oregon; Atlanta, Georgia; Prague, Czechoslovakia; Killarney, Ireland; Santa Clara, California; Manaus, Brazil, and Palm Springs, California. As the following lists indicate, many outstanding representatives of scientific, cultural, and political life have been among the presenters.

Christina and Stan Grof, Marilyn Hershenson, and Jerry Jampolsky with Mother Teresa at the ITA conference in Bombay in February 1982.

PSYCHOLOGY AND PSYCHIATRY: Frances Vaughan, Roger Walsh, Sandra Harner, June Singer, John Perry, James Fadiman, Arthur Hastings, Cecil Burney, Pierluigi Lattuada, David Lukoff, Francis Lu, Rashna Imhasly, R. D. Laing, Virginia Satir, Dora Kalff, Elisabeth Kuebler-Ross, Marie-Louise von Franz, Jean Shinoda Bolen, Claudio Naranjo, Ken Pelletier, Ralph Metzner, Angeles Arrien, Christopher Bache, Paul Grof, Stanislav Grof, Christina Grof, Charles Tart, Steven Larsen, Robin Larsen, Kenneth Ring, Judith Cornell, Richard Tarnas, Jean Houston, Steve Aizenstat, Arnold Mindell, Amy Mindell, Roger Woolger, Gilda Moura, Raymond Moody, John Bradshaw, Pierre Weil, Marion Woodman, Massimo Rosselli, Ann Armstrong, Paulo Rzezinski, Linda Leonard, Jane Middelton - Moz, Rokelle Lerner, Charles Whitfield, John Mack, Robert Jay Lifton, Robert McDermott, Stanley Krippner, Andrew Weil, Seymour Boorstein, Dean Shapiro, Charlene Spretnak, Marilyn Schlitz, Ingo Jahrsetz, Hércoles Jaci, John Beebe, Jenny Wade, Michael Mithoefer, Charles Grob, Richard Yensen, Kristina Maykov, Vladimir Maykov, Donna Dryer, Dennis Slattery, Rick Strassman, Phillippe Bandeira de Melo, Michael Grosso, David Ulansey, Don Juan Nuñez del Prado, Roberto Baruzzi, and others.

Stan and Christina Grof welcoming His Holiness the Dalai Lama to the ITA conference in Davos in 1983.

OTHER SCIENCES: David Bohm, Karl Pribram, Fritjof Capra, Rupert Sheldrake, Fred Alan Wolf, Ervin Laszlo, Elizabeth Kuebler-Ross, Willis Harman, Albert Hofmann, Orlando Villas-Boas, Vasily Nalimov, Ilya Prigogine, Lee Sannella, Igor Charkovsky, Elmer Green, Alice Green, Michael Harner, Peter Russell, Richard Katz, Russell Targ, Arthur Young, Jean Achterberg, Duane Elgin, Ivan Havel, Zdeněk Neubauer, Carl Simonton, Frederic Leboyer, Peter Schwartz, Bernard Lietaer, Brian McCusker, Terence McKenna, Brian Swimme, Amit Goswami, Arne Næss, Thomas Berry, Luiz Augusto de Queiroz, Michel Odent, Rachel Naomi Remen, and others.

Stan interviewing Ram Dass at the ITA conference in Palm Springs in 2004.

SPIRITUAL LIFE: Mother Teresa, His Holiness the Dalai Lama, Swami Muktananda, Brother David Steindl-Rast, Pir Vilayat Khan, Sheikh Muzaffer and the Halveti-Jerahi dervishes, Sogyal Rinpoche, Ram Dass, Chungliang Al Huang, Matthew Fox, Minocher Homji, Jack Kornfield, Wes Nisker, Nishitani Roshi, Gopi Krishna, Thomas Banyacya, Don Manuel Q'espi, Andrew Harvey, Lauren Artress, Alex Polari de Alverga, Huston Smith, Cecil Williams, Shairy Jose Quimbo, Brooke Medicine Eagle, Zalman Schachter, Olatunji Babatunde, Shlomo Carlebach, Credo Mutwa, and others.

ART AND CULTURAL LIFE: John Cleese, Alarmel Vali, Paul Horn, Mickey Hart, Steven Halpern, David Darling, Randall Bramblett, Michael Vetter, Gabrielle Roth, Nina Wise, Jiří Stivín, Patricia Ellsberg, Alex Grey, Silvia Nakkach, Lorin Hollander, Tara Tupper, Nina Simons, Jon Voight, Jai Uttal, Geoffrey Gordon, Russell Walder, Vishnu Tattva Das, Barbara Framm, Susan Griffin, Robert Bly, Robert Schwartz, Gloria Steinem, Isabel Allende, Jill Purce, Georgia Kelly, Steve Roach, Rusty Schweickart, Raizes Caboclas Orchestra, Mar Azul Capoeira group, Lost at Last, and others.

POLITICS: Karan Singh, Jerry Brown, John Vasconcellos, Jim Garrison, Burnum Burnum, Sulak Sivaraksa. The Czech president, Václav Havel, under whose auspices the 1992 ITA conference in Prague was held, was not able to address the participants of the conference because of an emergency meeting of the Czechoslovakian Parliament.

BIBLIOGRAPHY

Bibliography

Alexander, F. 1931. "Buddhist Training As Artificial Catatonia." Psychoanalyt. Rev. 18:129.

Anonymous. 1975. *A Course in Miracles*. New York, NY: Foundation for Inner Peace.

Appleby, L. 1998. "Violent Suicide and Obstetric Complications." British Medical Journal 14: 1333–1334.

Ardrey, R. 1961. *African Genesis*. New York, NY: Atheneum.

Assagioli, R. 1976. *Psychosynthesis*. New York, NY: Penguin Books.

Assagioli, R. 1977. "Self-Realization and Psychological Disturbances." Synthesis 3-4. Also in: Grof, S. and Grof, C. (eds) 1989. *Spiritual Emergency: When Personal Transformation Becomes a Crisis*. Los Angeles, CA: J. P. Tarcher.

Bache, C. 2000. *Dark Night, Early Dawn: Steps to a Deep Ecology of Mind*. Albany, NY: State University of New York (SUNY) Press.

Bacon, F. 1870. *De Dignitate and The Great Restauration*, Vol. 4, The Collected Works of Francis Bacon, eds. J. Spedding, L. Ellis, and D.D. Heath. London: Longmans Green.

Barrow, J. D. and Tipler, F. J. 1986. *The Anthropic Cosmological Principle*. Oxford: Clarendon Press.

Bastiaans, J. 1955. *Man in the Concentration Camp and the Concentration Camp in Man*. Unpublished manuscript. Leyden, Holland.

Bateson, G. 1972. *Steps to An Ecology of Mind*. San Francisco, CA: Chandler Publications.

Bateson, G. 1979. *Mind and Nature: A Necessary Unity*. New York, NY: E. P. Dutton.

Beringer, K. 1927. *Der Meskalinrausch* (Mescaline Intoxication). Berlin: Springer.

Bohm, D. 1980. *Wholeness and the Implicate Order*. London: Routledge & Kegan Paul.

Browne, I. 1990. "Psychological Trauma, or Unexperienced Experience." Re-Vision Journal 12(4):21-34.

Campbell, J. 1956. *The Hero with a Thousand Faces*. New York, NY: Meridian Books.

Capra, F. 1975. *The Tao of Physics*. Berkeley, CA: Shambhala Publications.

Capra, F. 1996. *The Web of Life*. New York: Anchor Books.

Cohen, S. 1960. "Lysergic Acid Diethylamide: Side Effects and Complications." Journal of Nervous and Mental Diseases 130:30.

Cohen, S. 1965. "LSD and the Anguish of Dying." Harper's Magazine 231:69-77.

Cohn, C. 1987. "Sex and Death in the Rational World of the Defense Intellectuals." Journal of Women in Culture and Society 12:687-718.

Corbin, H. 2000. "Mundus Imaginalis, Or the Imaginary and the Imaginal." In: *Working With Images* (B. Sells, ed.). Woodstock, CT: Spring Publications.

Dante, A. 1990. *Il Convivio, III. VI. 3.* (R. H. Lansing, transl.). New York, NY: Garland.

Darwin, C. 1952. *The Origin of Species and the Descent of Man.* Chicago, IL: Great Books of the Western World. Encyclopaedia Britannica. (Original work published 1859.)

Dawkins, R. 1976. *The Selfish Gene.* New York, NY: Oxford University Press.

des Près, T. 1976. *The Survivor: An Anatomy of Life in the Death Camps.* New York, NY: Oxford University Press.

Dollard, J. et al. 1939. *Frustration and Aggression.* New Haven, CN: Yale University Press.

Foerster, H. von. 1965. *Memory without a Record.* In: *The Anatomy of Memory* (D.P.Kimble, ed.). Palo Alto: Science and Behavior Books.

Forte, R. (ed) 1997. *Entheogens and the Future of Religion.* San Francisco, CA: Council on Spiritual Practices.

Frank, P. 1957. *Philosophy of Science: The Link Between Science and Philosophy.* Westport, CT: Greenwood Press.

Freud, S. and Breuer, J. 1936. *Studies in Hysteria.* New York, NY: Penguin Books.

Freud, S. 1955. *Beyond the Pleasure Principle.* In: *The Standard Edition of the Complete Works of Sigmund Freud, Vol. 18.* (J. Strachey, ed.). London: The Hogarth Press & The Institute of Psychoanalysis.

Fromm, E. 1973. *The Anatomy of Human Destructiveness.* New York, NY: Holt, Rinehart & Winson.

Frost, S. B. 2001. *SoulCollage.* Santa Cruz, CA: Hanford Mead.

Giger, H. R. 1977. *Necronomicon.* Basel: Sphinx Verlag.

Gleick, J. 1988. *Chaos: Making A New Science.* New York, NY: Penguin Books.

Goldman, D. 1952. "The Effect of Rhythmic Auditory Stimulation on the Human Electroencephalogram." EEG and Clinical Neurophysiology 4: 370.

Goleman, D. 1996. *Emotional Intelligence.* New York, NY: Bantam Books.

Goswami, A. 1995. *The Self-Aware Universe: How Consciousness Creates the Material World.* Los Angeles, CA: J. P. Tarcher.

Greyson, B. and Flynn, C. P. (eds.). 1984. *The Near-Death Experience: Problems, Prospects, Perspectives.* Springfield, IL: Charles C. Thomas.

Griffiths, R. R., Richards, W. A., McCann, U., and Jesse, R. 2006. "Psilocybin can Occasion Mystical Experiences Having Substantial and Sustained Personal Meaning and Spiritual Significance." Psychopharmacology 187:3, 268-283.

Grof, C. and Grof, S. 1990. *The Stormy Search for the Self: A Guide to Personal Growth Through Transformational Crisis.* Los Angeles, CA: J. P. Tarcher.

Grof, C. 1993. *The Thirst For Wholeness: Attachment, Addiction, and the Spiritual Path.* San Francisco, CA: Harper.

Grof, S. 1975. *Realms of the Human Unconscious: Observations from LSD Research.* New York, NY: Viking Press. (Republished in 2009 as *LSD: Doorway to the Numinous,* see Grof, S. 2009).

Grof, S. 1980. *LSD Psychotherapy.* Pomona, CA: Hunter House. (New editions: 1994 and 2001, Sarasota, Fl.: MAPS Publications).

Grof, S. 1985. *Beyond the Brain: Birth, Death, and Transcendence in Psychotherapy.* Albany, NY: State University New York (SUNY) Press.

Grof, S. 1987. "Spirituality, Addiction, and Western Science." Re-Vision Journal 10:5-18.

Grof, S. 1988. *The Adventure of Self-Discovery.* Albany, NY: State University of New York (SUNY) Press.

Grof, S. and Grof, C. 1989. *Spiritual Emergency: When Personal Transformation Becomes a Crisis.* Los Angeles, CA: J. P. Tarcher.

Grof, S. 1992. *The Holotropic Mind.* San Francisco, CA: Harper.

Grof, S. 1994. *Books of the Dead.* London: Thames and Hudson.

Grof, S. 1996. "Ken Wilber's Spectrum Psychology: Observations from Clinical Consciousness Research." In: Rothberg, D, and Kelly, S. (eds). 1998. *Ken Wilber in Dialogue: Conversations with Leading Transpersonal Thinkers.* Wheaton, IL: Theosophical Publishing House.

Grof, S. 1998. *The Cosmic Game: Explorations of the Frontiers of Human Consciousness.* Albany, NY: State University of New York (SUNY) Press.

Grof, S. 2000: *Psychology of the Future: Lessons from Modern Consciousness Research.* Albany, NY: State University of New York (SUNY) Press.

Grof, S. 2001. *LSD Psychotherapy.* Sarasota, FL: MAPS Publications.

Grof, S. 2006 a. *When the Impossible Happens: Adventures in Non-Ordinary Realities.* Louisville, CO: Sounds True.

Grof, S. 2006 b. *The Ultimate Journey: Consciousness and the Mystery of Death.* Sarasota, FL: MAPS.

Grof, S. 2007. "Psychology of the Future: Lessons from Modern Consciousness Research." In: *Nové perspektivy v psychiatrii, psychologii, a psychoterapii.* Břeclav: Moravia Press.

Grof, S. 2009. *LSD: Doorway to the Numinous: The Groundbreaking Psychedelic Research into Realms of the Human Unconscious.* Rochester, VT: Inner Traditions.

Grof, S. and Grof, C. 2010. *Holotropic Breathwork - A New Approach to Self-Exploration and Therapy.* Albany, NY: State University of New York (SUNY) Press.

Hagenbach, D. and Wertmueller, L. 2011. *Albert Hofmann und sein LSD: Ein bewegtes Leben und eine bedeutende Entdeckung (Albert Hofmann and his LSD: An Exciting Life and An Important Discovery).* Baden, Germany: AT-Verlag.

Harman, W. W. et al. 1966. "Psychedelic Agents in Creative Problem-Solving: A Pilot Study." Psychological Reports 19(1):211-212.

Harman, W. W. and Rheingold, H. 1984. *Higher Creativity: Liberating the Unconscious for Breakthrough Insights.* Los Angeles, CA: J. P.Tarcher.

Harner, M. 1980. *The Way of the Shaman: A Guide to Power and Healing.* New York, NY: Harper & Row.

Hastings, A. 1991. *With the Tongues of Men and Angels: A Study of Channeling.* New York, NY: Holt, Rinehart, and Winston.

Heisenberg, W. 1971. *Physics and Beyond: Encounters and Conversations.* New York, NY: Harper & Row.

Herbert, N. 1979. *Mind Science: A Physics of Consciousness Primer.* Boulder Creek, CA: C-Life Institute.

Hillman, J. 2004. *A Terrible Love of War*. New York, NY: The Penguin Press.

Hines, B. 1996. *God's Whisper, Creation's Thunder: Echoes of Ultimate Reality in the New Physics*. Threshold Books.

Hofmann, A. 2005. *LSD: My Problem Child*. Sarasota, FL: MAPS Publications.

Huxley, A. 1959. *The Doors of Perception and Heaven and Hell*. Harmondsworth, Middlesex, Great Britain: Penguin Books.

Jacobson, B. et al. 1987. "Perinatal Origin of Adult Self-Destructive Behavior." Acta psychiat. Scand. 76:364-371.

James, W. 1961. *The Varieties of Religious Experience*. New York, NY: Collier.

Jilek, W. J. 1974. *Salish Indian Mental Health and Culture Change: Psychohygienic and Therapeutic Aspects of the Guardian Spirit Ceremonial*. Toronto and Montreal: Holt, Rinehart, and Winston of Canada.

Jilek, W. 1982. "Altered States of Consciousness in North American Indian Ceremonials." Ethos 10:326-343.

Jung, C. G. 1957. "Wotan." In: Collected Works, Vol. 10, Bollingen Series XX. Princeton, NJ: Princeton University Press.

Jung, C. G. 1959. *Mandala Symbolism*. Translated by R.F.C. Hull. Bollingen Series. Princeton, NJ: Princeton University Press.

Jung, C. G. 1960. *Synchronicity: An Acausal Connecting Principle*. In: Collected Works, Vol. 8, Bollingen Series XX. Princeton, NJ: Princeton University Press.

Jung, C. G. 1964 a. *Flying Saucers: A Modern Myth of Things Seen in the Skies*. In: Collected Works, Vol. 10, Bollingen Series XX. Princeton, NJ: Princeton University Press.

Jung, C. G.: 1964 b. *Psychology of Religion: East and West*. In: Collected Works, Vol. 10, Bollingen Series XX. Princeton, NJ: Princeton University Press.

Jung, C. G. 1981. *The Archetypes and the Collective Unconscious*. In: Collected Works, Vol.9.1, Bollingen Series XX, 2nd Edition. Princeton, NJ: Princeton University Press.

Jung, C. G., 1999. *The Psychology of Kundalini Yoga: Notes of the Seminar Given in 1932*. Princeton, NJ: Princeton University Press.

Kalff, D. and Kalff, M. 2004. *Sandplay: A Psychotherapeutic Approach to the Psyche*. Cloverdale, CA: Temenos Press.

Ka-Tzetnik 135633. 1955. *The House of Dolls*. New York, NY: Pyramid Books.

Ka-Tzetnik 135633. 1977. *Sunrise Over Hell*. London: W.A. Allen.

Ka-Tzetnik 135633. 1989. *Shivitti: A Vision*. San Francisco, CA: Harper & Row.

Kandel, E. and Mednick S. A. 1991. " Perinatal Complications Predict Violent Offending." Criminology 29 (3): 519–529.

Kast, E. C. and Collins, V. J. 1966. "LSD and the Dying Patient." Chicago Med. School Quarterly 26:80.

Katz, R. 1976. "The Painful Ecstasy of Healing." Psychology Today, December.

Keen, S. 1988. *Faces of the Enemy: Reflections of the Hostile Imagination*. San Francisco, CA: Harper.

Kellogg, J. 1977. "The Use of the Mandala in Psychological Evaluation and Treatment." Amer. Journal of Art Therapy 16:123.

Kellogg, J. 1978. *Mandala: The Path of Beauty*. Baltimore: Mandala Assessment and Research Institute.

Klimo, J. 1998. *Channeling: Investigations on Receiving Information from Paranormal Sources*. Berkeley, CA: North Atlantic Books.

Kuhn, T. 1962. *The Structure of Scientific Revolutions*. Chicago, IL: University of Chicago Press.

Laszlo, E, 1993. *The Creative Cosmos: A Unified Science of Matter, Life and Mind*. Edinburgh, Scotland: Floris Books.

Laszlo, E. 1996. *Subtle Connections: Psi, Grof, Jung, and the Quantum Vacuum*. The International Society for the Systems Sciences and The Club of Budapest.

Laszlo, E., Grof, S., and Russell, P. 2003. *The Consciousness Revolution: A Transatlantic Dialogue*. London and Las Vegas, NV: Elf Rock Productions.

Laszlo, E. and Abraham, R. H. 2004. *The Connectivity Hypothesis: Foundations of An Integral Science of Quantum, Cosmos, Life, and Consciousness*. Albany, NY: State University of New York (SUNY) Press.

Laszlo, E. 2004. *Science and the Akashic Field: An Integral Theory of Everything*. Rochester, VT: Inner Traditions.

Lawson, A. 1984. "Perinatal Imagery In UFO Abduction Reports." Journal of Psychohistory 12:211.

Lee, R. B. and DeVore, I. (eds) 1976. *Kalahari Hunter-Gatherers: Studies of the !Kung San and Their Neighbors*. Cambridge, MA: Harvard University Press.

Litt, S. 1974. "A Study Of Perinatal Complications As A Factor In Criminal Behavior." Criminology 12 (1), 125–126.

Lorenz, K. 1963. *On Aggression*. New York, NY: Harcourt, Brace, and World.

Mack, J. 1994. *Abductions: Human Encounters with Aliens*. New York, NY: Charles Scribner Sons.

Mack, J. 1999. *Passport to the Cosmos: Human Transformation and Alien Encounters*. New York, NY: Crown Publishers.

MacLean, P. 1973. "A Triune Concept of the Brain and Behavior. Lecture I. Man's Reptilian and Limbic Inheritance; Lecture II. Man's Limbic System and the Psychoses; Lecture III. New Trends in Man's Evolution." In: The Hincks Memorial Lectures (T. Boag and D. Campbell, eds.). Toronto, Canada: University of Toronto Press.

Markoff, J. 2005. *What the Dormouse Said: How the Sixties Counterculture Shaped the Personal Computer Industry*. New York, NY: Viking Press, Penguin Group (USA) Inc.

Martin, J. 1965. *LSD Analysis*. Lecture and film presented at the Second International Conference on the Use of LSD in Psychotherapy held at South Oaks Hospital, May 8-12, Amityville, New York. Paper published in: H. A. Abramson (ed,) *The Use of LSD in Psychotherapy and Alcoholism*. Indianapolis, IN: Bobbs-Merrill. Pp. 223-238.

Mause, L. de. 1975. "The Independence of Psychohistory." In: *The New Psychohistory*. New York, NY: The Psychohistory Press.

McCririck, P. 1966. "*The Importance of Fusion in Therapy and Maturation.*" Unpublished paper.

McKenna, T. 1992. *Food of the Gods: The Search for the Original Tree of Knowledge*. New York, NY: Bantam Books.

Maslow, A. 1964. *Religions, Values, and Peak Experiences*. Cleveland, OH: Ohio State University.

Maslow, A. 1969. "The Farther Reaches of Human Nature." Journal of Transpersonal Psychology 1: 1-9.

Mithoefer, M. C., et al. 2010. "The Safety and Efficacy of ±3,4-methylenedioxy-methamphetamine - Assisted Psychotherapy in Subjects with Chronic Treatment-Resistant Posttraumatic Stress Disorder: The First Randomized Controlled Pilot Study." Journal of Psychopharmacology 25(4):439-452.

Moody, R.A. 1975. *Life After Life*. New York, NY: Bantam.

Mookerjee, A. and Khanna, M. 1977. *The Tantric Way*. London: Thames and Hudson.

Mookerjee, A. 1982. *Kundalini: Arousal of Inner Energy*. London: Thames and Hudson.

Moreno, J. L. 1948. "Psychodrama and Group Psychotherapy." Annals of the New York Academy of Sciences 49 (6):902-903.

Morris, D. 1967. *The Naked Ape*. New York, NY: McGraw-Hill.

Neher, A, 1961. "Auditory Driving Observed with Scalp Electrodes in Normal Subjects." Electroencephalography and Clinical Neurophysiology 13:449-451.

Neher, A. 1962. "A Physiological Explanation of Unusual Behavior Involving Drums." Human Biology 14:151-160.

Nevole, S. 1947. O čtyřrozměrném viděni: Studie z fysiopathologie smyslu prostorového, se zvláštním zřetelem k experimentální otravě mezkalinem (Apropos of Four-Dimesional Vision: Study of Physiopathology of the Spatial Sense with Special Regard to Experimental Intoxication with Mescaline.) Prague: Lékařské knihkupectví a nakladatelství.

Nevole, S. 1949. O smyslových ilusích a o jejich formální genese (Apropos of Sensory Illusions and Their Formal Genesis). Prague: Zdravotnické nakladatelství Spolku lékařů a vědeckých pracovníků J.E.Purkyně.

Odent, M. 1995. "Prevention of Violence or Genesis of Love? Which Perspective?" Presentation at the Fourteenth International Transpersonal Conference in Santa Clara, California.

Pahnke, W. N. 1963. "Drugs and Mysticism: An Analysis of the Relationship Between Psychedelic Drugs and the Mystical Consciousness." Ph. D. Dissertation, Harvard University.

Pahnke, W. N. and Richards, W. E. 1966. *"Implications of LSD and Experimental Mysticism."* Journal of Religion and Health 5:175.

Pahnke, W. N.. Kurland, A. A., Unger, S., Grof, S. 1970. "The Experimental Use of Psychedelic (LSD) Psychotherapy." Journal of the American Medical Association (JAMA) 212:856.

Perls, F. 1976. *The Gestalt Approach and Eye-Witness to Therapy*. New York, NY: Bantam books.

Perry, J. W. 1953. *The Self in the Psychotic Process*. Dallas, TX: Spring Publications.

Perry, J. W. 1974. *The Far Side of Madness*. Englewood Cliffs, NJ: Prentice Hall.

Perry, J. W. 1976. *Roots of Renewal in Myth and Madness*. San Francisco, CA: Jossey-Bass Publications.

Perry, J. W. 1991. *Lord of the Four Quarters: The Mythology of Kingship*. New York, NY: Holt, Rinehart, and Winston.

Perry, J. W. 1998. *Trials of the Visionary Mind: Spiritual Emergency and the Renewal Process*. Albany, NY: State University of New York (SUNY) Press.

Pribram, K. 1971. *Languages of the Brain*. Englewood Cliffs, NJ: Prentice Hall.

Prigogine, I. 1980. *From Being to Becoming: Time and Complexity in the Physical Sciences.* San Francisco, CA: W. H. Freeman.

Prigogine, I., and Stengers, I. 1984. *Order out of Chaos: Man's Dialogue with Nature.* New York, NY: Bantam Books.

Raine, A., Brennan, P., Mednick, S. A. 1995. "Birth Complications Combined with Early Maternal Rejection at Age 1 Year Predispose to Violent Crime at Age 18 Years." Obstetrical & Gynecological Survey 50 (11):775-776.

Ramacharaka (William Walker Atkinson). 1903. *The Science of Breath.* London: Fowler and Company, Ltd.

Reich, W. 1949. *Character Analysis.* New York, NY: Noonday Press.

Reich, W. 1961. *The Function of the Orgasm: Sex-Economic Problems of Biological Energy.* New York, NY: Farrar, Strauss, and Giroux.

Ring, K. 1982. *Life at Death: A Scientific Investigation of the Near-Death Experience.* New York, NY: Quill.

Ring, K. 1985. *Heading Toward Omega: In Search of the Meaning of the Near-Death Experience.* New York, NY: Quill.

Ring, K. and Valarino, E. E. 1998. *Lessons from the Light: What We Can Learn from the Near-Death Experience.* New York, NY: Plenum Press.

Ring, K. and Cooper, S. 1999. *Mindsight: Near-Death and Out-of-Body Experiences in the Blind.* Palo Alto, CA: William James Center for Consciousness Studies.

Roberts, T. B. (ed.) 2001. *Psychoactive Sacramentals: Essays on Entheogens and Religion.* San Francisco, CA: Council on Spiritual Practices.

Ross, C. A. 1989. *Multiple Personality Disorder: Diagnosis, Clinical Features, and Treatment.* New York, NY: Wiley.

Rothberg, D, and Kelly, S. (eds) 1998. *Ken Wilber in Dialogue: Conversations with Leading Transpersonal Thinkers.* Wheaton, IL: Theosophical Publishing House.

Roubíček, J. 1961. *Experimentální psychózy* (Experimental Psychoses). Prague: Statní zdravotnické nakladatelství .

Sabom, M. 1982. *Recollections of Death: A Medical Investigation.* New York, NY: Harper and Row.

Sannella, L. 1987. *The Kundalini Experience: Psychosis or Transcendence?* Lower Lake, CA: Integral Publishing.

Savage, C. and McCabe, L. 1971. "Psychedelic (LSD) Therapy of Drug Addiction." In: C. C. Brown and C. Savage, eds. *The Drug Abuse Controversy.* Baltimore, MD: Friends Medical Science Research Center.

Schroedinger, E. 1967. *What Is Life? and Mind and Matter.* Cambridge, MA: Cambridge University Press.

Schultes, R. E., Hofmann, A. and Rätsch, C. 2001. *Plants of the Gods: Their Sacred, Healing, and Hallucinogenic Powers.* Rochester, VT: Healing Arts Press.

Shapiro, F. 2001. *Eye Movement Desensitization and Reprocessing: Basic Principles, Protocols, and Procedures.* New York, NY: Guilford Press.

Sheldrake, R. 1981. *A New Science of Life: The Hypothesis of Formative Causation.* Los Angeles, CA: J. P. Tarcher.

Sparks, Tav 1993. *The Wide Open Door: The Twelve Steps, Spiritual Tradition, and the New Psychology.* Center City, MN: Hazelden Educational Materials.

Stoll, W. A. 1947. "LSD, ein Phantastikum aus der Mutterkorngruppe" (LSD, An Amazing Wonder from the Ergot Group). Schweiz.Arch. Neurol. Psychiat. 60:279.

Sutich, A. 1976. *The Founding of Humanistic and Transpersonal Psychology: A personal account*. Doctoral dissertation, Humanistic Psychology Institute, San Francisco, CA.

Sutich, A. 1976. "The Emergence of the Transpersonal Orientation: A personal account." Journal of Transpersonal Psychology 8: 5-19.

Talbot, M. 1991. *The Holographic Universe*. San Francisco, CA: Harper Collins.

Tarnas, R. 2006. *Cosmos and Psyche: Intimations of A New World View*. New York, NY: Viking Press.

Tinbergen, N. 1965. *Animal Behavior*. New York, NY: Time-Life.

Vithoulkas, G. 1980. *The Science of Homeopathy*. New York, NY: Grove Press.

Vondráček, V. 1935. *Farmakologie duše* (Pharmacology of the Soul). Prague: Lékařské knihkupectví a nakladatelství.

Washburn, M. 1988. *The Ego and the Dynamic Ground*. Albany, NY: State University of New York (SUNY) Press.

Wasson, G., Hofmann, A. and Ruck, C.A.P. 1978. *The Road to Eleusis: Unveiling the Secret of the Mysteries*. New York, NY: Harcourt, Brace, and Jovanovitch.

Weil, A. 1972. *The Natural Mind: An Investigation of Drugs and the Higher Consciousness*. Boston, MA: Houghton Mifflin Company.

Wilber, K. 1977. *The Spectrum of Consciousness*. Wheaton, IL: Theosophical Publishing House.

Wilber, K. 1980. *The Atman Project: A Transpersonal View of Human Development*. Wheaton, IL: Theosophical Publishing House.

Wilber, K. 1983. *A Sociable God: Brief Introduction to a Transcendental Sociology*. New York, NY: McGraw-Hill.

Wilber, K. 1995. *Sex, Ecology, and Spirituality: The Spirit of Evolution*. Boston, MA.: Shambhala Publications.

Wilber, K. 2000 a. *A Theory of Everything: An Integral Vision for Business, Politics, Science and Spirituality*. Berkeley, CA: Shambhala Publications.

Wilber, K. 2000 b. *Integral psychology: Consciousness, Spirit, Psychology, Therapy*, Boston: Shambhala (also part of volume IV of Collected Works).

Wilson, W. and Jung, C. G. 1963. *Mystical Quest, Attachment, and Addiction*. Letters republished in: Grof, S. (ed.): Special edition of the Re -Vision Journal 10 (2) 1987.

Wolf, F.A. 1981. *Taking the Quantum Leap*. San Francisco, CA: Harper & Row.

Woodroffe, Sir John (Arthur Avalon) 1974. *Serpent Power: The Secrets of Tantric and Shaktic Yoga*. New York, NY: Dover Publications.

Wrangham, R. and Peterson, D. 1996. *Apes and the Origins of Human Violence*. Boston, MA: Houghton Mifflin.

Index

Index

31131435R00156